VISUAL QUICKSTART GUIDE

FreeHand 5.5

FOR MACINTOSH

Sandee Cohen

Peachpit Press

FreeHand 5.5 for Macintosh
Visual QuickStart Guide
Sandee Cohen

Peachpit Press
2414 Sixth Street
Berkeley, CA 94710
510/548-4393
510/548-5991 (fax)
800/283-9444

Find us on the World Wide Web at:
http://www.peachpit.com
Peachpit Press is a division of Addison Wesley Longman

Copyright © 1996 by Sandee Cohen

Copyeditor: Liz Sizensky
Cover design: The Visual Group
Production: Sandee Cohen and Mary Littell

This book was created using QuarkXPress 3.3 for layout, Macromedia FreeHand 5.5 for illustrations, Mainstay Captivate 4.5 for screen shots, and Adobe Photoshop 3.0.4 for retouching on a Macintosh Quadra 840AV. The fonts used were ITC Garamond, Franklin Gothic, Franklin Gothic Condensed, and Futura from Adobe.

Notice of Rights
All rights reserved. No part of this book may be reproduced or transmitted in any form by any means, electronic, mechanical, photocopying, recording, or otherwise, without the prior written permission of the publisher. For information on getting permission for reprints and excerpts, contact Peachpit Press.

Notice of Liability
The information in this book is distributed on an "As Is" basis, without warranty. While every precaution has been taken in the preparation of the book, neither the author nor Peachpit Press shall have any liability to any person or entity with respect to any loss or damage caused or alleged to be caused directly or indirectly by the instructions contained in this book or by the computer software and hardware products described in it.

ISBN 0-201-88447-X

9 8 7 6 5 4 3 2 1

Printed and bound in the United States of America

♻ Printed on recycled paper

Dedicated to

Nathan Cohen
who has always told me to "put something new on the shelf."
I think this is a good start.

Terry DuPrât
who has taught me to have faith.

Bonnie Cohen
who has shown me her incredible strength through adversity.

Danny and Lizzie Wessel
who simply make me smile!

Thanks to

Roslyn Bullas and the rest of the Peachpit gang. You made it easy for my first time.

Pete Mason, Brian Schmidt, Doug Benson, John Dowdell, John Nosal, Rachel Schindler, Anna Sturvidant, and David Mendels of Macromedia for their help, encouragement, and technical advice.

Liz Sizensky, the copy editor with the microscopic eye! I couldn't have done it without you.

Mary Littell, who tested every one of the exercises, and found where I was vague or wrong.

Steve Rath, for his index—the most important part of any book.

Ted Alspach and Sharon Steuer, the most famous authors I know. You two have taught me more about writing and vectors than anyone else.

Jen Alspach, Erik Gibson, Mordy Golding, Sree Kotay, and the rest of my AOL vector friends for all their support and advice.

Ellen McKniely, Jackie McKee, Sandy McCarron, and the rest of the desktop publishing department at Random House for giving me the time to do this.

Peter Lowery, Joyce Chen, and Michael Callery of the New School for Social Research Computer Instruction Center. You've made it fun to come to work.

Elaine Weinmann and Peter Lourekas for their advice and for suggesting my name to Peachpit.

Table of Contents

Chapter 1: **The Basics** **1**
Introduction 1
FreeHand menu bar and document window 2
Toolbox 4
Menu commands 5
File menu 6
Edit menu 6
View menu 7
Arrange menu 7
Type menu 8
Window menu. 8
Xtras menu 8
Inspector palette 9
Align, Color List, Color Mixer, Halftone,
  Layers palettes 10
Operations, Styles, Transform, Type,
  Xtra Tools palettes 11
Sample dialog box 12

Chapter 2: **How FreeHand Works** **13**

Chapter 3: **Startup** **19**
Launch FreeHand. 19
Create a new document 20
Change unit of measurement 21
Change printer resolution. 21
Select page size 22
Change page orientation 23
Add pages 24
Arrange pages 25
Page magnification. 26
Set bleed size. 27
Save a document 28
Close a document 29
Revert to last saved version 30
Quit FreeHand 30

Chapter 4: **Display** **31**
Preview and Keyline modes. 31
Open document window rulers 33
Create guides. 34
Delete guides. 36
Add guides 37
Lock guides 38
Turn on Snap To Guides 38
View grid. 39
Change grid. 39

i

Table of Contents

                Turn on Snap To Grid 40
                Turn on Snap To Point. 41
                Zoom in or out with Magnifying tool 42
                Zoom in or out with Magnification menus. 43
                Enter exact magnification amounts 43
                Hide palettes 44
                Using the Zip feature 44

Chapter 5:   **Layers** **45**
                Move objects to front or back 46
                Move objects within a layer 47
                Paste behind 48
                View Layers palette 49
                Rename a layer 50
                Duplicate a layer 50
                Remove a layer 51
                Reorder layers 52
                Move objects between layers 53
                Make nonprinting layers. 54
                Make printing layers. 54
                Display layers 55
                Lock layers 56
                Lock objects 56

Chapter 6:   **Creation Tools** **57**
                Create Rectangles. 58
                Create Squares. 59
                Create Rounded-Corner rectangles 60
                Draw from center point 60
                Create Ellipses and circles 61
                Create Polygons. 62
                Create Stars 63
                Create Straight lines 64
                Use Freehand tool 65
                Choose Freehand settings. 65
                Draw with Freehand tool 66
                Choose Variable stroke settings. 67
                Draw with Variable stroke tool 68
                Choose Calligraphic pen settings 69
                Bézigon and Pen tools 69
                Choose Spiral tool settings 70
                Choose Arc tool settings. 72
                Place artwork for tracing 73
                Use Tracing tool. 74

Chapter 7:   **Points and Paths** **75**
                Select points by clicking. 75
                Select points with a marquee 76
                Select and move entire objects 77

Table of Contents

           Group paths 78
           Resize and reshape group objects. 78
           Select individual points in a group 79
           Nest objects. 80
           Work with nested groups 81
           Ungroup an object. 81
           Basics of points 82
           Corner points. 82
           Curve points 83
           Connector points 83
           One-third rule 83
           Convert points. 84
           Retract corner point handles. 86
           Extend point handles 86
           Retract handles manually 87
           Extend handles manually 87
           Delete an object. 88
           Delete a point from a path 88
           Add a point to a path. 89
           Close a path 89
           Close a previously drawn path 90
           Open or close paths with Inspector palette. 90
           Move points and groups numerically 91
           Change group size numerically. 92

Chapter 8:   **Pen and Bézigon Tools** **93**
           Create an object with straight sides. 94
           Draw smooth curved path with Bézigon 95
           Draw smooth curved path with Pen 96
           Draw bumpy curved path with Bézigon 97
           Draw bumpy curved path with Pen 98
           Draw straight-to-bumpy path with Bézigon. 99
           Draw traight-to-bumpy path with Pen 100
           Create connector points using Bézigon or Pen. . . 101
           Add points to end of path 102

Chapter 9:   **Move and Transform** **103**
           Read Info Bar. 103
           Cut, copy, or paste objects 105
           Move and copy an object 105
           Rotate an object by eye 106
           Scale an object by eye 107
           Reflect an object by eye 108
           Skew an object by eye 109
           Copy as you transform 110
           Power Duplicating 110
           View the Transform palette. 112
           Move object using Transform palette. 112
           Rotate object using Transform palette 113

iii

Table of Contents

                Scale object using Transform palette 114
                Skew object using Transform palette 115
                Reflect object using Transform palette 116

Chapter 10: Color **117**
                Color Mixer 117
                Define a color 119
                Add a color to the Color List 120
                Rename a color 122
                Convert process and spot colors 123
                Move color names 124
                Duplicate a color 124
                Remove a color 124
                Make a tint 125
                Add multiple colors to the Color List 126
                Color-matching libraries 126
                Export custom color library 128

Chapter 11: Fills **129**
                Apply Basic fills 130
                Change color of a Basic fill 130
                Apply Graduated fills 132
                Create 3-D button with Graduated fills 132
                Apply Graduated fill by dragging color 133
                Apply Radial fills 134
                Create 3-D button with Radial fills 135
                Apply Radial fill by dragging color 135
                Create and apply Tiled fills 137
                Adjust Tiled fills 138
                Apply Custom fills 140
                Apply Textured fills 141
                Apply Pattern fills 142
                Apply PostScript fills 143
                Create and apply Multi-Color fills 144
                Create Graduated Multi-Color fills 145
                Create Radial Multi-Color fills 145
                Apply a None fill 145
                Overprint 146

Chapter 12: Strokes **147**
                Apply Basic strokes 147
                Change color of a stroke 148
                Change width of a stroke 148
                Apply Stroke caps 149
                Apply Stroke joins 150
                Change Miter limit 151
                Apply Dash patterns 151
                Edit dash patterns 152
                Create multi-colored dash 153

Create "string of pearls" 153
Apply Arrowheads 154
Edit arrowheads. 155
Create arrowheads 155
Apply Custom stroke patterns. 156
Apply Pattern strokes 157
Apply PostScript strokes 158

Chapter 13: Blends **159**
Create a blend 160
Change number of steps in a blend. 161
Change number of steps in a document 162
Create Live Blends 162
Rules of blends 163
View blends. 163
Print blends 164

Chapter 14: Text **165**
Create text block by dragging. 165
Create text block by clicking. 166
Change size of dragged text block 166
Change the auto-expansion settings of
 a text block 167
Automatically shrink a text block 168
Apply a border to a text block 168
Inset text 169
Position a text block. 169
Import text. 170
Use Link box 171
Change typeface, type size, or style 171
Use Character Inspector 172
Use Paragraph Inspector. 174
Change margin indents. 175
Keep lines together 175
Create hanging punctuation 175
Change paragraph alignment 176
Use tab alignment 176
Set tabs 177
Change tabs. 177
Turn on hyphenation 178
Create columns and rows 178
Add rules to columns and rows 179
Link text between objects. 180

Chapter 15: Special Text Effects **181**
Bind text to a path 181
Change text flow direction 182
Move text along a path. 182
Text on a path options 183

Table of Contents

    Highlight, Inline, Shadow, Strikethrough,
        Underline, and Zoom special text effects 184
    Apply special text effects 185
    Edit Inline effect.......................... 186
    Edit Zoom effect 187
    Edit Highlight, Underline and
        Strikethrough effects.................. 188
    Use Shadow effect 188
    Wrap text around a graphic 189
    Create Inline graphics..................... 190
    Convert text to paths 192

Chapter 16: **Edit Text** **193**
    Use Text editor 193
    Use Spelling checker 194
    Use Special Characters 197
    Use Find Text dialog box 199

Chapter 17: **Styles**............................ **201**
    View Styles palette....................... 201
    View default styles....................... 201
    Define a style by example 202
    Rename a style........................... 203
    Apply a style 203
    Define a style by attributes 204
    Redefine a style 205
    Edit Style dialog box 206
    Base one style on another 207
    Work with Parent and Child styles......... 208
    Duplicate styles 209
    Copy styles between documents............ 209
    Remove a style........................... 210
    Change default styles 210

Chapter 18: **Path Operations**................... **211**
    Create Composite paths 211
    Release composite paths.................. 213
    Create a mask 213
    Release a mask 214
    Close an open path 214
    Open a closed path 215
    Split paths jaggedly 215
    Split paths evenly....................... 216
    Punch holes............................. 217
    Erase parts of paths 217
    Use Reverse Direction command with blends ... 218
    Use Remove Overlap command 219
    Use Simplify command................... 220
    Use Intersect command 221

Table of Contents

	Use Punch command 222
	Use Union command 223
	Use Transparency command. 224
	Use Expand Stroke command. 225
	Use Inset Path command 226
	Use Crop command 228
	Use Command-Shift-Plus command. 228
Chapter 19:	**Xtras** **229**
	Use 3D Rotation tool 230
	Use Fisheye Lens tool. 231
	Use Smudge tool 232
	Use Eyedropper tool 233
	Use Color Control dialog box 233
	Darken or Lighten Colors 234
	Saturate or Desaturate Colors 234
	Name All Colors. 235
	Sort Color List By Name 235
	Use Unused Named Colors command 235
	Randomize Named Colors 235
	Fractalize. 236
	Trap 237
	Create Blend 238
	Use Empty Text Blocks command. 238
	Add Xtras from other companies. 238
	Use Xtras from other companies 238
Chapter 20:	**Other Applications** **239**
	Place artwork. 239
	Resize placed images 240
	Transform a placed image 241
	Modify a placed image. 241
	Install Photoshop filters 242
	Apply Photoshop filters 243
	Extract an embedded placed image. 243
	Export files 244
	Export as an EPS file 244
	Export as an Adobe Illustrator file. 246
	Export as a FreeHand file. 247
	Export as other formats 247
	Create a PICT image. 248
	PICT image options 249
	Open Acrobat PDF. 250
	Add Fetch info 250
Chapter 21:	**Printing**. **251**
	Basic printing. 252
	Open Printer dialog box. 252
	Set up Printer dialog box 252

vii

Table of Contents

    Tile an oversized illustration 254
    Advanced printing 255
    Change print options 255
    Add printer marks 255
    Add page labels 255
    Choose imaging options 256
    Choose spread size 256
    Select the PPD 257
    Set the halftone screen 257
    Set the Transfer function 258
    Set the separations 259
    Open Output Options dialog box 260
    Choose output options 260
    Create a document report 261
    Send a file for imagesetting 262

Chapter 22: Preferences **263**
    Change Color preferences 263
    Change Document preferences 265
    Change Editing general preferences 266
    Change Object editing preferences 267
    Change Text editing preferences 268
    Change Importing/Exporting preferences 269
    Change Palettes preferences 270
    Change Redraw preferences 271
    Install snap sounds 273
    Change Snap sounds preferences 273
    Change Spelling preferences 274
    Change Expert document preferences 275
    Change Expert editing preferences 276
    Change Expert import/output preferences 277
    Save Preferences settings 277
    Change FreeHand defaults file 278

Appendix A: Keyboard Shortcuts **279**
    Menu commands 279
    General commands 280
    Text commands 280

Appendix B: Fills and Strokes **281**
    Custom fills 281
    Textured fills 282
    Pattern fills and strokes 283
    Custom strokes 284

Index **285**

THE BASICS 1

Welcome to Macromedia FreeHand. If you're like most people who are just starting out with the program, you may find it a little overwhelming. For instance, there are over 26 different variations of the Inspector palette, FreeHand's main control device. There are 12 other palettes, each with its own variations. There are over 70 different menu commands spread out on seven different menus. Finally, there are sixteen different tools, many of which have their own control settings. This *Visual QuickStart Guide* has been written to help sort out the features.

The first few chapters are overviews of the program. You may find that you don't create any artwork in those chapters. Don't skip them. They contain information that will help you later.

The middle chapters of the book contain the most artistic information. This is where you can see how easy it is to create sophisticated artwork using FreeHand.

The final chapters are about printing, preferences, and using your artwork with other applications. Some of this information refers to technical printing terms. If you are not familiar with these terms, speak to the print shop that will be printing your artwork.

With a program as extensive as FreeHand, there will be many features that you never use. Don't worry. It's hard to believe that even the experts use all of FreeHand's features.

Find the areas you wish to master, and then follow the exercises. If you are patient, you will find yourself creating your own work in no time. And don't forget to have fun!

Chapter 1

The FreeHand menu bar and document window

1 Menu bar

File   Edit   View   Arrange   Type   Window   Xtras

2 Close box
3 Title bar
4 Zoom box/zip box

My artwork

units: inches

5 Zero point settings
7 Horizontal ruler
8 Info bar
6 Vertical ruler
9 Ruler guides
10 Document grid
14 Scroll arrow
11 Magnification pop-up menu
30%
Preview
12 Page icons
13 Display mode pop-up menu
15 Resize box

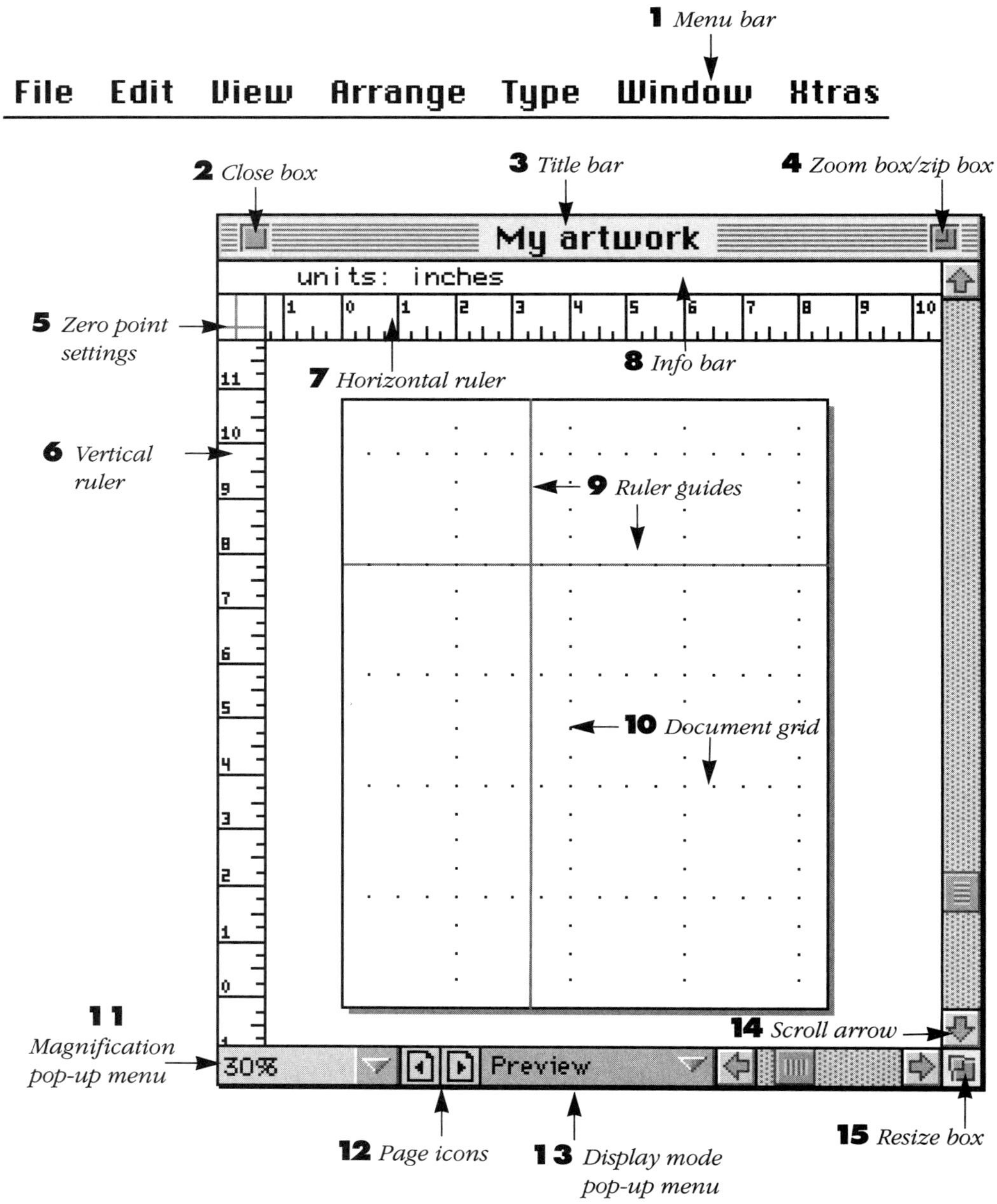

Figure 1. *The **menu bar** and **document window**.*

2

The Basics

Key to the FreeHand menu bar and document window

1 *Menu bar*
Press and choose any menu to access commands, dialog boxes, and submenus.

2 *Close box*
Click to close a window or palette. (Palette close boxes are smaller than window close boxes.)

3 *Title bar*
Displays the name of the file.

4 *Zoom box/zip box*
A click of a window's zoom box will expand the window to its full size or contract it to its previous size. A click of a palette's zip box will expand the palette to its full size or contract it so that only its title bar is visible.

5 *Zero point settings*
Drag to reset the lower-left corner of the illustration page to a new position.

6 *Vertical ruler*
Shows the vertical measurements.

7 *Horizontal ruler*
Shows the horizontal measurements.

8 *Info bar*
Displays various measurements and information about the position of the mouse, object sizes, movement lengths, angles, etc.

9 *Ruler guides*
Created by dragging from the horizontal or vertical rulers.

10 *Document grid*
Displayed from the View menu. The visible part of the document grid consists of dots evenly spaced into squares along your page. The invisible part of the document grid connects those dots.

11 *Magnification pop-up menu*
Press to choose one of the preset magnification levels or enter a custom magnification level.

12 *Page icons*
Click to change the active page. The right arrow moves forward. The left arrow moves backward.

13 *Display mode pop-up menu*
Press to choose between the Preview or Keyline modes.

14 *Scroll arrow*
Press to move the illustration page to a new position in the window.

15 *Resize box*
Press and drag to resize the document window.

Chapter 1

Toolbox

The toolbox contains 16 different tools that perform selection, creation, text, transformation, and magnification functions. Click with the mouse to select each tool, or use the keyboard commands to access the tools. Double-click on tools with a corner symbol to access their dialog box settings.

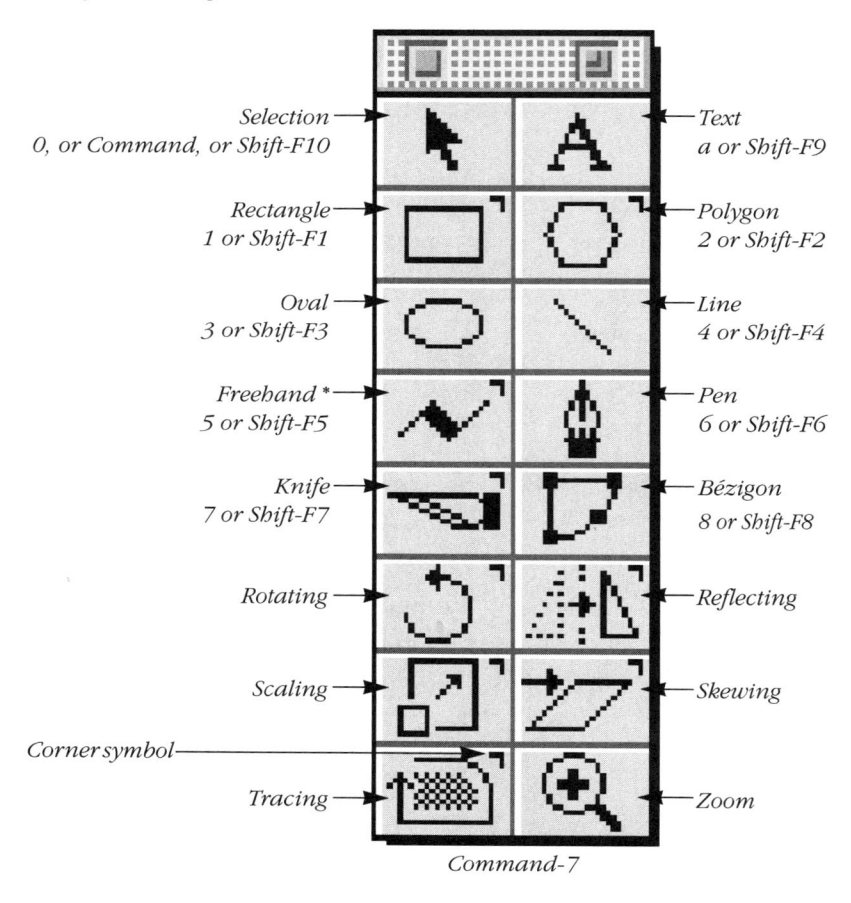

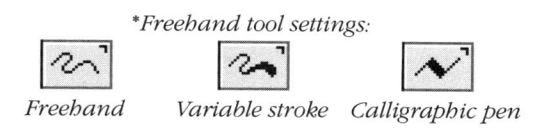

Selection — 0, or Command, or Shift-F10
Text — a or Shift-F9
Rectangle — 1 or Shift-F1
Polygon — 2 or Shift-F2
Oval — 3 or Shift-F3
Line — 4 or Shift-F4
Freehand* — 5 or Shift-F5
Pen — 6 or Shift-F6
Knife — 7 or Shift-F7
Bézigon — 8 or Shift-F8
Rotating
Reflecting
Scaling
Skewing
Corner symbol
Tracing
Zoom
Command-7

*Freehand tool settings:
Freehand   Variable stroke   Calligraphic pen

Figure 2. The **toolbox**.

The Basics

Menu commands

To choose from a menu, press on the name of the menu, and still pressing, drag down through the menu to the command. Release to activate the command.

The seven FreeHand menus are listed on the following pages.

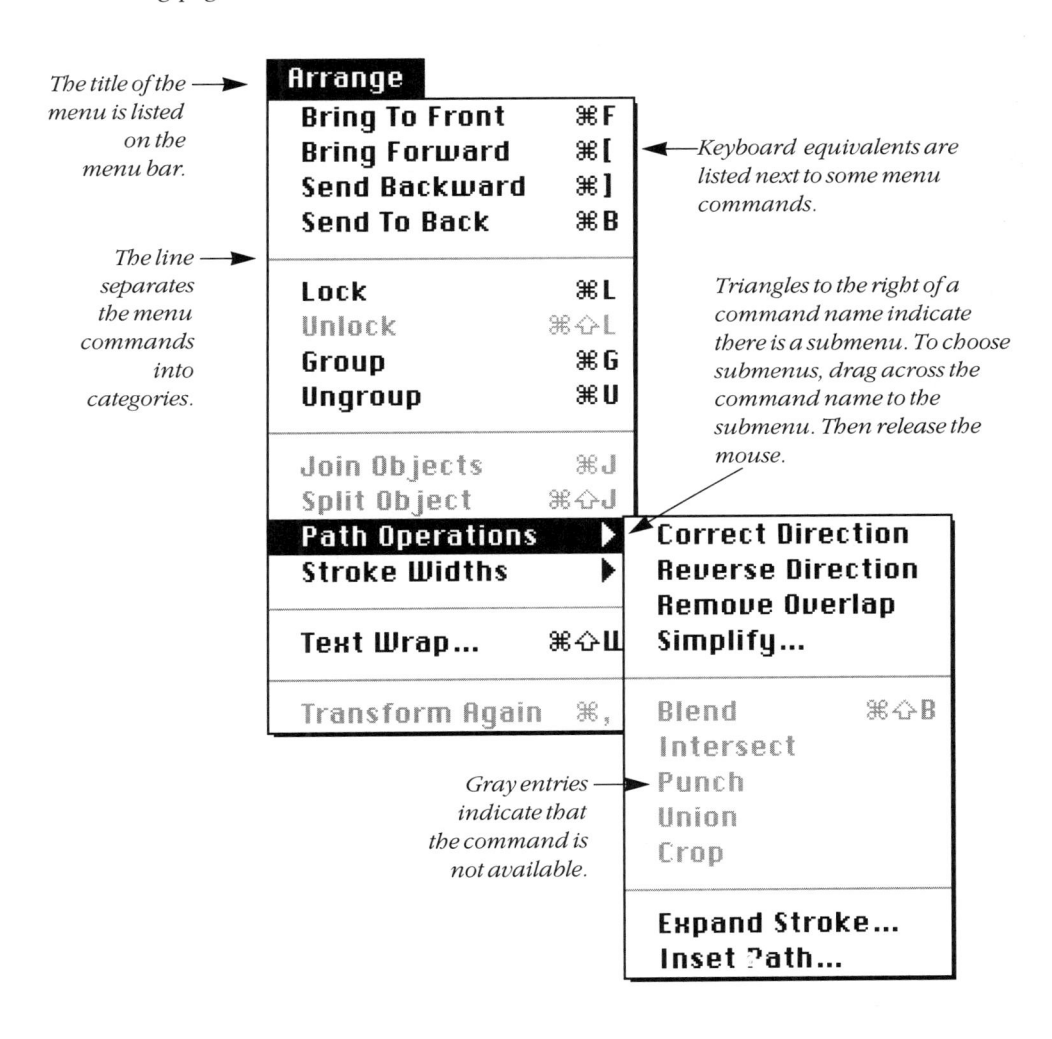

The title of the menu is listed on the menu bar. →

Keyboard equivalents are listed next to some menu commands.

The line separates the menu commands into categories. →

Triangles to the right of a command name indicate there is a submenu. To choose submenus, drag across the command name to the submenu. Then release the mouse.

Arrange
Bring To Front	⌘F
Bring Forward	⌘[
Send Backward	⌘]
Send To Back	⌘B
Lock	⌘L
Unlock	⌘⇧L
Group	⌘G
Ungroup	⌘U
Join Objects	⌘J
Split Object	⌘⇧J
Path Operations	▶
Stroke Widths	▶
Text Wrap...	⌘⇧W
Transform Again	⌘,

Path Operations submenu:
- Correct Direction
- Reverse Direction
- Remove Overlap
- Simplify...
- Blend ⌘⇧B
- Intersect
- Punch
- Union
- Crop
- Expand Stroke...
- Inset Path...

Gray entries indicate that the command is not available.

Figure 3. *A typical **menu**.*

Chapter 1

File and Edit Menus

File menu

The File menu is used to create, open, close, save, rename, revert, set print and output options and print an illustration. It also allows you to access the Preferences settings, create a report about the file, place artwork, export the file information, and add Fetch Info. Finally, it lets you quit FreeHand.

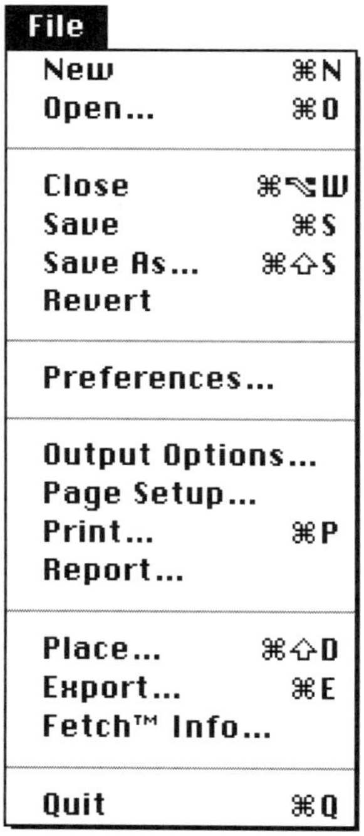

File	
New	⌘N
Open...	⌘O
Close	⌘⌥W
Save	⌘S
Save As...	⌘⇧S
Revert	
Preferences...	
Output Options...	
Page Setup...	
Print...	⌘P
Report...	
Place...	⌘⇧D
Export...	⌘E
Fetch™ Info...	
Quit	⌘Q

Figure 4. *The **File** menu.*

Edit menu

The Edit menu is used to undo commands and to cut, copy, and clear items. In addition, it lets you perform several different paste functions: paste, paste behind, paste attributes, and paste inside. It also lets you choose editions for publish and subscribe functions. It allows you to cut and paste the contents of objects. Finally, it lets you select, duplicate, and clone objects.

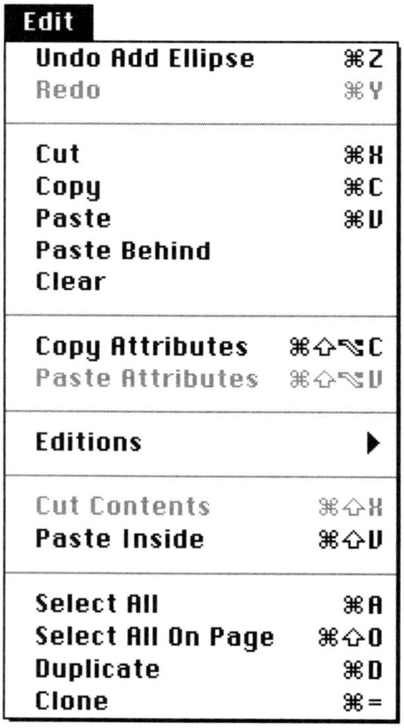

Edit	
Undo Add Ellipse	⌘Z
Redo	⌘Y
Cut	⌘X
Copy	⌘C
Paste	⌘V
Paste Behind	
Clear	
Copy Attributes	⌘⇧⌥C
Paste Attributes	⌘⇧⌥V
Editions	▶
Cut Contents	⌘⇧X
Paste Inside	⌘⇧V
Select All	⌘A
Select All On Page	⌘⇧A
Duplicate	⌘D
Clone	⌘=

Figure 5. *The **Edit** menu.*

6

View menu

The View menu lets you change the magnifications and display settings. It lets you see the utility features such as rulers, info bar, grid, guides, and palettes. It provides access to the edit guides function. It also turns on and off the "snap to" functions.

Arrange menu

The Arrange menu lets you move objects within layers. It lets you lock and unlock, group and ungroup, and join and split objects. It also lets you access the path operations functions and stroke widths, and make text wrap around objects. Finally, it lets you repeat the last transformations made with the transformation tools.

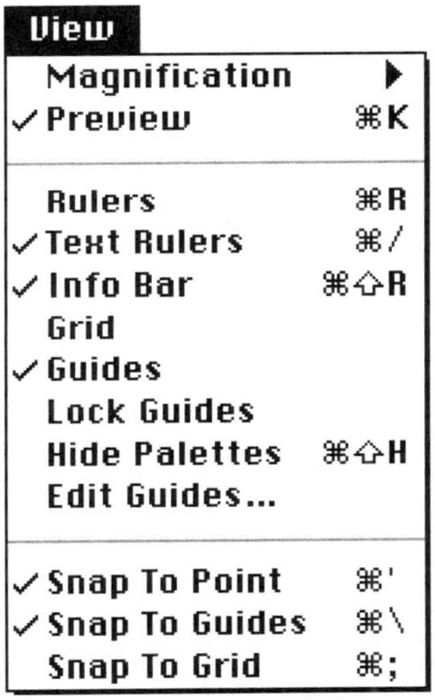

View

Magnification	▶
✓ Preview	⌘K
Rulers	⌘R
✓ Text Rulers	⌘/
✓ Info Bar	⌘⇧R
Grid	
✓ Guides	
Lock Guides	
Hide Palettes	⌘⇧H
Edit Guides...	
✓ Snap To Point	⌘'
✓ Snap To Guides	⌘\
Snap To Grid	⌘;

Figure 6. *The **View** menu.*

Arrange

Bring To Front	⌘F
Bring Forward	⌘[
Send Backward	⌘]
Send To Back	⌘B
Lock	⌘L
Unlock	⌘⇧L
Group	⌘G
Ungroup	⌘U
Join Objects	⌘J
Split Object	⌘⇧J
Path Operations	▶
Stroke Widths	▶
Text Wrap...	⌘⇧W
Transform Again	⌘,

Figure 7. *The **Arrange** menu.*

Chapter 1

Type menu

The Type menu lets you make changes to the font, size, and type style. It accesses the spell checker, the text find and change functions, and the text editor. It lets you access special text characters. It also provides the special text effects of binding text to a path, flowing text inside a path, and removing text from a path. Finally, it converts type from text to artwork paths.

Window menu

The Window menu lets you create new windows for your documents. It lets you access the various utility palettes such as the toolbox, Inspector palette, etc. Finally, when multiple documents are open, it lets you choose which document you want to be active.

Type	
Font	▶
Size	▶
Type Style	▶
Spelling...	⌘⇧G
Text Find...	⌘⇧F
Text Editor...	⌘⇧E
Special Characters	▶
Bind To Path	⌘⇧Y
Flow Inside Path	⌘⇧U
Remove From Path	
Convert To Paths	⌘⇧P

Figure 8. *The **Type** menu.*

Window	
New Window	⌘⌥N
✓Toolbox...	⌘7
Inspector...	⌘I
Color Mixer...	⌘⇧C
Color List...	⌘9
Type...	⌘T
Align...	⌘⇧A
Halftone...	⌘H
✓Layers...	⌘6
Styles...	⌘3
✓Transform...	⌘M
Other	▶
✓My artwork	

Figure 9. *The **Window** menu.*

Xtras menu

The Xtras menu lets you access the various Xtra features. In addition to the Xtras that come with FreeHand, Xtras from third-party vendors, when installed, are added to the Xtras menu.

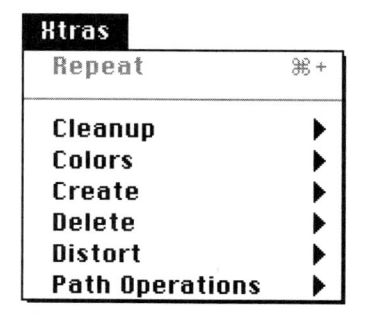

Xtras	
Repeat	⌘+
Cleanup	▶
Colors	▶
Create	▶
Delete	▶
Distort	▶
Path Operations	▶

Figure 10. *The **Xtras** menu.*

The Basics

Inspector palette

The Inspector palette has different functions depending on which of the five icons in the top row are chosen. When the Object icon is selected, the palette is called the Object Inspector. When the Document icon is selected, the palette is called the Document Inspector. And so on for each of the other icons. When the Text, Text Object, or Document icons are chosen, two additional rows of icons are displayed. The keyboard commands will call up the Inspector palette as well as switch between icons.

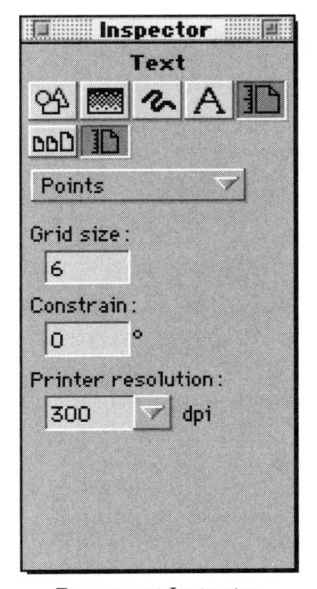

Document Inspector 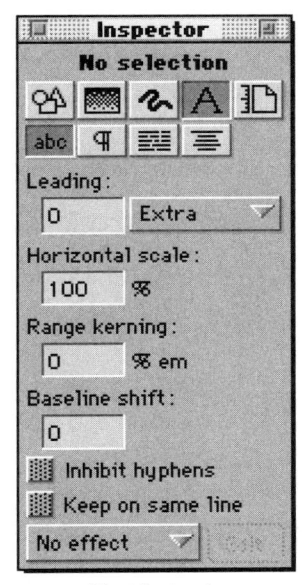   *Text Inspector* 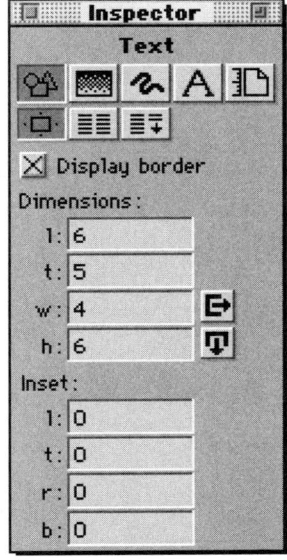   *Object Inspector*

	Object icon (Command-Option-I)
	Fill icon (Command-Option-F)
	Stroke icon (Command-Option-L)
	Text icon (Command-Option-T)
	*Document icon* (Command-Option-D)
	*Pages icon*
	*Document Setup icon*

	Character icon (Command-Option-T)
	Paragraph icon (Command-Option-P)
	Spacing-and-Hyphenation icon (Command-Option-K)
	Alignment icon (Command-Option-A)
	Inset icon (Command-Option-B)
	Column-and-Row icon (Command-Option-R)
	Copyfit icon (Command-Option-C)

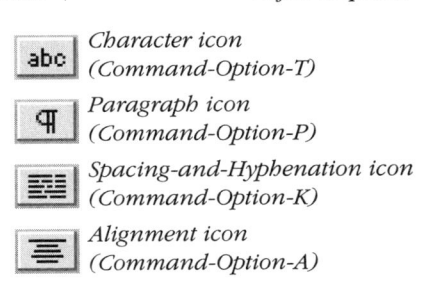

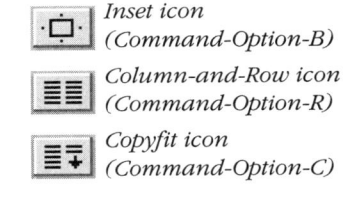

Figure 11. *Three versions of the* **Inspector** *palette and their icons.*

Chapter 1

The other FreeHand palettes

In addition to the Toolbox and the Inspector palette, FreeHand has ten other palettes. The Align palette arranges objects. The Color List organizes colors. The Color Mixer creates colors and tints. The Halftone palette controls the screen values of objects. The Layers palette controls layers and guides. The Operations palette lets you apply operations to objects. The Styles palette lets you define and apply object and paragraph styles. The Transform palette controls object transformations. The Type palette controls some type features. The Xtra Tools palette contains additional drawing and modification tools. The keyboard commands will show or hide the palettes.

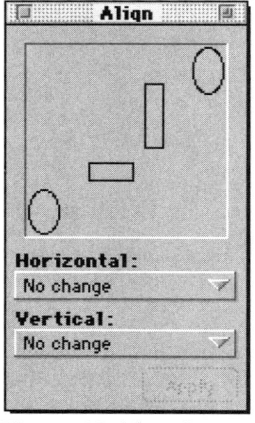

Figure 12. The **Align** palette (Command-Shift-A).

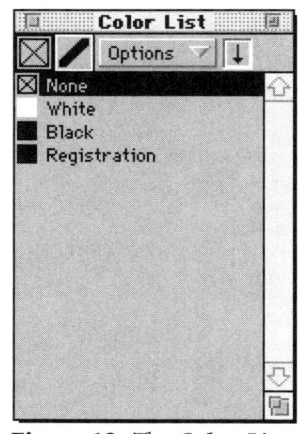

Figure 13. The **Color List** (Command-9).

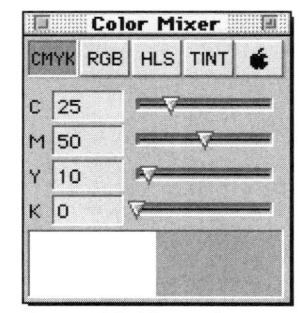

Figure 14. The **Color Mixer** (Command-Shift-C; tint: Command-Shift-Z).

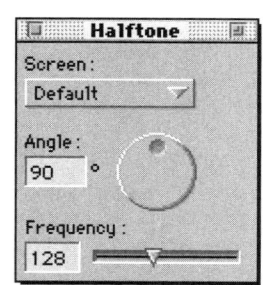

Figure 15. The **Halftone** palette (Command-H).

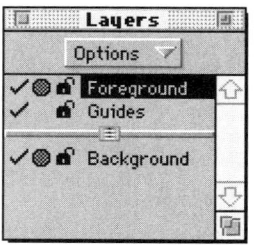

Figure 16. The **Layers** palette (Command-6).

Align, Color List, Color Mixer, Halftone, and Layers Palettes

10

The Basics

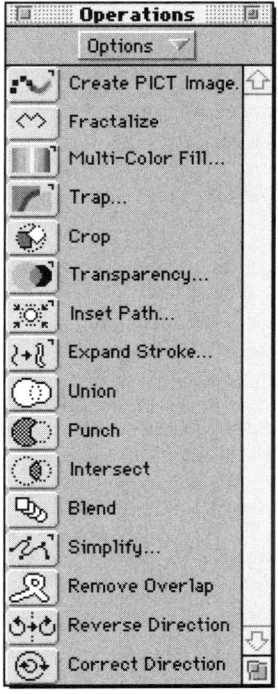

Figure 17. The **Operations** palette (Command-Shift-D).

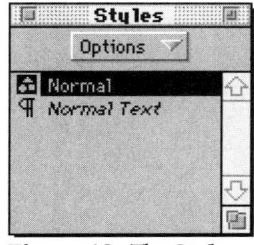

Figure 18. The **Style** palette (Command-3).

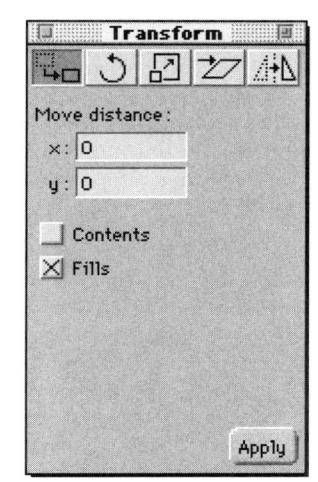

Figure 19. The **Transform** palette (Command-M).

Figure 20. The **Type** palette (Command-T).

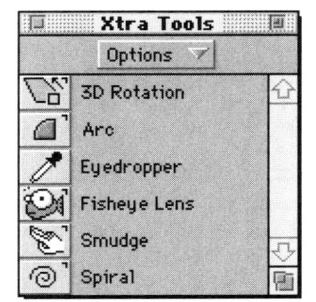

Figure 21. The **Xtra Tools** palette (Command-Shift-K).

Operations, Styles, Transform, Type, and Xtra Tools Palettes

11

Chapter 1

Sample dialog box

Many of FreeHand's features are set using dialog boxes. Though each dialog box differs, they all use similar setting devices: pop-up menus, fields in which to enter numbers, sliders, wheels, color drop boxes, checkboxes, icons, and buttons.

Sample Dialog Box

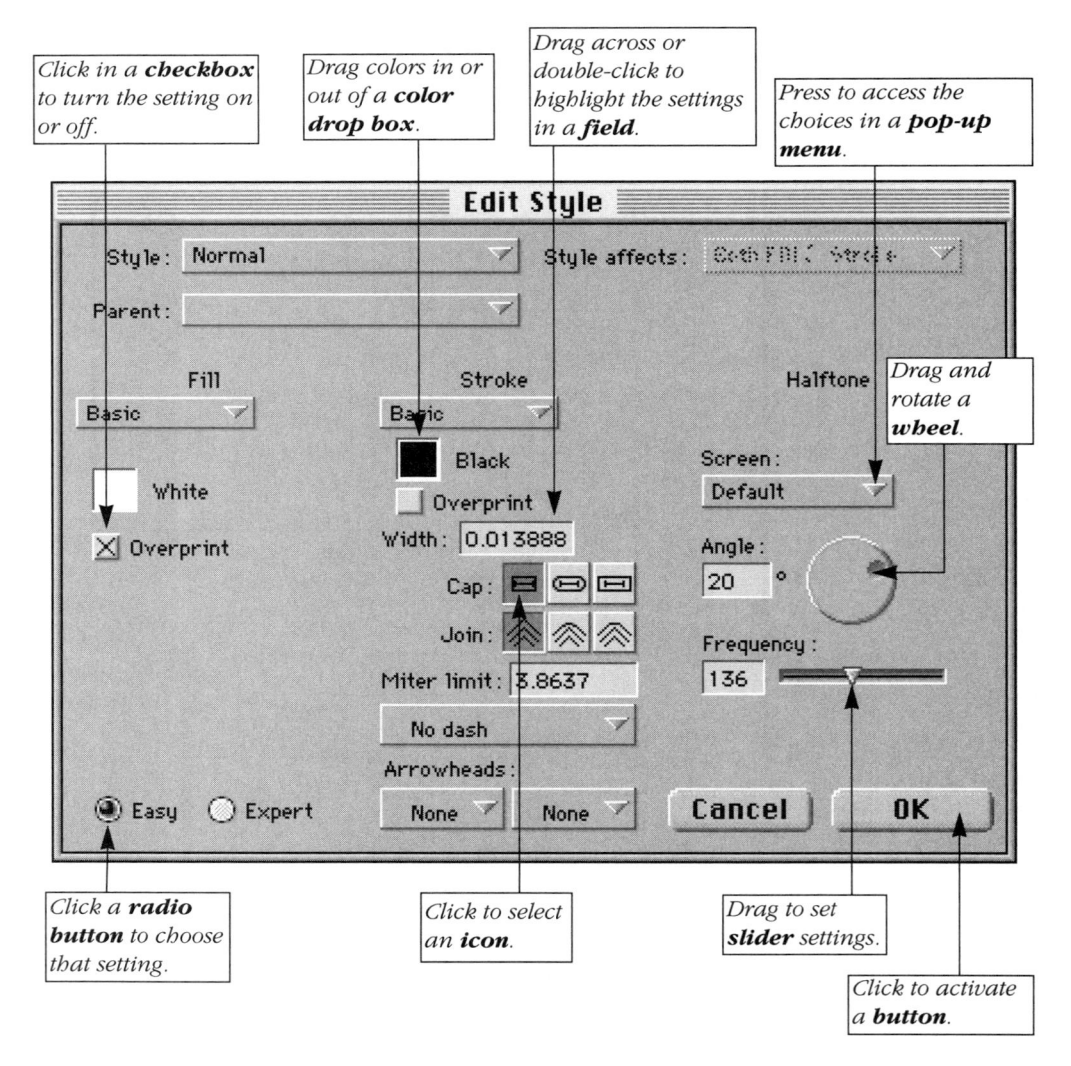

Callouts around the Edit Style dialog box:
- *Click in a **checkbox** to turn the setting on or off.*
- *Drag colors in or out of a **color drop box**.*
- *Drag across or double-click to highlight the settings in a **field**.*
- *Press to access the choices in a **pop-up menu**.*
- *Drag and rotate a **wheel**.*
- *Click a **radio button** to choose that setting.*
- *Click to select an **icon**.*
- *Drag to set **slider** settings.*
- *Click to activate a **button**.*

Figure 22. *The **setting devices** of a typical **dialog box**.*

12

HOW FREEHAND WORKS 2

FreeHand is one of the most versatile programs for the Macintosh. At its simplest, FreeHand is a graphics or drawing program. It allows you to create artwork such as drawings, logos, and illustrations. But because FreeHand lets you bring in scanned artwork from programs such as Photoshop or Painter, it is also an excellent layout program. This allows you to create ads, book covers, and posters. Finally, because FreeHand has a very sophisticated multiple-page feature, it is also a multipage document program. This allows you to create newsletters and flyers, as well as multipage presentations with differently sized pages.

FreeHand as a graphics or drawing program

There are two main types of computer graphics programs: bitmapped and object-oriented. FreeHand is an object-oriented, or vector-based, graphics program. Other object-oriented programs are Adobe Illustrator, MacDraft from Innovative Data Design, and part of Deneba Canvas. All of these programs, including FreeHand, create illustrations by a series of differently shaped objects. This is similar to cutting out many different pieces of paper and layering them into position.

The other type of graphics program is the bitmapped, or pixel-based, drawing program. Pixel-based programs include Adobe Photoshop, Fractal Design Painter, and the grandparent of all Macintosh graphics programs, MacPaint. These programs create their illustrations by coloring hundreds of thousands of tiny squares. This is similar to the images created on television screens. If you get real close to the image, you can see the individual colored squares, or pixels. But if you stand back, the colors all merge together into one image.

Advantages of object-oriented programs

When you work in FreeHand, every object that you create stays a distinct element that can be moved, reshaped, or recolored at any time while you are working on it. This means that if you have been working on an illustration and later decide you want to change a color or change the size of an object, you just open up the file, select the object, and make the changes.

This is in distinct contrast to the bitmapped, or pixel-based, programs. When you're using these programs, you have to be very careful when you set the color or shape of an object. It is not so simple to go in later and make changes to your artwork.

When you work in FreeHand, the artwork you create is called "resolution-independent." This is a technical term that means you don't have to worry about scaling the artwork to a new size. In an object-oriented program such as FreeHand there is practically no limit to how big or small you can scale the object.

In the bitmapped, or pixel-based, programs, you have to be careful that your image is the right size for final output. This means that if you've been working on an illustration that is 2" by 2" and you discover that you now need it at 4" by 4", you will need to rescan or redraw your illustration to make it the correct size. If you try to scale up a pixel-based illustration, you run the risk of creating a rough or jagged edge (**Figure 1**).

Another advantage of object-oriented programs is that the files tend to be smaller than the equivalent bitmapped artwork. If you draw a 1" square at a resolution of 300 pixels per inch using a bitmapped program, there are 90,000 pixels in that drawing. Each one of those pixels takes up disk space. And if the square is in color, there are actually four channels of 90,000 pixels each. This will mean a file of about 352K.

The same 1" square in object-oriented programs is created by four anchor points. The set of instructions defining the type and position of these points is all that takes up disk space. In addition, the color is defined by a set of instructions, not by four different layers. So a plain 1" square created in FreeHand takes up only 8K—far less disk space than the square created in a pixel-based program.

FreeHand as a layout program

Some people use FreeHand to create artwork that is then saved in a certain format and brought into layout programs such as Adobe PageMaker or QuarkXPress. However, FreeHand itself is quite capable of performing as a layout program. Instead of taking the artwork into another program and then adding text

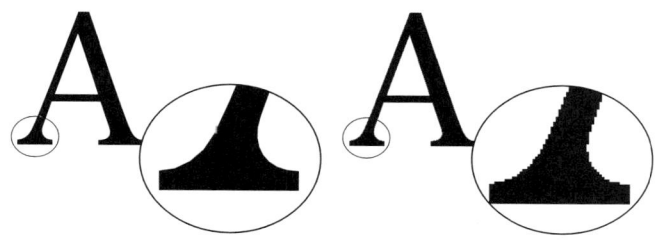

Figure 1. *The shape of an object drawn in FreeHand (left) stays smooth no matter how much it is scaled up or down. The shape of an object drawn in a bitmapped program (right) can get rough or jagged when it is scaled.*

and scanned pictures, you can use FreeHand for your final layout. This makes FreeHand an excellent choice for working on projects in which you need to combine artwork with scanned photos, copy, display text, and so on. FreeHand lets you place the photos on the page and then add all the other elements.

FreeHand as a multipage program

Finally, FreeHand lets you work on multiple pages in one document. This means that if you are working on a three-fold brochure with information on the front and back, you can create individual pages and arrange them together as a front unit and a back unit.

Also, unlike other programs that have to have their pages all the same size and shape, FreeHand lets you create multiple-page documents in which the pages are different sizes. This makes FreeHand an excellent choice for creating sophisticated presentations of differently sized pages such as letterheads, envelopes, and business cards. Using FreeHand's custom-size pages, each object will be on a page that is the correct size.

Objects in FreeHand

The objects you create in FreeHand are all created using the same principles. Each object is really a path, or outline. Along the path are elements called anchor points. These anchor points allow you to change the direction of a path. The different types of FreeHand points are corner points, curve points, and connector points. If a path starts at one point and ends at another, it is considered to be an open path. This is similar to a piece of string. The string can be arranged in any shape, but its ends are not connected. If a path starts and ends at the same point, it is considered to be a closed path. This is similar to a rubber band. The path can also be arranged in any shape, but it must be a shape that is self-contained.

Each of the tools in FreeHand is used to create different types of points or objects. The type and number of points in the object is determined by the tool used, by the settings in the dialog box for the tool, and by any modifier keys that may have been pressed. For instance, the Rectangle tool creates four-sided objects with corner points. The Oval tool creates four arcs that are joined with curve points. The Polygon tool creates multisided objects with as many sides as you select in its dialog box. The Line tool creates straight open paths. The FreeHand tool lets you create different types of paths that can look like lines, brush strokes, or the strokes of a calligraphic pen. The Tracing tool is used to create paths that follow the shape of imported artwork. The Pen and and the Bézigon tools let you draw paths with combinations of curve, corner, and connector points. Finally, FreeHand has additional features, called Xtras, that allow you to create other, sophisticatedly shaped objects.

Modifying the shape of objects

Any object in FreeHand can have its shape altered by either manipulating the anchor points, changing the type of points it has, or manipulating its Bézier handles. Bézier handles are nonprinting lines that come out of the anchor points of a path. Moving the Bézier handles will change the shape of the curve.

Filling and stroking objects

Once you have created an object in FreeHand, you have a wide variety of choices about its appearance. By stroking and filling an object, you create its look. The stroke of the object is applied along the path. Both open and closed paths can have visible strokes. The fill of the object is applied inside the path. Only closed paths can have fills. If a closed path has a fill of "None," then it will be an object that you can see through.

FreeHand offers a wide variety of strokes and fills. Some, such as basic colors, graduated fills, and radial fills, can be seen onscreen. Others, such as the custom or textured fills and strokes, can only be seen when the file is printed.

An object can have only one fill and only one stroke applied to it. If you wanted to have one path change from red to blue, you would actually need to have two separate paths: One path would be stroked red and the other, connected path would be stroked blue.

Text in FreeHand

FreeHand gives you several options for working with text. You can have a single line of text; this is very useful for creating headlines or other short text. You can also have paragraphs of text that are contained in a block. This text block governs the width of the paragraph. Changing the width of the block will cause the copy within the block to rewrap. You can also divide this text block into columns and rows, and the text will flow from one column to another. And text can be made to flow into irregularly shaped objects.

There are also a couple of special text effects that are very useful. You can make text flow along a path, or you can convert the text into outlines. When text is converted into outlines, it can then be reshaped and altered in many different ways.

Transforming objects in FreeHand

Once you have created an object, it can be modified by using one of the transformation tools. The basic transformation tools are the Rotating, Scaling, Reflecting, and Skewing tools. There are also special effects tools in the Xtra Tools palette that give you further options. These include the 3D Rotation, Fisheye Lens, and Smudge tools.

In addition to changing the shape of objects, FreeHand lets you modify how two or more objects relate to each other. These are called path operations. Some of the more common path operations are to make one object punch a hole in another object, to join two separate objects together into one path, to simplify the number of anchor points in a path, and to remove the overlap between two objects.

Third-party Xtras

When you are working in FreeHand, you are not limited to just those features that shipped with the program. FreeHand allows you to use the filters or plug-ins from Adobe Illustrator. Recently, there have been various third-party companies that have been creating their own Xtras for use in FreeHand. These include KPT Vector Effects, Infinite FX, and the Letraset Envelopes.

Working with colors

FreeHand offers a very extensive choice of color systems. If you are using commercial printers, you can choose the process color CMYK mode, or one of several spot color models such as Pantone or Toyo. If you are going to use your artwork for video or multimedia presentations, you can choose your colors via the RGB (Red, Green, Blue) color system or the HLS (Hue, Lightness, Saturation) system. You can also pick colors using the traditional Apple color wheel. Finally, tints can be created from any color.

FreeHand utilities

Some tools and commands are used not to create or modify objects, but to help you move around or view your work. The zoom tool lets you zoom in to get a closer look at your work, or you can zoom out to see the whole thing at once. It's not in the toolbox, but there is also a Hand tool, or grabber, that lets you move around your window without using the window scrollbars.

Working with other applications

FreeHand also lets you place pixel-based artwork that's been scanned or created by programs such as Photoshop and Painter. In addition, FreeHand lets you modify those placed images, either by coloring them or by applying filters that are used with Photoshop. These may be the built-in filters that came with Photoshop, or third-party filters such as Kai's Power Tools and Adobe Gallery Effects. FreeHand, however, is not a substitute for working with those programs—it is an auxiliary tool.

FreeHand also offers you a way to convert your vector-based artwork into pixels. This allows you to create images using FreeHand tools and then convert them so they can be manipulated by pixel filters while still in FreeHand.

FreeHand menus, submenus, and palettes

As you have seen in Chapter 1, FreeHand offers a wealth of palettes and menus to control its commands and functions. Many times, these palettes and menus perform the same functions; this way, FreeHand gives you a choice as to how you execute a command.

Most of FreeHand's functions are contained in the Inspector palette. This palette changes its features depending on which type of object is selected and which of the Inspector icons is selected. The wealth of choices in the Inspector palette may seem daunting. You do not have to memorize them. Many times, the best way to learn is to "keep clicking" until you find the features you are looking for.

Outputting your work

Once you have created your FreeHand file, you will want to output it. FreeHand offers you several choices. You can print your file to a low-resolution printer or to a high-resolution imagesetter. You can also export your FreeHand file so it can be used in other programs.

STARTUP 3

You're now ready to actually start working. In this chapter you will learn how to: launch FreeHand; start a blank document or continue working on an old document; change the units of measurement for your document; change the size of your pages; change the orientation of your pages from tall to wide; add pages to your document; use the Document Inspector to move pages together; change the page magnification; add a "bleed" area to your work page; save your work as a document or a template; close your document; and quit FreeHand.

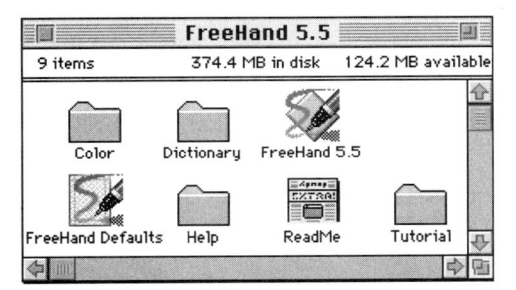

Figure 1. *Double-click on the **FreeHand icon** to launch the program.*

To launch FreeHand:

In the Finder, open the folder that holds the FreeHand application. If you used the default settings during the installation, that folder is called FreeHand 5.5. Double-click on the FreeHand application icon (**Figure 1**). This will launch FreeHand.

Tip

■ If you have a previously saved FreeHand document, you can double-click on it. This will launch FreeHand and bring you directly to that document, where you can continue working.

If you double-clicked on the FreeHand icon, you will see the FreeHand menus and palettes on your screen, but you won't have an actual document open (**Figure 2**).

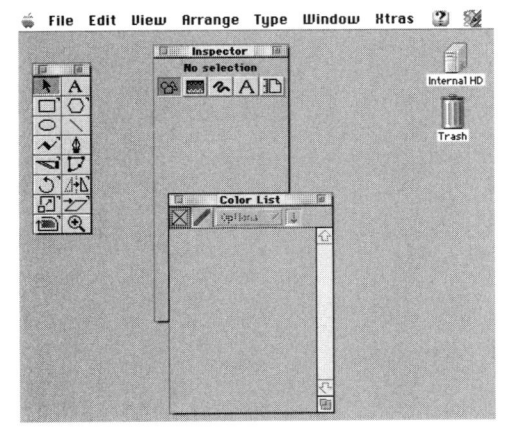

Figure 2. *Double-clicking on the FreeHand icon brings you into the **application**, but you will not have a document open.*

19

Chapter 3

To create a new document:

To start working, you need to create a new document. To do so, choose New from the File menu (**Figure 3**). This will create a window containing an untitled document.

Tips

- To tell whether or not FreeHand is the active application, look for the FreeHand application icon in the upper right corner of your screen. This lets you know you're actually in the program.

- If you want to open a previously saved document, you can switch back to the Finder and double-click on the document, or you can choose Open from the File menu (**Figure 4**).

You now have an untitled document window on your screen. Inside it is the rectangular work page. This is the actual area where you will be creating your work. Around the rectangular illustration page is a plain white area that is called the "pasteboard" (**Figure 5**). You can place objects in the pasteboard that you need to use, but don't want to print.

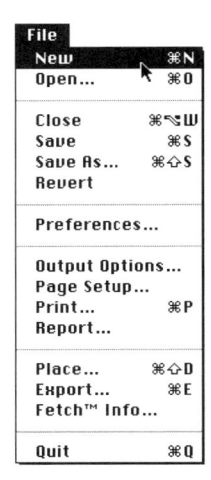

Figure 3. *To start a new document, choose **New** from the **File** menu or press **Command-N**.*

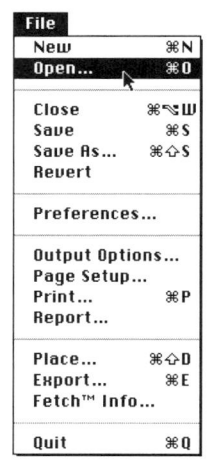

Figure 4. *To open a previously saved document, choose **Open** from the **File** menu or press **Command-O**.*

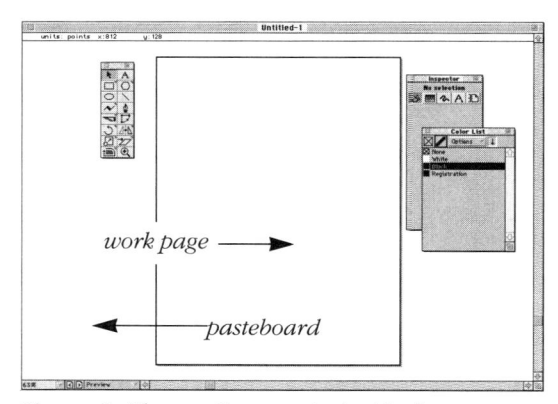

Figure 5. *The **work page** sits inside the **pasteboard** area.*

20

Startup

Figure 6. *To put the **Document Inspector** palette on your screen, choose **Inspector** from the **Window** menu.*

Document Setup icon

Document Inspector icon

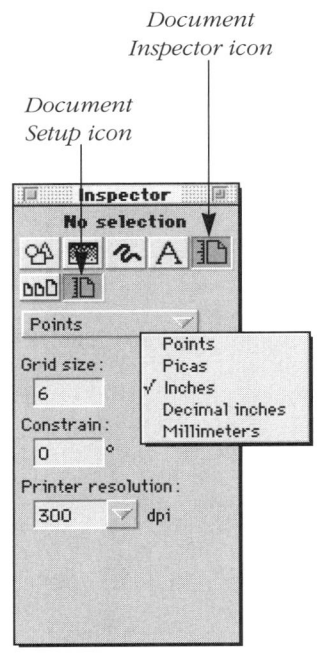

Figure 7. *In the **Document Inspector** palette, choose the **Document Setup** icon to bring you to where you can change the units of measurement for your document.*

Once you have a new document open, you may need to change the unit of measurement and the printer resolution.

To change the unit of measurement:

1. Make sure the Inspector palette is open. If it is not open, choose Inspector from the Window menu (**Figure 6**).

2. Click on the Document icon of the Inspector palette. Two more icons will appear, creating a second row.

3. Click on the Document Setup icon.

4. To change the unit of measurement from points to inches, press on the pop-up menu and choose inches (**Figure 7**).

Tip

■ No matter which unit of measurement your document is in, you can still enter sizes in whatever units you want. To enter points, type "p" before the number. To enter picas, type "p" after the number. To enter inches, type "i" after the number. To enter millimeters, type "m" after the number.

To change the printer resolution:

1. Make sure the Document Inspector palette is open and the Document Setup icon is chosen.

2. Drag across the field for the Printer resolution and enter the amount for the type of printer you will be sending your document to for printing.

Tip

■ If you are unsure about what printer resolution you will need for your final artwork, you can leave the setting low, and then change the resolution later.

Chapter 3

The next thing you need to do is make sure the work page is the correct size. Your work page is not necessarily the same size as the paper you are printing on. For instance, you may need to change your work page to a Tabloid or a Legal size.

To select a new work page size:

1. Click on the Document Inspector icon in the top row of the Inspector palette. Two more icons will appear, creating a second row.

2. Click on the Pages icon in the second row. To change the size of the work page to one of the preset page sizes, press on the pop-up menu (**Figure 8**).

If one of the preset sizes is not right for your job, you will need to create a work page with custom measurements. For instance, if you were creating business cards, you would want your work page to be the trim size of the card.

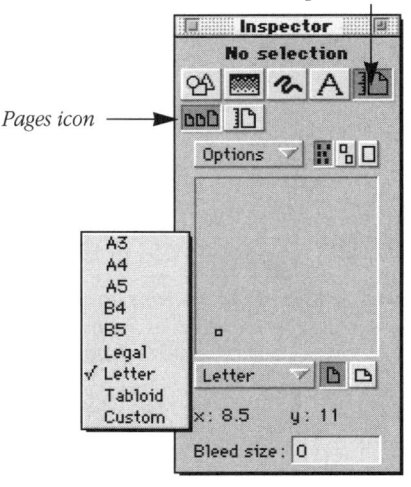

Figure 8. *There are eight different preset page sizes, plus* **Custom**, *which lets you enter the exact measurements for any work page size.*

To create a custom-size work page:

1. Click on the Pages icon in the second row of the Inspector palette and choose Custom from the pop-up menu.

2. Click in the area next to the x and type the horizontal measurement of your page. In this case, type "2."

3. Click in the area next to the y and type the vertical measurement of your page. In this case, type "3.5" (**Figure 9**).

4. Press the Return key. Your page size will now be the custom size.

Tip

■ If you are entering numbers in the same unit of measurement that your document is in, you do not need to type "i" after the number for inches, "p" after the number for picas, etc.

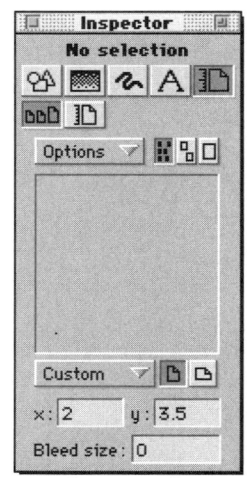

Figure 9. *When you choose* **Custom** *from the* **Page Size** *pop-up menu, you can enter your exact measurements in the x (horizontal) and y (vertical) fields.*

Startup

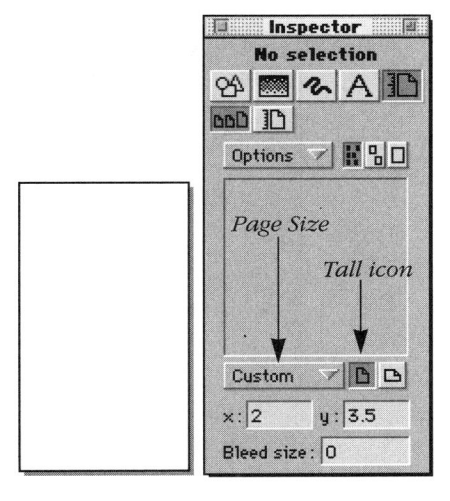

Figure 10a. *A **Custom-size page** with the **Tall** orientation selected.*

In the previous example, you will notice that the custom-size page you created is taller than it is wide. You may decide that you want to reverse the horizontal and vertical sizes of your document. In this case, we would like our business card to be wider than it is tall.

To change the orientation of your page:

1. In the Document Inspector palette, click on the Pages icon.

2. Click on the Wide icon next to the Page Size. This will swap your horizontal and vertical measurements (**Figures 10a–b**).

Tip

- If you have the Tall icon selected and you enter your measurements in the wrong order, FreeHand will automatically correct your mistake. Therefore, you can never have a work page that is wider than it is tall with the Tall icon selected. You can also never have a work page that is taller than it is wide with the Wide icon selected.

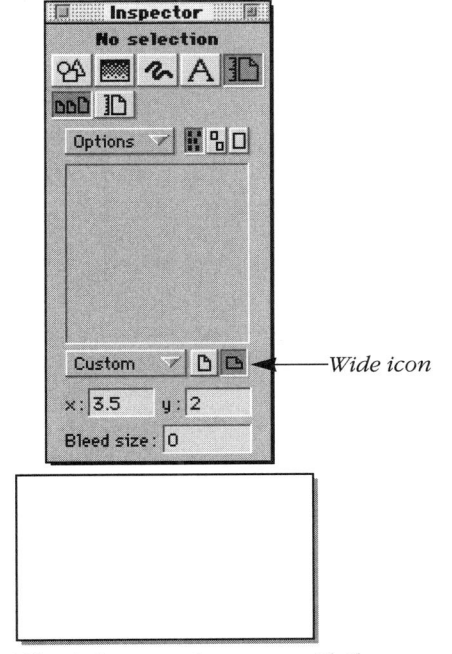

Figure 10b. *A **Custom-size page** with the **Wide** orientation selected.*

23

Chapter 3

Now that you've set your page size, you may need to create additional work pages. For instance, if you are creating a series of layouts for your client to choose from, you would need multiple work pages.

To create additional work pages:

1. In the Document Inspector palette, click on the Pages icon. Under the Options pop-up menu, choose Duplicate. This will create a new work page that is the exact size as your first page (**Figure 11a**).

or

Choose Add Pages from the Options menu. The Add Pages dialog box will appear. Type the number of pages you want. Use the pop-up menu to pick the page size. Click on the Tall or Wide icon for the proper orientation (**Figure 11b**).

2. Click on the OK button or press the Return key on your keyboard. You will now have additional pages on your pasteboard.

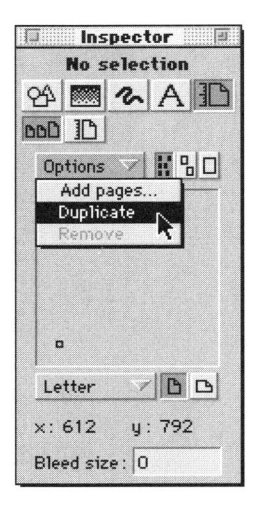

Figure 11a. *Choosing **Duplicate** from the **Options** pop-up menu of the **Document Inspector** palette will create a new work page the same size as the page selected.*

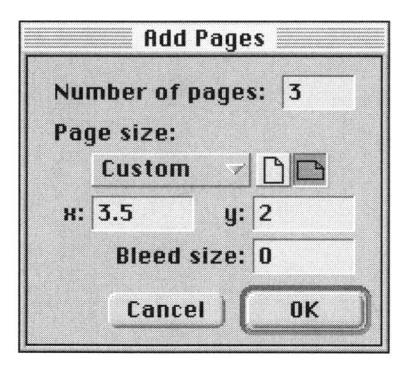

Figure 11b. *The **Add Pages** dialog box lets you specify how many pages you want to add, their size, their orientation, and the bleed area. This allows you to quickly create a FreeHand document with many work pages.*

Startup

Magnification icon

page thumbnails

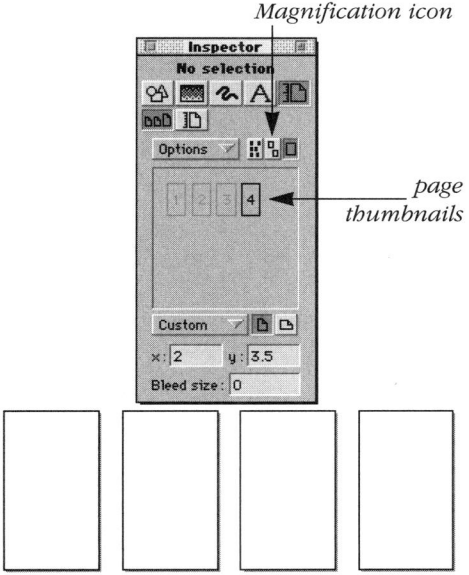

Figure 12a. *Four pages on the pasteboard next to each other. Notice there are spaces between both the page thumbnails and the actual pages on the pasteboard.*

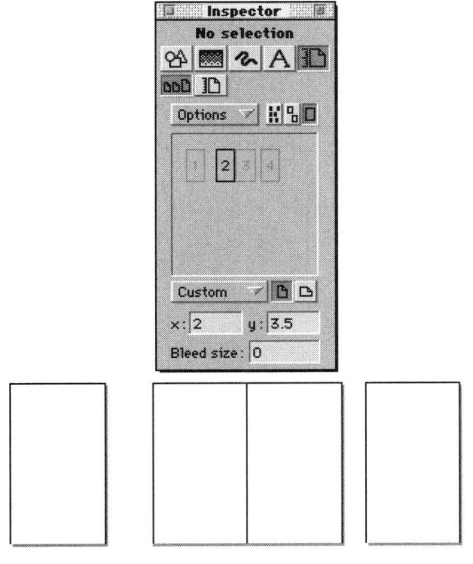

Figure 12b. *Two of those four pages have been positioned so that they touch each other. This allows graphics to stretch from one page to another.*

If you are working with multiple pages, you might want to move your pages around the pasteboard area. For instance, you might want two pages to touch each other so that you can bleed graphics from one page to another. This is extremely helpful if you are doing something like a three-page brochure. You might want each of the three pages to be next to each other so you can place artwork across the fold lines. In order to do this, you will need to use the Magnification icon in the Document Inspector.

To arrange pages next to each other:

1. Make sure you are working on a document that has at least two pages.

2. In the Document Inspector, click on the middle Magnification icon. Boxes should appear in the rectangular area of the Document Inspector. These are the page thumbnails in your document.

3. Drag one of the Page icons right next to the other. Look at the pasteboard area of your document. Notice how the pages now are right next to each other. (**Figures 12a–b**).

Arrange Pages

25

Chapter 3

If you have many different work pages, you may find that the middle Magnification icon does not show you enough of your pages. You may need to change the magnification.

To change the page magnification:

1. Click on the first Magnification icon. This shrinks the size of the Page icons so that you can see more of them at once.
2. Click on the middle Magnification icon. This expands the size of the Page icons so that you can see them more clearly.
3. Click on the third Magnification icon. This expands the size of the Page icons so that you can move them around more precisely (**Figures 13a–c**).

Tips

- If you are working on a single-page document, you will probably find the largest magnification setting the most useful.
- If you are working on a two- or three-page document, you will probably find the middle magnification setting the most useful.
- If you are working on a multipage document with many pages, such as a newsletter, you will probably find the smallest magnification setting the most useful.
- If you double-click on the Page icon in the Document Inspector, you will instantly go to that page and zoom out so that the whole page fits in the window.

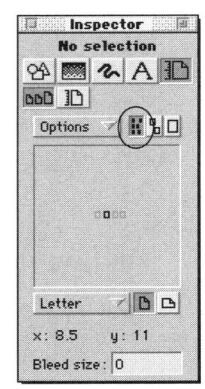

Figure 13a. *The **Magnification** icon for the **smallest size** setting.*

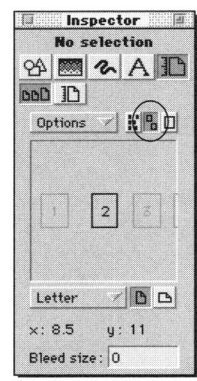

Figure 13b. *The **Magnification** icon for the **middle size** setting.*

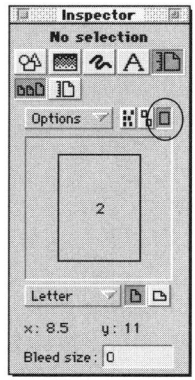

Figure 13c. *The **Magnification** icon for the **largest size** setting.*

Figure 14. *The light-gray line around the work page indicates the **bleed area**. Any artwork or graphics in the bleed area will print on your finished page.*

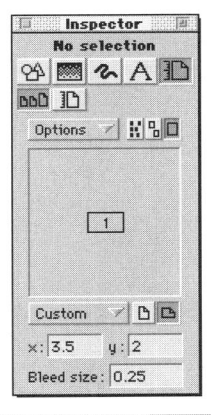

Figure 15. *The bleed area of this illustration contains notes about the layout and a "bleed" of the gray background. As long as these elements are in the bleed area, they will print on the final document.*

You may find that you need a "bleed" for your layout. A bleed is any artwork or graphic that extends off the side of the work page. In order for you to have artwork bleed off the page, you will have to set a bleed size.

To set a bleed size:

1. Click on the Pages icon in the Document Inspector.
2. At the bottom of the palette, enter your desired bleed size. Press Return.
3. A light-gray line will appear around your work page. This is the bleed area (**Figure 14**).

Tips

- Any object sitting in the bleed area will print. This allows you to use the bleed area to create fold marks, or to note special instructions. These marks or instructions will print on your finished artwork but will not be inside the live area of your artwork (**Figure 15**).

- You do not have to use the bleed area to hold the crop marks or registration marks that your print shop may ask you for. FreeHand's print options let you create those automatically *(see page 255)*.

- One of the most common errors people make is to set a bleed area for an 8½-by-11-inch document and then try to print that page on a letter-size piece of paper. You need a paper size bigger than 8½-by-11 inches to print into the bleed area.

Chapter 3

Now that you've created your pages in the correct size, you will want to save your work. This is not too different from the usual way of saving on the Macintosh. You do have a choice, however, between saving your work as a FreeHand document or as a FreeHand template.

Saving as a FreeHand document means that each time you open the document, you will be working on that document. Saving as a FreeHand template means that whenever you open the document, you will actually be working on an untitled copy of the original document. This protects your document from inadvertent changes.

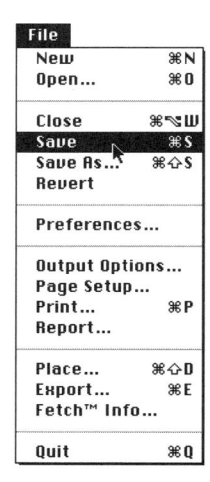

Figure 16. Choose **Save** from the **File** menu to save your work.

To save your document:

1. Choose Save from the File menu or type Command-S (**Figure 16**). The Save dialog box appears (**Figure 17**).

2. If you are just working on ordinary artwork, save your file as a FreeHand document.

or

If you want to protect your document from inadvertent changes, save your file as a FreeHand template.

Tips

■ You can tell the difference between a FreeHand document and a FreeHand template by looking at their icons. FreeHand documents have no "page corner" in their icon. FreeHand templates do have a lower-right-hand page corner in their icon (**Figure 18**).

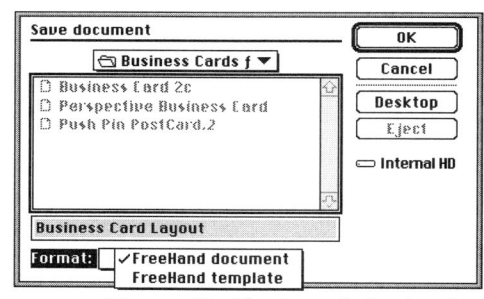

Figure 17. The **Save** dialog box lets you choose between a FreeHand document and a FreeHand template.

Figure 18. The difference between the FreeHand **document** and the FreeHand **template** icons.

Startup

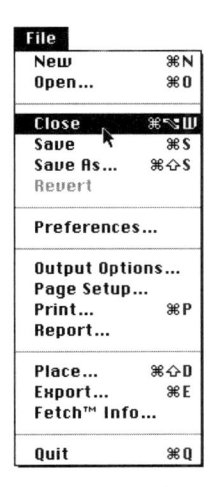

Figure 19. *To close a document, you can choose **Close** from the **File** menu or type **Command-Option-W**.*

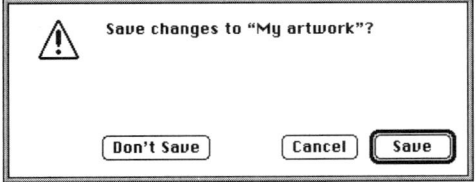

Figure 20. *The **Save Changes** dialog box alerts you that you are trying to close a document that has unsaved work in it.*

- If you want to make changes to a template, open it and make the changes. Save your document with the same name as the original template. When the Macintosh asks if you would like to replace the old template, click on the Replace button.
- FreeHand uses the term template like most applications and the Macintosh finder. This means a template in FreeHand is *not* a layer that lets you trace over a drawing. That is done by the use of the nonprinting layer *(see page 54).*

To close a document:

Once you have saved your work, you can close your document by choosing Close from the File menu or by typing Command-Option-W (**Figure 19**).

Tip

- If you try to close a document that has unsaved work on it, you will see a dialog box asking you if you want to save changes to the document (**Figure 20**). If you click on the Save button, your changes will be saved and the document will be closed. If you click on the Don't Save button, any changes since your last save will be discarded and the document will be closed. If you click on the Cancel button, your command to close the document will be canceled and you can continue working on the document.

29

Chapter 3

To revert to last saved version:

Choose Revert from the File menu (**Figure 21**). You will see a dialog box asking you if you want to revert the changes to your document. Clicking on the Revert button will restore you to the last version you saved (**Figure 22**).

Tip

- You can also close the document without saving changes and then reopen it.

To quit FreeHand:

When you are finished working in FreeHand, you can quit the application by choosing Quit from the File menu or typing Command-Q. If you have more than one document open with unsaved work, you will see a dialog box telling you that there are documents with unsaved work and asking if you would like to review them (**Figure 23**). If you click the Review button, you will then be shown each document along with the Save Changes dialog box. If you click on the Quit Anyway button, all documents will be closed and unsaved work will be lost. If you click on the Cancel button, you will cancel your command to quit FreeHand.

Tip

- By changing the Preferences settings, you can turn the Review feature on or off (*see page 275*).

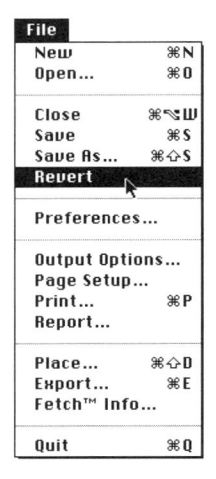

Figure 21. *If you would like to go back to the last saved version of your document, choose **Revert** from the **File** menu.*

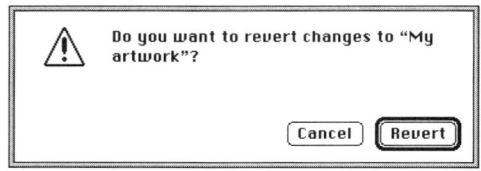

Figure 22. *Choosing **Revert** from the **File** menu brings you to the **Revert Changes** dialog box. This allows you to restore your work to the last version you saved.*

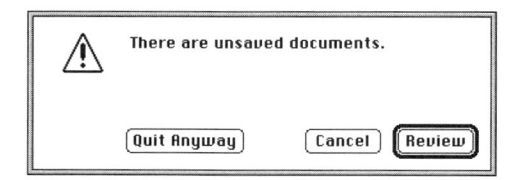

Figure 23. ***Quitting** FreeHand when you have unsaved work presents you with the **Review** dialog box. Click on the **Review** button to review each of the documents and save changes. Click on the **Quit Anyway** button to quit and discard the unsaved work. Click on the **Cancel** button to cancel the command to quit FreeHand.*

DISPLAY 4

There are many different features that affect what you see on the screen and how you work. In this chapter you will learn about the features found in the View menu: the Preview and Keyline modes; the document window rulers; guides; grids; the "snap to" settings; the Magnification menus; and the Hide Palettes feature. You will also learn about the Magnifying tool and the "zip" feature.

Once you have a document open, there are two different ways that your artwork can be displayed. The first is the Preview mode. In the Preview mode you will see a very close likeness of your final artwork, including fills, strokes, colors, patterns, placed art, etc. The second is the Keyline mode. In the Keyline mode all you see is the outline that defines the path; you do not see any fills, strokes, colors, patterns, placed art, etc. (**Figures 1a–b**)

Preview and Keyline Modes

Figure 1a. *When you view artwork in the **Preview** mode, you see the fills, strokes, and other elements that will print.*

Figure 1b. *When you view artwork in the **Keyline** mode, all you see are the outline paths that define the shape of the objects. You do not see the actual fills, strokes, and other elements that will print.*

Chapter 4

To view your artwork in the Preview mode:

Choose Preview from the View menu (**Figure 2**). If Preview is checked, you're already in the Preview mode.

or

Press on the pop-up menu at the bottom left of your document window. Choose Preview from the choices (**Figure 3**). If Preview is in the field or is checked, you're already in the Preview mode.

Sometimes you may find it necessary to view your artwork in the Keyline mode. This may be so that you can see an object that is sitting behind another.

To view your artwork in the Keyline mode:

If Preview is checked in the View menu, choose it. This switches you out of Preview and into Keyline.

or

Press on the pop-up menu at the bottom left of your document window. Choose Keyline. If Keyline is in the field or is checked, you're already in the Keyline mode.

Tips

- Pressing Command-K will toggle you in and out of the Preview and Keyline modes.

- You will find that the time it takes your screen to redraw is much less when you're working in the Keyline mode. This is especially true if you have artwork with complicated fills such as gradients or artwork that has been made into blends *(see Chapter 11, "Fills," and Chapter 13, "Blends")*.

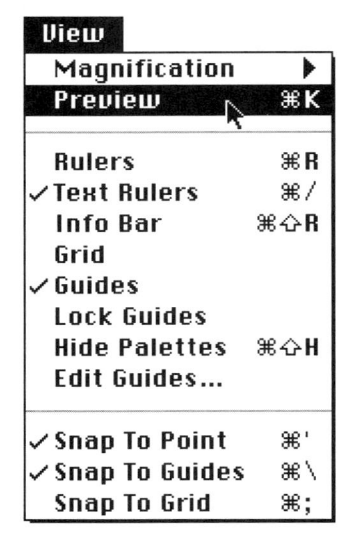

Figure 2. *Choosing* **Preview** *from the* **File** *menu will switch you to the Preview mode. If Preview is already checked, then choosing it will switch you to the Keyline mode.*

Figure 3. *Choosing* **Preview** *from the pop-up menu at the bottom left corner of the document window will switch you to the Preview mode. Choosing* **Keyline** *from the pop-up menu will switch you to the Keyline mode.*

Display

Once you're working on your document, you may find that you need some help making your work more precise. FreeHand offers you several different features to help you work more precisely. The first is the document window rulers. These are two rulers that extend along the top and left sides of your document window (**Figure 4**).

To open the document window rulers:

Unless you have already changed your FreeHand settings, your document probably does not show the document window rulers. To make the rulers visible, choose Rulers from the View menu (**Figure 5**). If Rulers is already checked, the rulers are visible. If you choose Rulers when it is checked, you will turn off the document window rulers.

Tip

- Pressing Command-R will toggle you in and out of viewing your document window rulers.

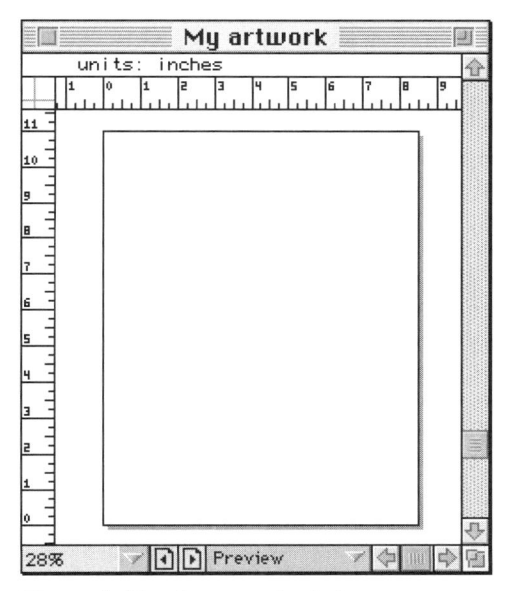

Figure 4. The **document window rulers** run down the left and top sides of the document window.

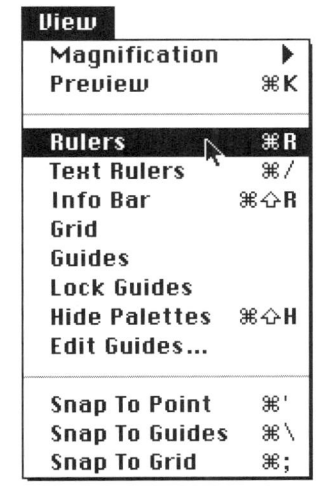

Figure 5. To see the document window rulers, choose **Rulers** from the **View** menu.

Chapter 4

Once you have the rulers visible, you can use them to create guides at specific places on your document.

To create Guides:

1. Check in the View menu to make sure that Guides is checked. If Guides is not checked, then choose it. This will allow you to see the guides that you are creating (**Figure 6**).

2. Move your arrow so that it touches either the top (horizontal) ruler or the left (vertical) ruler.

3. For a horizontal guide, press and drag the arrow down onto the page (**Figures 7a–b**). For a vertical guide, press and drag the arrow to the right onto the page.

4. Let go. If you are in the Preview mode, you will see a colored line on your page. If you are in the Keyline mode, you will see a dotted line on your page (**Figures 8a–b**).

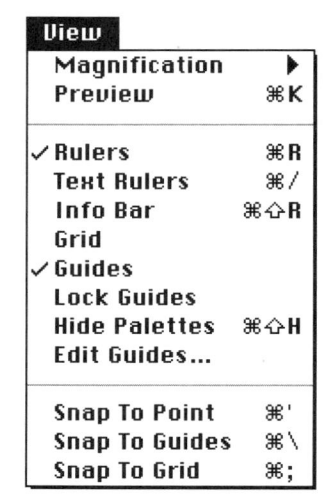

Figure 6. *In order to see the guides you create, make sure that **Guides** is checked in the **View** menu.*

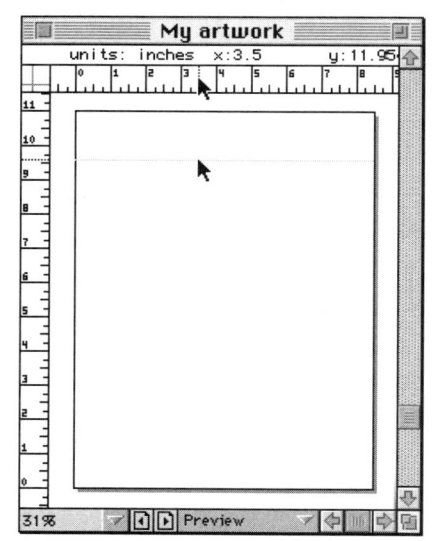

Figure 7a. *To drag a horizontal **Guide** from the **Rulers**, place your arrow on the top ruler and drag down onto the page.*

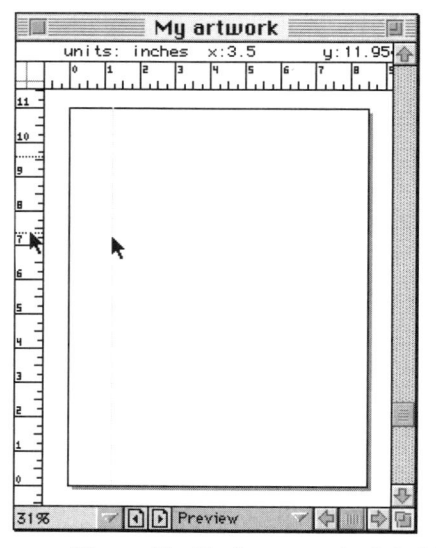

Figure 7b. *To drag a vertical **Guide** from the **Rulers**, place your arrow on the left ruler and drag to the right.*

34

Display

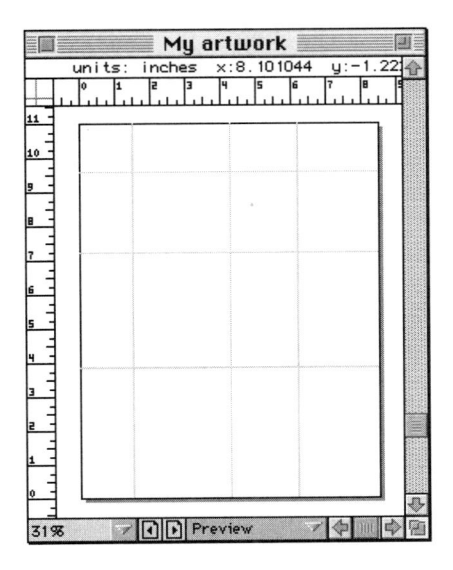

Figure 8a. ***Guides*** *in the* ***Preview*** *mode appear as colored lines.*

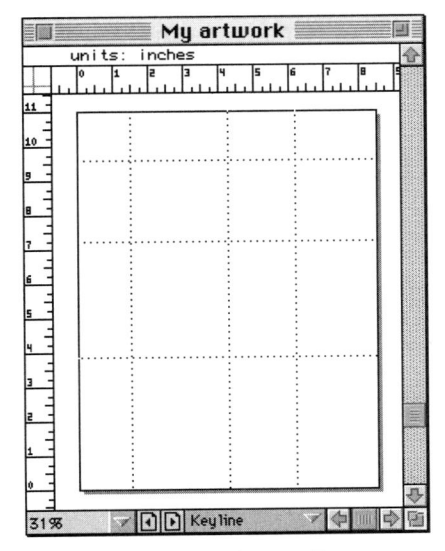

Figure 8b. ***Guides*** *in the* ***Keyline*** *mode appear as dotted lines.*

Tips

- If you are dragging a horizontal guide down from the top ruler, look at the vertical ruler on the left. There is a little line that will show you the measurement point where your guide will be if you let go.
- If you are dragging a vertical guide from the left ruler, look at the horizontal ruler at the top of the window. A line will show the measurement point where your guide will be if you let go.
- To move guides you have already positioned on the page, use the Selection tool from the toolbox. Press on the guide and drag it into position.
- To get rid of a guide you don't want, use the Selection tool to drag the guide back into the ruler it came from. If you want to delete many guides at once, see the section on the Edit Guides commands later in this chapter.
- You must drag your arrow from the ruler onto the page, not the pasteboard. If you drag onto the pasteboard, you will not create a guide.

Create Guides

35

Chapter 4

Sometimes you may find that you need to fill the page with many guides at exact intervals or you need to position guides more precisely. While you could create or modify each guide one at a time, it is easier to use the Edit Guides commands.

To delete guides:

1. Choose Edit Guides from the View menu (**Figure 9**). You will see the Guides dialog box that lists the type of guides you have and their position on the page (**Figure 10**).
2. To delete a guide, click on the name of the guide in the dialog box. You should see the guide highlighted.
3. Click on the Delete key. This deletes the guide from the list. If you need to delete other guides, click on their names and then click the Delete key.
4. When you have finished deleting your guides, press the OK button.

Tips

- If you need to delete many guides at once, click on the the name of the first guide you want deleted. Hold the Shift key down and then click on the name of the last guide you want deleted. The first and last guides and all the guides in between will now be selected. You can then press the Delete key and all the selected guides will be deleted.

- The Release button in the Guides dialog box will release the path from being a guide and turn it into a regular path *(see Chapter 7, "Points and Paths")* that can be filled *(see Chapter 11, "Fills")* or stroked *(see Chapter 12, "Strokes")*.

Figure 9. *To adjust many guides at one time, choose **Edit Guides** from the **View** menu.*

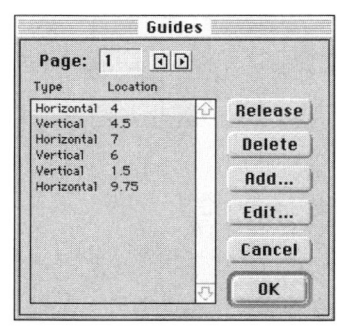

Figure 10. *The **Guides** dialog box gives you a list of all the guides on each page and their position.*

Display

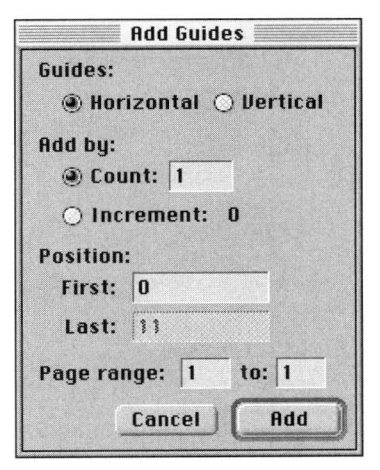

Figure 11. *The **Add Guides** dialog box allows you to create many guides at regular intervals down or across your work pages.*

To add guides numerically:

1. Choose Edit Guides from the View menu. Click on the Add button. This opens the Add Guides dialog box (**Figure 11**).

2. Choose either Horizontal or Vertical. (To make both horizontal and vertical guides, you need to make one type first and then the other.)

3. If you want a specific number of guides, click the Count button. Type the number you want.

4. If you want a specific distance between each guide, click the Increment button. Type the distance you want between the guides.

5. Press the Add button. This will bring you back to the Edit Guides dialog box. If you want another set of guides in the other direction, click the Add button, and create the second set.

6. When you are finished, click the OK button in the Guides dialog box. Your page will be filled with the guides you added.

Tips

- If you want to create guides at regular intervals down or across your work pages, the First field under Position lets you specify from which point on the page you want your guides to start. The Last field lets you specify at which point on the page you want your guides to stop.

- If you are working with a multiple page document, set the page range for the pages you want to have guides.

- You can switch which page you are adding guides to by entering the page number at the top of the Guides dialog box or clicking the little page icons to move from one page to another.

Add Guides

37

Chapter 4

You may want to make sure your guides don't get moved inadvertently. To do so, you will need to lock them into position.

To lock guides:
From the View menu, choose Lock Guides (**Figure 12**). If you choose Lock Guides when it is checked, you will then unlock your guides. You can also lock guides using the Layers palette *(see page 56)*.

Tips
- If you want the guides in front of the artwork, you will need to change the order of the Guides layer *(see page 52)*.
- If you want to turn any path into guides, you will need to place the path on the Guides layer *(see page 53)*.

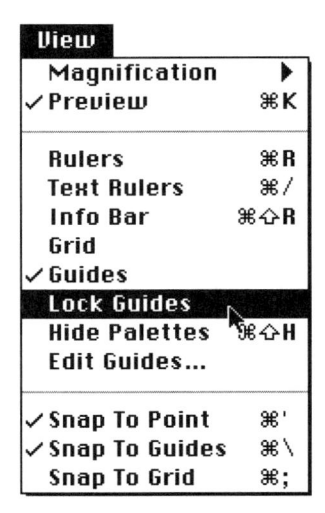

Figure 12. *Choosing* **Lock Guides** *from the* **View** *menu locks the guides so that they cannot be moved.*

You may want all your objects to automatically align themselves or "snap to" the guide lines that you have created.

To turn on the Snap To Guides:
Choose Snap To Guides from the View menu (**Figure 13**). If it is checked, the Snap To Guides feature is already turned on. If you choose Snap To Guides when it is already checked, then you will be turning off the Snap To Guides feature. When the Snap To Guides is turned on, any objects coming close to any guide will automatically jump or snap to that guide.

Tip
- By using the Preferences settings, you can change how close the object has to come to the guide before it will "snap to" *(see page 266)*.

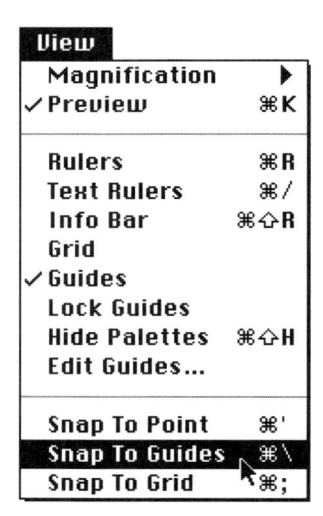

Figure 13. *Choosing* **Snap To Guides** *from the* **View** *menu will cause any object to jump to the guides when that object is moved or created.*

Display

Another feature that helps you work precisely is the document grid. First, it is a visible grid of nonprinting dots spaced at regular intervals. Second, it is an invisible grid of lines that connect the visible dots. You can have objects, points, and text "snap to" the invisible grid (**Figure 14**).

To view the document grid:

Choose Grid from the View menu (**Figure 15**). If Grid is checked then it is already visible. If you choose Grid when it is checked, you will turn off the grid.

To change the document grid intervals:

1. Click on the Document icon of the Document Inspector.
2. Click on the Document Setup icon of the Document Inspector.
3. In the Grid size field, type the distance you want between sections of your grid (**Figure 16**).
4. Press Return.

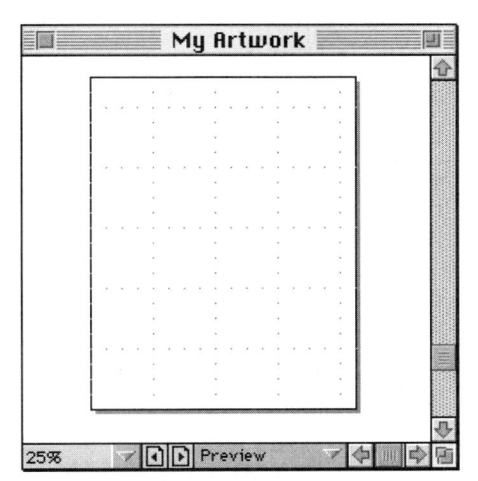

Figure 14. *The **visible grid** consists of dots evenly spaced into squares along your page. The **invisible grid** connects those dots.*

Figure 15. *Choosing **Grid** from the **View** menu allows you to see the visible part of the document grid.*

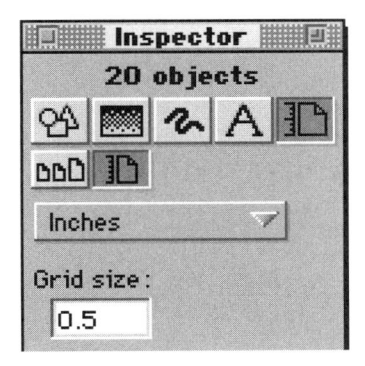

Figure 16. *The Grid interval size is entered by going to the **Grid size** field of the **Document Inspector** palette.*

Chapter 4

To Turn on the Snap To Grid feature:

Choose Snap To Grid from the View menu (**Figure 17**). If Snap To Grid is checked, the Snap To Grid feature is already turned on. If you choose Snap To Grid when it is already checked, you will turn off the Snap To Grid feature.

Tips

- If you turn on the Snap To Grid in the middle of working, all previously drawn objects will remain where they were positioned. Only those objects that are newly drawn, moved, or resized will then snap to the grid.

- If you have the Snap To Grid feature turned on, you may find it impossible to draw certain objects. For instance, if your grid is set in .5″ intervals, and the Snap To Grid feature is turned on, you will not be able to draw a rectangle that measures 2.25″ wide. The Snap To Grid feature will force your rectangle to be 2″ or 2.5″ (**Figure 18**).

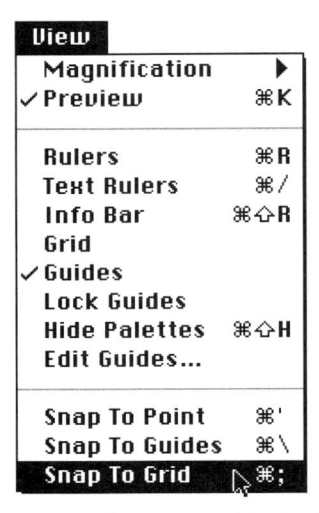

Figure 17. *Choose **Snap To Grid** from the **View** menu to turn on the Snap To Grid feature.*

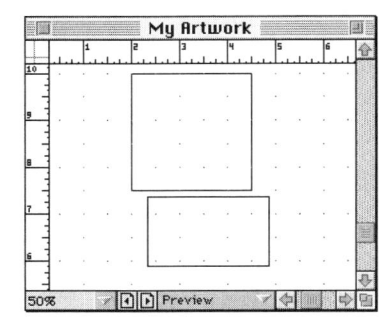

Figure 18. *When the **Snap To Grid** is turned on, you cannot draw objects with dimensions that are in between the grid intervals. The top rectangle was drawn with the Snap To Grid turned on. Its sides fall on the grid intervals. The bottom rectangle was drawn with the Snap To Grid turned off. Its sides fall between the intervals.*

Display

Figure 19. *To turn on the Snap To Point feature, choose **Snap To Point** from the **View** menu.*

In addition to snapping to guides and the grid, FreeHand lets you snap to points. This lets you move one object so that it aligns precisely on the point of another object.

To turn on Snap To Point:

Choose Snap To Point from the View menu (**Figure 19**). If Snap To Point is checked, the Snap To Point feature is already turned on. If you choose Snap To Point when it is checked, you will turn off the Snap To Point feature.

Tip

- You may find that you would like a signal when your object has actually snapped to a grid, a guide, or a point. FreeHand offers a series of audible "snap to" sounds that will play when the object snaps. These sounds are set in the Preferences settings *(see page 273).*

Chapter 4

When you work on your document, you may find that you need to zoom in for a closer look at your artwork. Or you may need to zoom out so that you can see more of the whole page at once. FreeHand lets you zoom in to magnify your artwork up to 25,600% of its actual size or you can zoom out to view your artwork at 6% of its actual size. There are several different ways to zoom in and out of your document.

To zoom in or out using the Magnifying tool:

1. Click on the Magnifying tool in the toolbox.

2. Click the Magnifying tool on the object that you wish to zoom in on. Keep clicking as many times as necessary to zoom in.

or

Drag the Magnifying tool around the area that you wish to zoom in on. When you let go of your mouse you will zoom in to the magnification necessary to see the area you dragged a marquee around in the document window (**Figures 20a–b**).

Tip

■ Holding the Command-Spacebar keys gives you the Magnifying tool without leaving the current tool in the toolbox.

■ Hold the Option key while you are in the Magnifying tool. This turns the icon from a plus sign (+) to a minus sign (-). When you click with the minus sign Magnifying tool, you will zoom out (**Figure 21**).

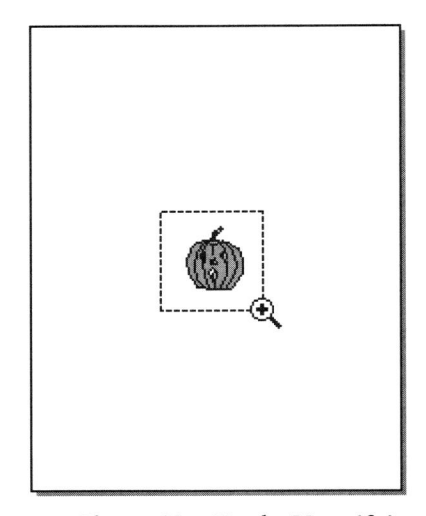

Figure 20a. *Use the **Magnifying** tool to zoom in on a specific object by **dragging a marquee** around the specific object you want to see. The dashed line shows the area being marqueed.*

Figure 20b. *After dragging, the area that's been marqueed fills up the entire window.*

Figure 21. *Holding the **Option** key while you are in the Magnifying tool will let you zoom out from an object.*

Display

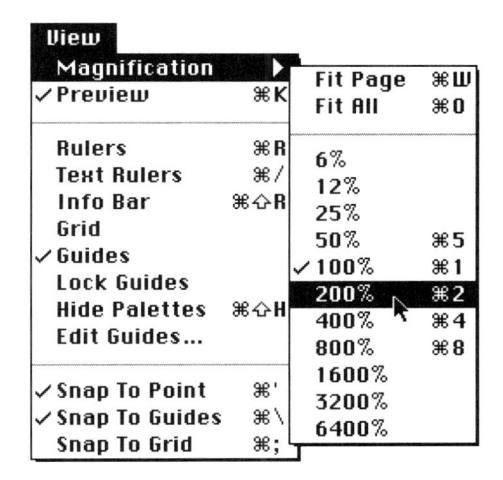

Figure 22a. *Choosing the **Magnification** submenu of the **View** menu allows you to choose one of 11 preset magnifications.*

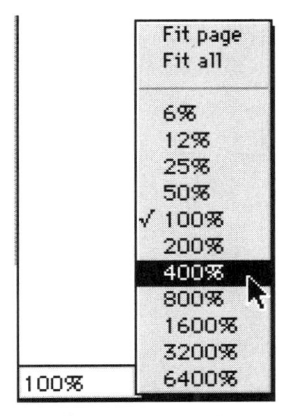

Figure 22b. *The **Magnification** pop-up menu allows you to choose one of 11 preset magnifications.*

Figure 23. *Double-clicking or dragging across the number in the **Magnification** pop-up menu allows you to enter an exact magnification amount.*

To zoom in or out using the Magnification submenu or pop-up menu:

1. From the View menu, choose one of the magnification amounts from the Magnification submenu (**Figure 22a**) or from the Magnification pop-up menu at the bottom of the document window (**Figure 22b**). Choosing a specific magnification will zoom you in or out to that exact magnification.

or

Type one of the following:
Command-1 for 100%
Command-2 for 200%
Command-4 for 400%
Command-8 for 800%
Command-5 for 50%

2. Choosing Fit Page (Command-W) will zoom you in or out so that the page you are working on fits completely in the document window.

3. Choosing Fit All (Command-0) will fit all document pages in the window.

Tip

■ When you choose one of the magnification settings from the Magnification submenu or the Magnification pop-up menu, FreeHand uses the center of your page as the center of the zoom.

To enter exact magnification amounts:

1. Double-click or drag across the number in the Magnification pop-up menu document window (**Figure 23**).

2. Type in the percentage at which you would like to view your page. (You do not need to type the "%" character.)

3. Press the Return or Enter key.

Magnification Menus

43

Chapter 4

Unless you have a large monitor, you may find that all the palettes get in the way. FreeHand lets you hide palettes.

To hide all the palettes:

1. Choose Hide Palettes from the View menu or press Command-Shift-H or the F12 key (**Figure 24**). If Hide Palettes is checked, the feature is already turned on. If you choose Hide Palettes when it is checked, then you will make the palettes reappear.

Tips

- The toolbox will not be hidden using Hide Palettes. To hide it, press Command-7.

- When palettes are hidden, a diamond will appear next to their names in the Window menu (**Figure 25**). Choosing any one of the palettes, hidden or not, will result in showing all the palettes.

In addition to hiding palettes, FreeHand lets you "zip" or close up the palettes.

To use the zip feature:

1. Click on the zip box in the upper-left-hand corner of the palette (**Figure 26a**). This will collapse the palette.

2. Click again on the zip box (**Figure 26b**). This will expand the palette.

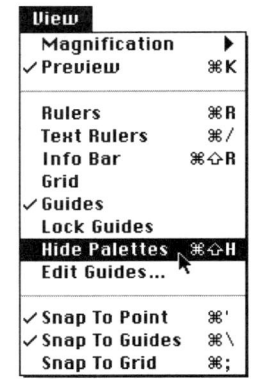

Figure 24. *Choosing* **Hide Palettes** *from the* **View** *menu allows you to hide any palettes that might be in the way of viewing your artwork.*

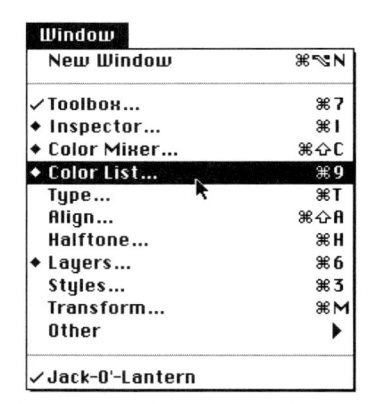

Figure 25. *When* **Hide Palettes** *has been chosen, a diamond will appear next to all the hidden palettes in the* **Window** *menu.*

Figure 26b. *Clicking on the* **zip box** *of a collapsed palette will expand that palette.*

Figure 26a. *Clicking on the* **zip box** *will collapse a palette.*

LAYERS 5

As soon as you put more than one path on your page, you've already started working in layers. Since you can easily generate hundreds of paths in your document, you will very quickly need to manage the layers and the layering of your objects. In this chapter you will learn: the difference between the layering of objects and the layers in the Layers palette; how to move objects within their own layer and between layers; how to create, rename, remove, reorder, display, and lock layers; and how to lock objects. You will also learn the difference between Foreground (printing) and Background (nonprinting) layers.

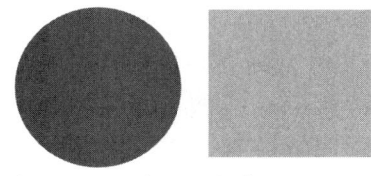

Figure 1a. *When two objects are side by side, it may not be obvious but one object is layered in front of the other.*

Every object in FreeHand sits either above or below the other objects. The order in which the objects are layered follows the order in which they were created. If you create a red circle and then a blue square, the red circle will be behind the blue square. Though you may not see this when the two objects are sitting side by side, it is immediately apparent when one object overlaps the other (**Figures 1a–b**).
Once you have objects in a certain order, you can move them to different positions on the layer.

Figure 1b. *When two objects overlap, it is obvious which object is in front of the other.*

45

Chapter 5

To move objects to the front or back of a layer:

1. Click on an object in your artwork.

2. If you want the object to be moved to the very front of its layer, choose Bring To Front (Command-F) from the Arrange menu (**Figure 2**). Any objects in that layer that were in front of the object will now be behind the object (**Figures 3a–b**).

3. If you want the object to be moved to the very back of its layer, choose Send To Back (Command-B) from the Arrange menu (**Figure 4**).

Figure 2. *To move an object to the front of its layers, choose **Bring To Front** from the **Arrange** menu.*

Figure 3a. *The circle in this illustration was selected to be moved to the front.*

Figure 3b. *The same illustration after the circle was moved using the **Bring To Front** command.*

Figure 4. *To move an object to the back of its layer, choose **Send To Back** from the **Arrange** menu.*

Layers

Figure 5. *To move an object in front of the first object it was behind, choose **Bring Forward** from the **Arrange** menu.*

Figure 6a. *In this illustration, the circle needs to be put in front of the triangle and square but behind the oval and the rectangle.*

Figure 6b. *The same illustration after the **Bring Forward** command was applied twice to the circle.*

Sometimes you may want to move an object somewhere in the middle of a layer. To do this, you need to use a different set of commands.

To move objects within a layer:

1. Click on an object in your artwork.
2. If you want the object to be moved forward within its layer, choose Bring Forward (Command-[) from the Arrange menu (**Figure 5**). This will move the object in front of the first object it was behind.
3. If you want the object to be moved farther up, choose Bring Forward (Command-[) again. Repeat until the object is where you want it to be (**Figures 6a–b**).
4. If you want the object to be moved backward within its layer, choose Send Backward (Command-]) from the Arrange menu.
5. If you want the object to be moved farther back, choose Send Backward (Command-]) again. Repeat until the object is where you want it to be.

Chapter 5

If you have an object that needs to be moved behind or in front of many other objects, it may not be feasible to choose Send Backward or Bring Forward over and over. FreeHand offers you another way to move an object within its layer.

To move objects using Paste Behind:

1. Choose an object that you would like to move behind another object (**Figure 7a**).

2. Choose Cut from the Edit menu (**Figure 7b**).

3. Click on the object that you would like to be in front of the original object (**Figure 7c**).

4. Choose Paste Behind from the Edit menu. Your original object will be layered behind the object you chose (**Figure 7d**).

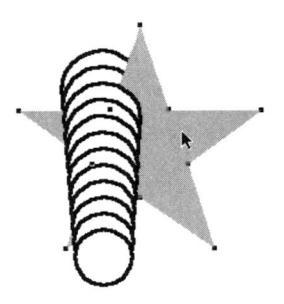

Figure 7a. *To move an object using* **Paste Behind***, start by selecting the object you want to move. In this illustration, the star has been selected.*

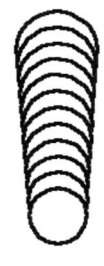

Figure 7b. *Choose* **Cut (Command-X)** *from the* **Edit** *menu. In this illustration, the star has been cut.*

Figure 7c. *Select the object you want the original object to be behind. In this illustration, a circle farther up the row has been selected.*

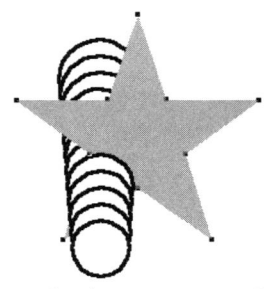

Figure 7d. *Choose* **Paste Behind** *from the* **Edit** *menu. In this illustration, the star has been moved up within its layer.*

48

Layers

Figure 8. To work with the Layers palette, choose **Layers** from the **Window** menu.

Tips

- If you choose Bring To Front or Send To Back on the single object of a group *(see Chapter 7, "Points and Paths," for working with groups)* the object will be moved to the front of or back of the group.

- Locked objects cannot be moved within their layer.

- Other objects can, however, be sent to the front or back of locked objects or moved forward or backward of locked objects.

Since FreeHand documents can easily contain hundreds, if not thousands, of objects, you may find that moving objects within their layers is not enough. In that case, you will need to use FreeHand's Layers palette.

To view the Layers Palette:

1. If you do not see the Layers palette on your screen, choose Layers from the Window menu (**Figure 8**).

2. If you have not changed the default layers for your document, you should see three layers: Foreground, Guides, and Background (**Figure 9**).

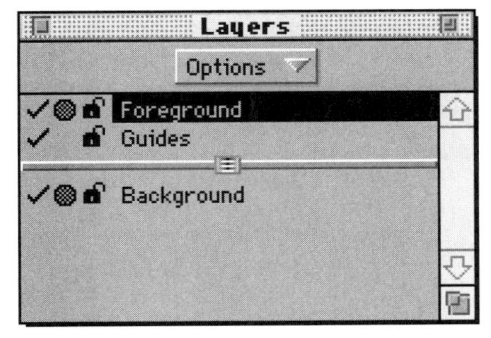

Figure 9. The Layers palette with the three **default layers: Foreground**, **Guides**, and **Background**.

49

Chapter 5

Once you have created a layer, you may want to rename it so that it reflects the items on that layer. For instance, if you have an illustration of a farm scene, you may want to put the barn on a layer named "barn," the sky on a layer named "sky," and so on.

To rename a layer:

1. In the Layers palette, double-click on the name of the layer you wish to rename (**Figure 10**).

2. Type the new name of the layer.

3. Press Return or Enter, or click with the mouse anywhere on the Layers palette.

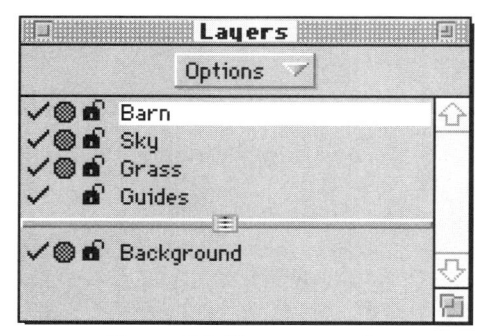

Figure 10. *To rename a layer, double-click on the name to highlight it.*

You may find that you would like to duplicate a layer, including all the objects on that layer. To do so, you can use the Options pop-up menu of the Layers palette.

To duplicate a layer:

1. Click on the name of the layer that you want to duplicate.

2. Press on the Options pop-up menu in the Layers palette.

3. Choose Duplicate (**Figure 11**). The layer and the objects on it will be duplicated.

Tip

- The Guides layer cannot be renamed or duplicated.

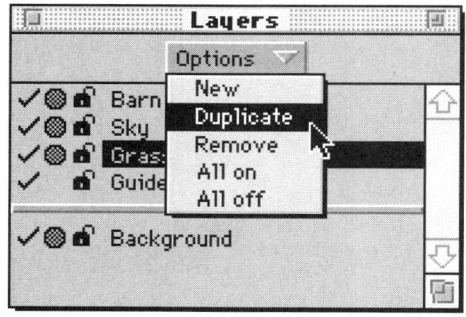

Figure 11. *The **Options** pop-up menu lets you **Duplicate** a layer and the objects on that layer.*

Layers

To remove a Layer:

1. Click on the name of the layer that you wish to remove.

2. Press on the Options pop-up menu. Choose Remove (**Figure 12**). The layer and the objects on it will be removed.

Tips

- You cannot delete the very last drawing layer of a document.
- You cannot remove the Guides layer.
- If you try to remove a layer that has an object on it, you will see an alert box stating "Layer 'X' contains data. Remove it anyway?" If you click OK, the layer and any objects on it will be removed (**Figure 13**).

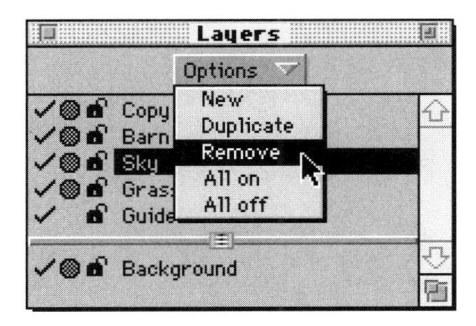

Figure 12. *The **Options** pop-up menu of the Layers palette allows you to **Remove** a layer and its contents.*

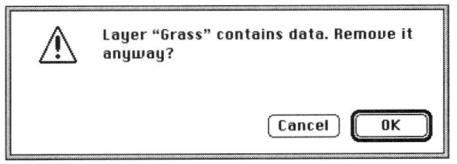

Figure 13. *The alert box lets you know that the layer you are trying to remove has objects or paths on it. This gives you an opportunity to **Cancel** the request to remove the layer.*

Chapter 5

If a layer's name appears under another layer, then the objects on that layer will appear behind the objects on the other layer. But layers do not have to remain in the order in which you created them; you can reorder them.

To reorder layers:

1. Press on the name of the layer that you want to reorder.

2. Drag the name of the layer to the spot where you would like it to be.

3. Let go. The name of the layer will disappear from where it was and reappear in its new position in the Layers palette (**Figure 14**). All objects on the layer will now be repositioned in the document (**Figures 15a–b**).

Tip

- If you want your guides to appear in front of your artwork, drag the Guides layer above the layer that contains the artwork.

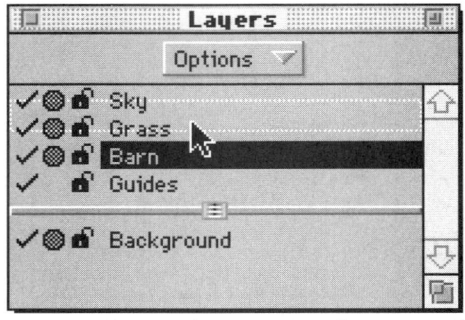

Figure 14. *Dragging the name of a layer from one position to another will change the order in which the layers appear in the Layers palette.*

Figure 15a. *Changing the order of a layer will change how objects are displayed. In this illustration, the objects for the grass need to be positioned behind the barn and the sky.*

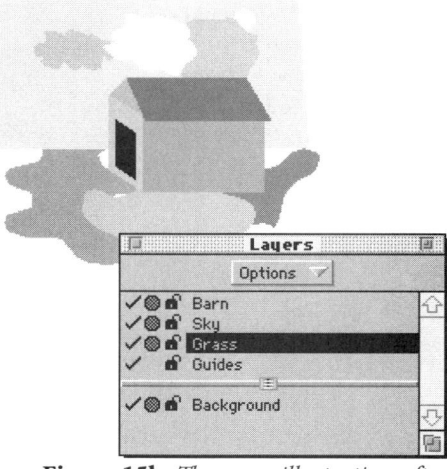

Figure 15b. *The same illustration after dragging the grass layer below the sky layer.*

Layers

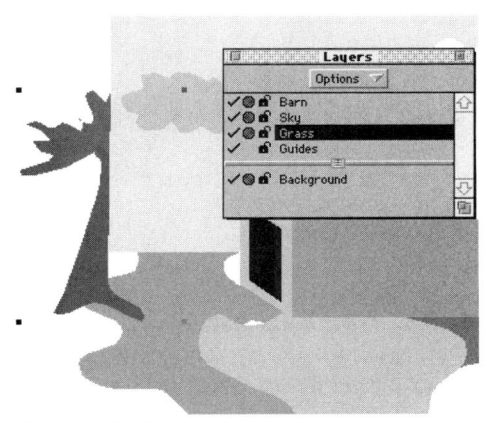

Figure 16a. *In this illustration, the tree needs to be moved from the grass layer. The tree has been selected.*

When you are working, the objects that you create will be placed on whichever layer is the active or highlighted layer. You may want to move artwork from one layer to another.

To move objects between layers:

1. Select the artwork that you would like to move (**Figure 16a**).

2. Click on the name of the layer that you want to move the artwork onto. The artwork will now be located on a new layer (**Figure 16b**).

Tip

- You cannot move artwork onto a locked layer.

Figure 16b. *The same illustration after clicking on the name of the sky layer. The tree has been moved from the grass layer to the sky layer.*

53

Chapter 5

There is a horizontal line that divides the Layers palette into two areas, top and bottom. Objects on layers above the line will appear normal and will print. Objects on layers below the line will appear dimmed and will not print (**Figure 17**). If you have done nothing to change the default settings, you will have one layer called "Background" below the line. As you work, you may find that you want to move layers between the two areas of the Layers palette.

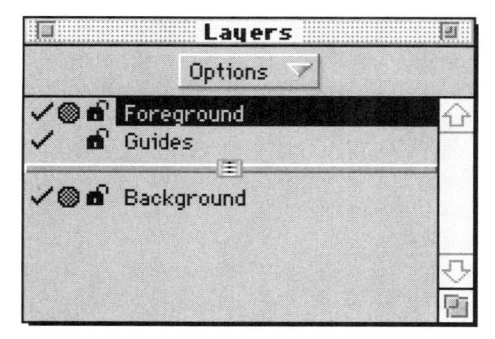

Figure 17. *The default settings of the Layers palette. The **horizontal line** divides the layers into **printing** and **nonprinting** layers.*

To make a layer nonprinting layer:

1. Press on the name of the layer that you wish to make nonprinting (**Figure 18a**).

2. Drag the name of the layer below the dividing line in the Layers palette.

3. Release the mouse. The layer will now be positioned below the line and any objects on the layer will be dimmed and will not print (**Figure 18b**).

To make a layer a printing layer:

1. Press on the name of the layer that you wish to make a printing layer.

2. Drag the name of the layer above the dividing line in the Layers palette.

3. Release the mouse. The layer will now be positioned above the dividing line and any objects on the layer will print.

Tips

- Objects on the Guides layer will not print regardless of where the Guides layer is, either above or below the line.

- Use nonprinting layers to hold images that have been placed for tracing *(see page 73)*.

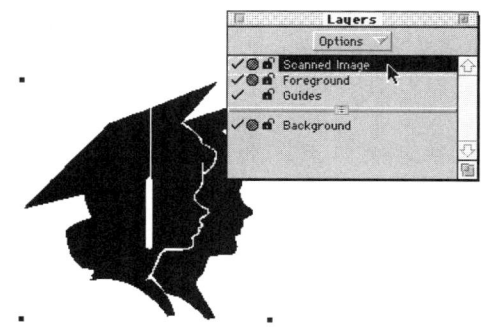

Figure 18a. *To make a layer nonprinting, drag the name of the layer below the horizontal line.*

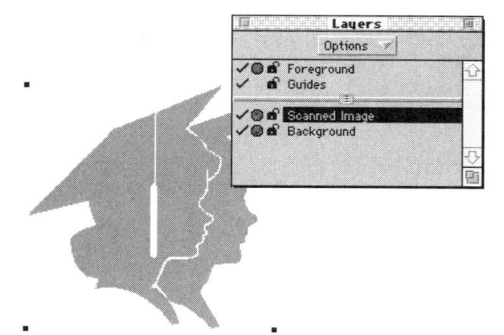

Figure 18b. *The results of dragging the name of the layer below the line.*

Layers

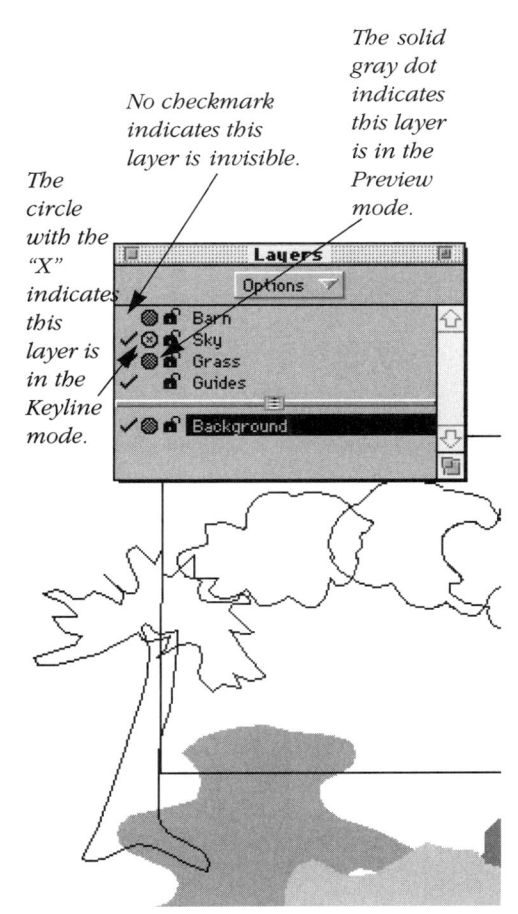

The circle with the "X" indicates this layer is in the Keyline mode.

No checkmark indicates this layer is invisible.

The solid gray dot indicates this layer is in the Preview mode.

Figure 19. *The different ways layers can be set for **display** in the **Layers** palette.*

You can also use the Layers palette to change how the objects on each layer are seen (**Figure 19**).

To change the display of a layer:

1. If there is a checkmark to the left of the layer name, click on the checkmark. This will delete the checkmark and make all the objects on the layer invisible.

2. If there is no checkmark to the left of the layer name, click on the blank space. This will bring back the checkmark and make all the objects on the layer visible.

3. If there is a solid gray dot to the left of the layer name, click on the dot. This will change the dot into a circle with an "X" in it and make any objects on the layer visible in the Keyline mode.

4. If there is a circle with an "X" to the left of the layer name, click on the circle. This will change the circle into a gray dot and make any objects on the layer visible in the Preview mode.

(See pages 31–32 for more information about the difference between the Keyline and Preview modes.)

Tips

- If you have a layer that is invisible, any objects on that layer will still print. Check to make sure no layers are holding invisible objects before you send the file to be printed.

- If you hold the Option key as you click on the gray dot for any layer, you will make all the layers in your document appear in the Keyline mode.

Display Layers

Chapter 5

There may be times when you want to see the objects on a layer, but you don't want to be able to select those objects. In this case, you need to lock the layer.

To lock a layer:

1. Look at the padlock to the left of the layer name. If the padlock is in the open position, it means the layer is unlocked.

2. Click on the padlock. This will cause the padlock to change to the closed position and will lock all objects on the layer (**Figure 20**).

3. If the padlock is already in the closed position, click on it. This will cause the padlock to change to the open position and will unlock all objects on the layer.

To lock an object on a layer:

1. Select the object or objects you wish to lock.

2. Choose Lock (Command-L) from the Arrange menu (**Figure 21**).

To unlock an object on a layer:

1. Select the object or objects you wish to unlock.

2. Choose Unlock (Command-Shift-L) from the Arrange menu.

Tips

- Locked objects can be selected and their fills and strokes can be changed, but locked objects cannot be deleted.

- Locked objects cannot be moved, resized, or transformed.

- Locked text objects can have their text attributes changed or the text edited.

- Locked objects can be copied but they cannot be cut.

The closed padlock indicates this is a locked layer.

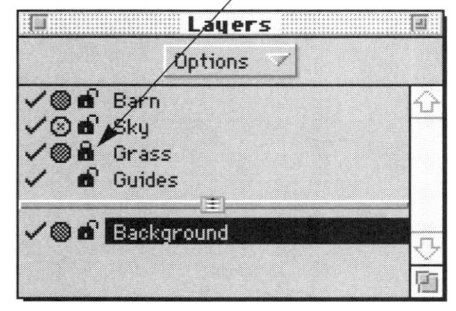

Figure 20. *Clicking on the **padlock** will turn it to the **locked** or **closed** position. This will lock all objects on the layer, preventing them from being selected, resized, or transformed.*

Figure 21. *Choosing **Lock** from the **Arrange** menu will lock individual objects on a layer without locking the entire layer.*

CREATION TOOLS 6

Once you've got your document open, you will want to use FreeHand's creation tools to construct the different objects that will make up your artwork. In this chapter you will learn how to create rectangles, squares, rounded-corner rectangles, ellipses and circles, polygons, stars, and lines. You will also learn how to use the Freehand, Variable stroke, and Calligraphic pen tools. You will learn the basics of the Pen and Bézigon tools and how these two tools let you draw more precisely. (Because these two tools are not as simple to use as the other creation tools, they are covered in detail in Chapter 8.) You will also learn how to use FreeHand's Spiral and Arc tools to easily make sophisticated spirals and arcs. Finally, you will learn how to use FreeHand's Tracing tool to automatically trace scanned artwork.

One of the most basic objects to create is a rectangle. This includes regular rectangles, squares, and rounded-corner rectangles (**Figure 1**).

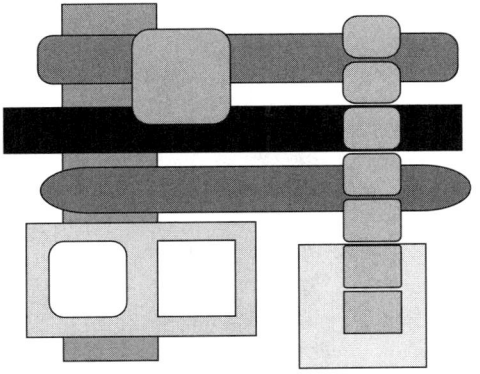

Figure 1. *The **Rectangle** tool will create rectangles, squares, and rounded-corner rectangles.*

Chapter 6

To create a rectangle:

1. With a document open, click on the Rectangle tool in the toolbox (**Figure 2**).
2. Bring your arrow over your work page area. You should see a plus sign (+) cursor (**Figure 3**).
3. Press and drag along the diagonal line that would reach across your rectangle (**Figure 4**).
4. As you drag, you will see the four sides that define your rectangle. Let go of the mouse when you are satisfied with the size of the rectangle (**Figure 5**).

Tip

- If you let go too soon, you can change the dimensions of the rectangle *(see page 92)*.

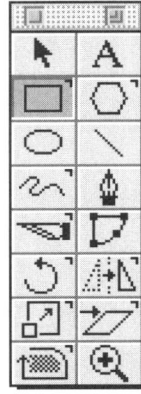

Figure 2. *When the **Rectangle** tool has been selected in the toolbox, the tool becomes shaded so that it looks recessed. (If your toolbox does not look like this, you need to change the Preferences settings for your palettes. See Chapter 22, "Preferences.")*

Figure 3. *When the **Rectangle** tool is chosen, the arrow becomes a plus sign (+) cursor.*

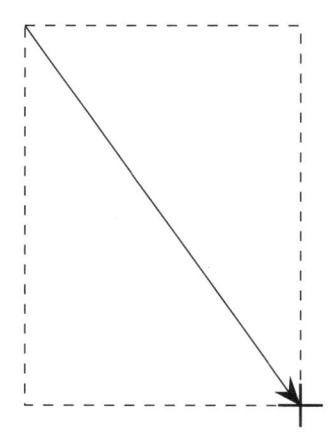

Figure 4. *When you draw a rectangle, drag down along the diagonal line that would run from the upper-left corner to the lower-right corner.*

Figure 5. *When you let go of the mouse after dragging with the rectangle tool, you will see the rectangle you have created.*

Creation Tools

Path of the drag.

Correct diagonal.

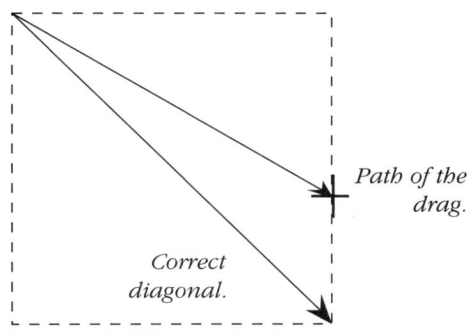

Figure 6. *Holding the **Shift** key constrains your rectangle into a square. Even if the path of your drag moves away from the correct diagonal, the object will still be a square.*

Figure 7. *When you let go of the mouse after dragging with the rectangle tool, you will see the square you have created.*

You may think of a square as different from a rectangle, but FreeHand doesn't. You use the same tool. You just add the Shift key to your procedure.

To create a square:

1. With a document open, click on the Rectangle tool in the toolbox.

2. Bring your arrow over your work page area. You should see a plus sign (+) cursor.

3. With one finger on the Shift key, use the other hand to press and drag along the diagonal line that would reach across your square. Notice that even if your hand is unsteady, your rectangle must be a square. This is because you are holding the Shift key (**Figure 6**).

4. As you drag, you will see the line that defines your square. Let go of the mouse first, then the Shift key, when you are satisfied with the size of the square. If you let go of the Shift key first, you may not draw a square (**Figure 7**).

Tip

- If you let go too soon, you can always change the dimensions of the square (*see page 92*).

Squares

Chapter 6

Another type of rectangle has curved or rounded corners. The amount of the curve depends on the Corner radius (**Figure 8**).

To set the Corner radius for a rounded-corner rectangle:

1. Double-click on the Rectangle tool in the toolbox. The Rectangle Tool dialog box will appear (**Figure 9**).

2. In the Corner radius field, type the amount you want for the rounded corner.

or

Press and drag on the triangle slider to set the number you want for the Corner radius.

3. Once you have set the Corner radius, follow the steps for drawing a rectangle or a square.

Tip

■ Once you draw an object, you can use the Object Inspector to change a rectangle's corner radius.

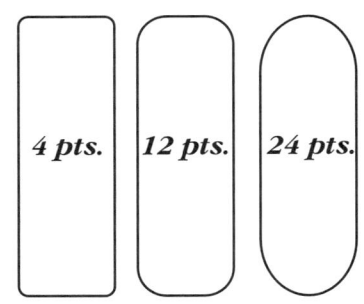

Figure 8. *Different **Corner radius** settings will result in different looks for rounded-corner rectangles.*

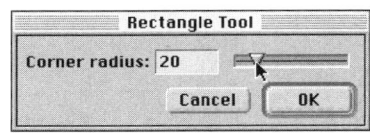

Figure 9. *Double-click on the Rectangle tool in the toolbox. The **Rectangle Tool** dialog box will appear and will let you set the amount of the Corner radius.*

You can also draw your rectangle from the center point outward.

To create a rectangle from the center point outward:

1. Choose the Rectangle tool from the toolbox.

2. Hold the Option key and press where you would like the center point of the rectangle to be positioned (**Figure 10**).

3. As you drag, you will see the line that defines your rectangle. Let go of the mouse first, then the Option key, when you are satisfied with the size.

Tip

■ If you hold both the Option and the Shift keys as you drag, you will draw a square outward from the center point.

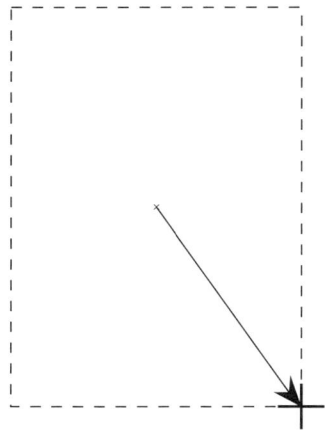

Figure 10. *Holding the **Option** key will cause your rectangle to be drawn from the center point outward.*

Creation Tools

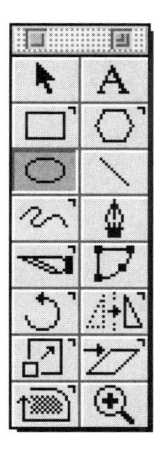

Figure 11. *The **Ellipse** tool when selected in the toolbox.*

Another type of object you can create is the ellipse or oval. Since circles are perfect ovals, the Ellipse tool will also create circles.

To create an ellipse or circle:

1. Click on the Ellipse tool in the toolbox (**Figure 11**).

2. Press and drag along the diagonal line that would reach across your ellipse.

3. If you want to make a circle, hold the Shift key as you drag.

4. As you drag, you will see the line that defines your ellipse or circle. Let go of the mouse first, then the Shift key, when you are satisfied with the size of the object (**Figure 12**).

Tip

- If you let go too soon, you can change the dimensions of the object *(see page 92)*.

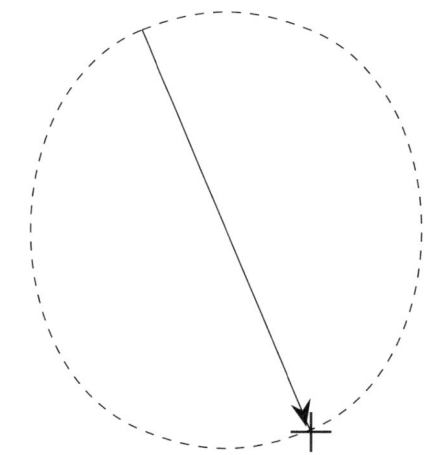

Figure 12. *When you let go of the mouse after dragging with the Ellipse tool, you will see the ellipse or circle you have created.*

Ellipses and Circles

61

Chapter 6

While ellipses and rectangles are the basic objects of drawing, you will probably want to create other objects: triangles, stars, octagons, etc. (**Figure 13**). Fortunately FreeHand has the Polygon tool.

To create a polygon:

1. Double-click on the Polygon tool in the toolbox (**Figure 14**).
2. You should now see the Polygon tool dialog box (**Figure 15**).
3. Enter the number of sides for your polygon by typing the number in the field or dragging the triangle slider.
4. Click OK or press the Return or Enter key on your keyboard. This will return you to your work page.
5. Drag with the plus sign (+) cursor. You will be drawing your polygon from the center outward.
6. As you drag, you will see the shape that defines your polygon. Drag your mouse to rotate the polygon to the position you want. Let go of the mouse when you are satisfied with the size and position of the polygon (**Figure 16**).

Tips

- If you let go too soon, you can still change the dimensions of the polygon *(see page 92)*.
- If you do not like the orientation, you can use the Rotating tool to change it *(see page 106)*.
- Hold the Shift key as you drag your polygon to constrain it to an upright position.
- Use the polygon set at 4 sides to draw rectangles that can be rotated as you draw them.

Figure 13. *Various objects that can be drawn using the **Polygon** tool.*

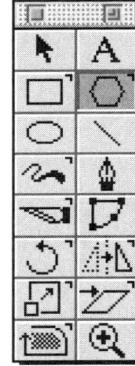

Figure 14. *Selecting the **Polygon** tool lets you draw different polygons and stars.*

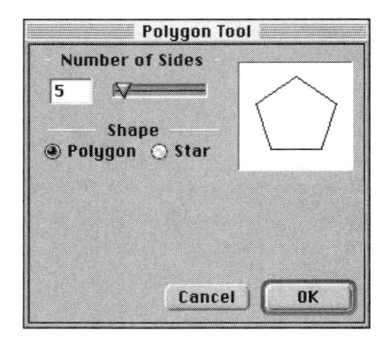

Figure 15. *Double-clicking on the **Polygon** tool opens the dialog box, where you can set the type and number of sides for your polygon or star.*

Creation Tools

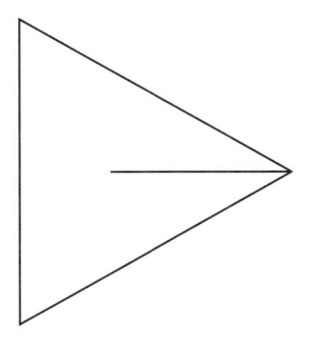

Figure 16. *A triangle drawn by dragging along the line indicated.*

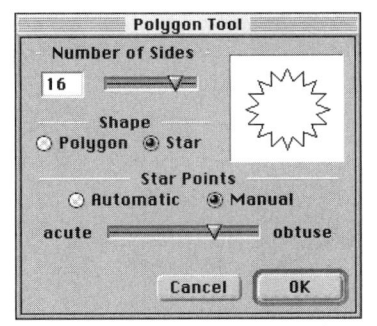

Figure 17. *Choosing the **Star** shape in the **Polygon Tool** dialog box gives you additional choices about the type of star points you want.*

To create a star:

1. Double-click on the Polygon tool in the toolbox. Click on the radio button for the Star shape. You should now see the additional choices in the Polygon Tool dialog box (**Figure 17**).

2. Enter the number of points you want for your star in the field for number of sides. (This is a slightly incorrect label by FreeHand, since a star with 5 points actually has 10 sides.)

3. If you want your star to have its segments automatically aligned, choose the Automatic radio button. If you want to shape the star yourself, choose the Manual button and then adjust the slider from acute to obtuse. The preview window will show you what your changes will do to the star (**Figures 18a–c**).

Tip

- When you set the Polygon Tool dialog box to a certain setting, that setting will remain in effect until you reset the dialog box.

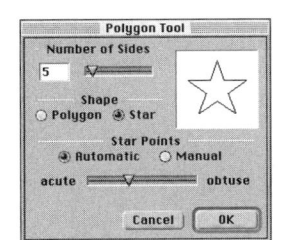

Figure 18a. *The Polygon Tool dialog box for an **Automatic** five-pointed star.*

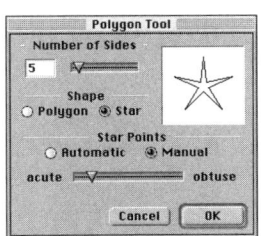

Figure 18b. *The Polygon Tool dialog box for a **Manual** five-pointed star at a high **acute** setting.*

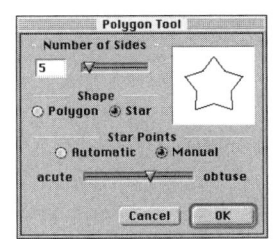

Figure 18c. *The Polygon Tool dialog box for a **Manual** five-pointed star at a high **obtuse** setting.*

63

Chapter 6

FreeHand is definitely the program for anyone who has said they can't even draw a straight line. With the Line tool, you can.

To create a straight line:

1. Click on the Line tool in the toolbox (**Figure 19**).
2. Press at the point where you would like your line to start.
3. Drag along the direction you would like your line to follow.
4. Move your mouse to change the length and direction of the line.
5. Let go of the mouse when you are satisfied (**Figure 20**).

Tip

- If you hold the Shift key as you use the Line tool, your lines will be constrained to 45° or 90° angles.

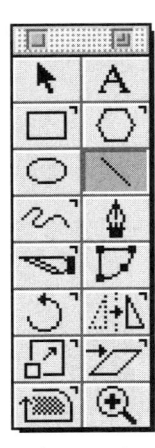

Figure 19. *Selecting the **Line** tool lets you draw straight lines.*

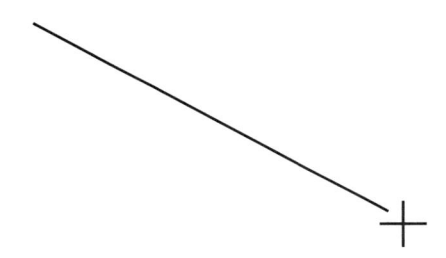

Figure 20. *A straight line drawn with the **Line** tool.*

Straight Lines

64

Creation Tools

Figure 21. *The Freehand tool settings:* **Freehand** *(top),* **Variable stroke** *(middle), and* **Calligraphic pen** *(bottom).*

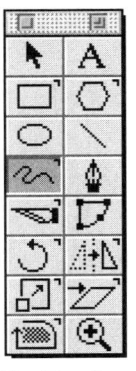

Figure 22. *The* **Freehand** *tool in the toolbox.*

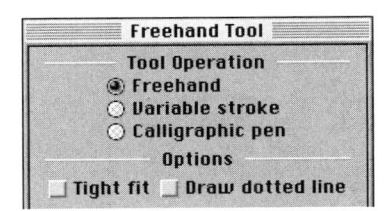

Figure 23. *Double-clicking on the* **Freehand** *tool opens the* **Freehand Tool** *dialog box.*

While it may be a little confusing, there is a Freehand tool in the FreeHand program. The Freehand tool has three different settings: Freehand, Variable stroke, and Calligraphic pen. Each one creates different types of looks (**Figure 21**).

The Freehand setting is very useful for tracing over scanned images. The Variable stroke setting creates an object that resembles a brushstroke. The Calligraphic pen setting creates an object that resembles the stroke of a calligraphy pen. Both the Variable stroke and Calligraphic pen settings are especially effective if you have a pressure-sensitive tablet that lets you vary the width of the stroke depending on how much pressure you exert on the tablet.

To choose the Freehand settings:

1. Double-click on the Freehand tool in the toolbox (**Figure 22**). This will bring you to the Freehand Tool dialog box (**Figure 23**).

2. To work with the Freehand tool, make sure that the Freehand radio button is chosen.

3. If you want your path to follow any minor variables as you drag, choose Tight fit.

4. If you want your path to smooth out any minor variables as you drag, make sure Tight fit is unchecked.

5. Click OK, which will return you to your work page.

Chapter 6

To draw with the Freehand tool:

1. Make sure the Freehand tool is selected.
2. Drag with the plus sign (+) cursor along the path you want to create.
3. Let go of the mouse when you have completed your path (**Figure 24**).

Tips

- If you draw quickly and have a slow machine, you may find your stroke cannot keep up with your dragging. Open the Freehand Tool dialog box and check the box for Draw dotted line. As you drag, you will see a dotted line that follows your path. FreeHand will then fill in that dotted line with the actual path.
- If you need to erase the part of the path you have just drawn, hold the Command key and drag backward over the part you want to erase.
- If you want part of the path you draw with the Freehand tool to be straight, hold the Option key as you drag. A straight line will appear along the path. When you've had enough of the straight line, let go of the Option key (but not the mouse) and continue your drag (**Figure 25**).

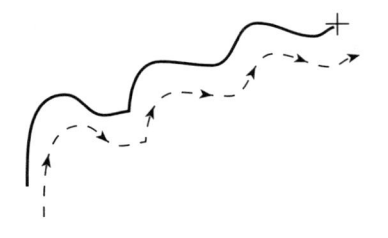

Figure 24. *Dragging with the **Freehand** tool will create a line that follows the path you dragged.*

Path starts with an ordinary drag.

Option key was held here.

Option key was released...

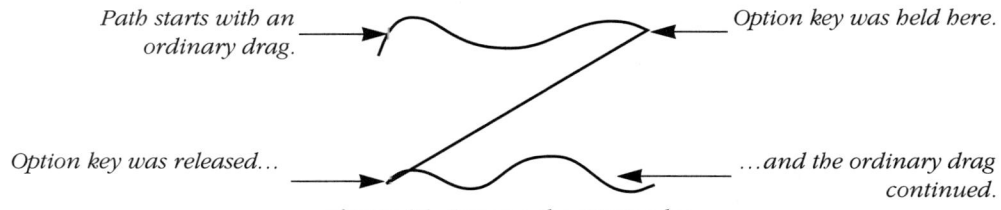

...and the ordinary drag continued.

Figure 25. *Pressing the **Option** key as you drag with the **Freehand** tool will create straight lines.*

Creation Tools

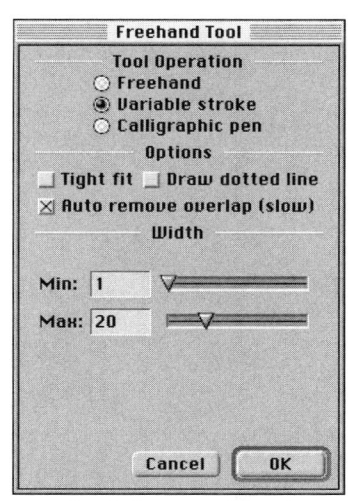

Figure 26. *Clicking on the radio button for **Variable stroke** gives you these options.*

To choose the Variable stroke settings:

1. Double-click on the Freehand tool in the toolbox. The Freehand Tool dialog box will appear.

2. Click on the radio button for Variable stroke (**Figure 26**).

3. In the Min field, enter the size for the thinnest part of your brush stroke. (Any size from 1 point to 72 points.)

4. In the Max field, enter the size for the thickest part of your brush stroke. (Any size from 1 point to 72 points.)

5. If you want to eliminate any parts of the path that cross over each other, choose Auto remove overlap (slow). This cleans up the path and makes it easier to reshape; it can also help you avoid printing problems later on. (You may notice a slight hesitation after you let go of your mouse as FreeHand performs the calculations necessary to remove any overlap.)

6. Click OK, which returns you to your work page.

Chapter 6

To draw with the Variable stroke tool:

1. If you have chosen the Variable stroke tool in the dialog box, you should see the Variable stroke icon in the toolbox (**Figure 27**).

2. Drag with the plus sign (+) cursor to create the path.

3. If you have a pressure-sensitive tablet, any changes in the pressure you exert on the tablet will change the thickness of your stroke (**Figure 28**).

Tips

- The object created by the Variable stroke tool is a closed path. This means that to change the color of the object you change the Fill, not the Stroke.

- If you do not have a tablet, you can still vary the thickness of your stroke by pressing the following modifier keys: To increase the thickness, press the right arrow, the right bracket (]), or the number 2.
To decrease the thickness, press the left arrow, the left bracket ([), or the number 1.

- If you draw with a mouse without using modifier keys, FreeHand will use the Min field setting as the width of your stroke.

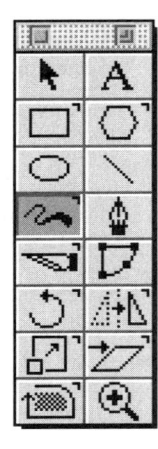

Figure 27. *When the radio button for the* **Variable stroke** *tool is chosen in the Freehand Tool dialog box, its icon appears in the toolbox.*

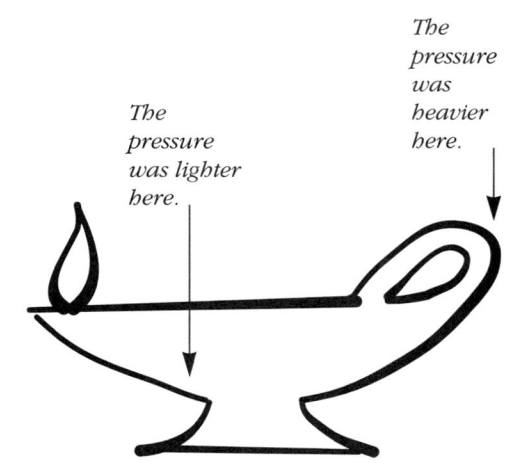

Figure 28. *Changing the pressure while drawing with the Variable stroke tool will create strokes that change their thickness.*

Creation Tools

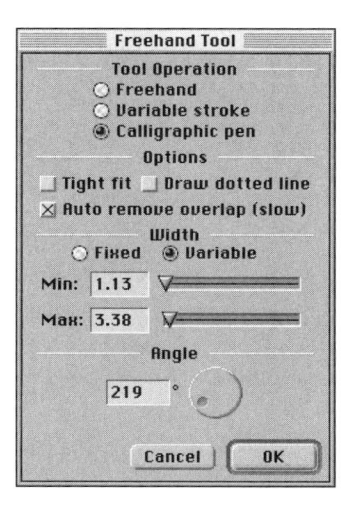

Figure 29. *Clicking on the radio button for **Calligraphic pen** gives you these options.*

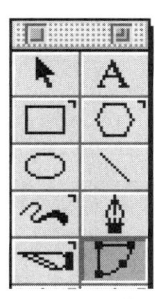

Figure 30. *The **Bézigon** tool in the toolbox.*

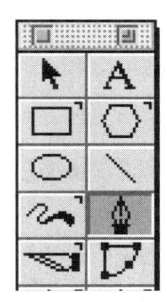

Figure 31. *The **Pen** tool in the toolbox.*

Figure 32. *The same illustration drawn with the **Freehand** tool (top) and the **Pen** tool (bottom).*

To choose the Calligraphic pen settings:

1. Double-click on the Freehand tool in the toolbox. The Freehand Tool dialog box will appear.
2. Click on the radio button for Calligraphic pen (**Figure 29**).
3. Click on the Fixed radio button under the Width option if you want to use a pressure-sensitive tablet without changing the thickness of your stroke.
4. Under the Angle options, type in the degree of the angle or rotate the wheel to set the angle that your stroke uses for its calligraphic lines.
5. Click OK, which returns you to your work page.

Tip

- True calligraphers are constantly adjusting the angle of their pens. Don't forget to go back to the Freehand Tool dialog box to change your angle.

The final two creation tools are the Bézigon (**Figure 30**) and the Pen (**Figure 31**) tools. Both of these tools allow you much greater control over the shape of the path that you are drawing. This is especially true when they are compared to the Freehand tool (**Figure 32**). Both the Pen and the Bézigon tools create much more precise, uniform, and exact paths. This makes either tool extremely useful for working on precision drawings such as architectural illustrations, logos, technical illustrations, etc. Because these two tools are not as simple to use as the other creation tools, they are covered separately in Chapter 8.

69

Chapter 6

Finally, FreeHand provides you with two more creation tools that are not in the toolbox—the Spiral tool and the Arc tool. With these two tools, it is very easy to draw a wide variety of paths (**Figure 33**).

To choose settings for the Spiral tool:

1. To open the Xtra Tools toolbox, choose Xtra Tools from the Other submenu of the Window menu or press Command-Shift-K (**Figure 34**).
2. Double-click on the Spiral tool in the Xtra Tools toolbox (**Figure 35**).
3. You should now see the Spiral dialog box (**Figure 36**).
4. Choose between the nonexpanding and expanding Spiral type. The expanding type gives you a spiral in which the space between the rotations increases as the spiral rotates from the center. The nonexpanding type gives you a spiral where the space remains constant between the rotations.
5. If you have chosen an expanding spiral, you will see an Expansion field (**Figure 36**). This controls how fast your spiral expands (**Figure 37**). The higher the number, the greater the expansion rate. Enter this amount by typing in the field or dragging the triangle slider.

Figure 33. *The **Spiral** and **Arc** tools let you easily create different types of spiral and arc paths.*

Figure 34. *Choose **Xtra Tools** from the **Other** submenu of the **Window** menu to open the Xtra Tools toolbox.*

Figure 35. *The **Xtra Tools** toolbox with the **Spiral** tool selected.*

Spiral Tool Settings

70

Creation Tools

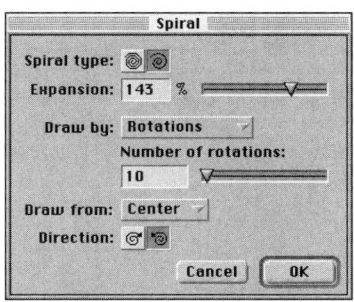

Figure 36. *The **Spiral** dialog box allows you to choose the type of spiral, the rate of expansion, the width increments, the number of rotations, the direction from which to draw the spiral, and the direction of the spiral.*

6. Press on the Draw by pop-up menu to choose between drawing by increments or by rotations. Drawing by increments lets you specify the increment width for nonexpanding spirals or the starting radius for expanding spirals. Drawing by rotations lets you specify the number of rotations.

7. Press on the Draw from pop-up menu to choose between drawing from the Center, the Edge, or the Corner of the location of the Spiral tool (**Figure 38**).

8. Click on one of the Direction icons to choose either a counterclockwise or a clockwise spiral. Click OK to implement all your settings.

Figure 37. *A comparison between a spiral drawn with an **Expansion** rate of 50% (left) and one drawn with a rate of 100% (right).*

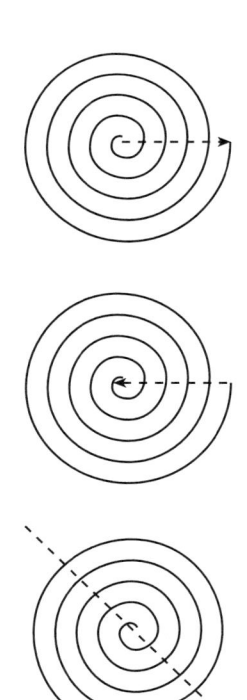

Figure 38. *Three spirals drawn from the **Center** (top), the **Edge** (middle), and the **Corner** (bottom). The dashed lines show the length and direction of the drags.*

Chapter 6

To choose settings for the Arc tool:

1. Open the Xtra Tools toolbox. (Choose Xtra Tools from the Other submenu of the Window menu or press Command-Shift-K).
2. Double-click on the Arc tool in the Xtra Tools toolbox (**Figure 39**).
3. You should now see the Arc dialog box (**Figure 40**).
4. Choose Create open arc if you want your arc to remain open. Deselect this option if you want your arc to be closed (**Figure 41**).
5. Choose Create flipped arc to flip your arc from one direction to another (**Figure 42**).
6. Choose Create concave arc to create an arc that sits concave inside a corner (**Figure 43**).

Tips

- Holding the Option key after you start the drag with the Arc tool will create a flipped arc.
- Holding the Command key after you start the drag with the Arc tool will create a closed arc.
- Holding the Control key after you start the drag with the Arc tool will create a concave arc.

Figure 39. *The* **Arc** *tool selected in the* **Xtra Tools** *toolbox.*

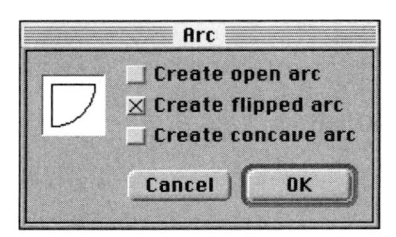

Figure 40. *The* **Arc** *dialog box allows you to choose the type of arc: open or closed, flipped, or concave.*

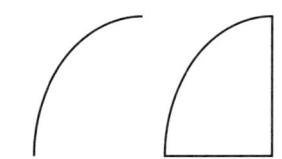

Figure 41. *The difference between an* **open arc** *(left) and a* **closed arc** *(right).*

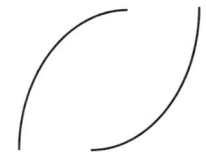

Figure 42. *An open arc (left) and the same arc set to be* ***flipped*** *(right).*

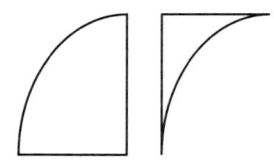

Figure 43. *A closed arc (left) and the same arc set to be* ***concave*** *(right).*

Creation Tools

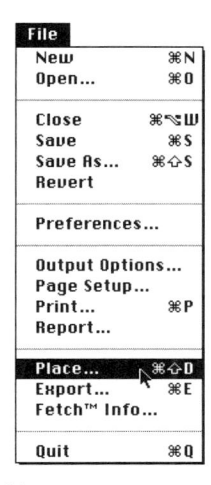

Figure 44a. *To trace an image, choose **Place** from the **File** menu.*

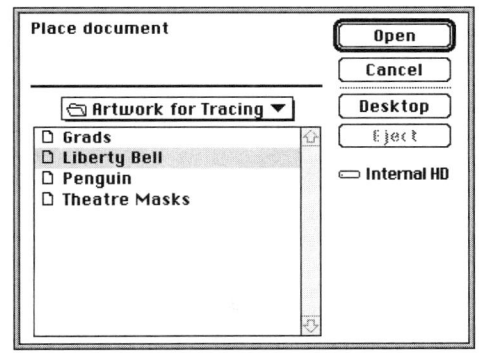

Figure 44b. *Any **PICT, TIFF,** or **EPS** file may be selected in the **Place** dialog box.*

Figure 44c. *A **placed** image with its **four anchor points**.*

There may be times when you have a piece of scanned artwork that you want to convert into FreeHand paths. You may want to be able to scale the artwork up or down without worrying about resolution, or to be able to apply spot colors to certain parts of the artwork, or to make a rough sketch more precise. In these situations, you can use FreeHand's Tracing tool.

To place artwork for tracing:

1. With your document open, choose Place from the File menu or press Command-Shift-D (**Figure 44a**).

2. Use the navigational tools to find the PICT, TIFF, or EPS file that you would like to trace. Click the Open button (**Figure 44b**).

3. After you choose the file you want to place, you will see your cursor change to a corner symbol.

4. Click with the corner symbol. The image will be placed with four anchor points surrounding it (**Figure 44c**).

Tips

- Though you can trace artwork on any layer, most people put their placed images on layers below the horizontal line of the Layers palette so the placed images will not print *(see page 54)*.

- Once you have placed the image on a layer, lock that layer so that you do not inadvertently select the placed image. You can then select a printing layer to be the layer for the traced artwork.

- For best results using the Tracing tool, turn on the High-Resolution TIFF display *(see page 271)*.

Chapter 6

Tracing Tool

To trace an image:

1. Double-click on the Tracing tool in the toolbox (**Figure 45a**).
2. The Tracing Tool dialog box will open (**Figure 45b**). After choosing your settings, click OK to go back to your work page.
3. Drag with the Tracing tool around the part of the image you want to trace (**Figure 45c**).
4. Depending on the artwork, it will take a few seconds or so for your artwork to be traced (**Figure 45d**).

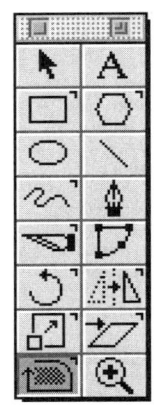

Figure 45a. *The **Tracing** tool in the toolbox. Double-click on the Tracing tool to open the **Tracing Tool** dialog box.*

Figure 45b. *The **Tracing Tool** dialog box. The **Tight** setting controls how detailed your trace will be. The **Trace foreground** and **Trace background** settings control which layers will be traced.*

Figure 45c. *Drag a marquee* *with the **Tracing** tool to trace your image. Let go of the mouse when you have finished dragging.*

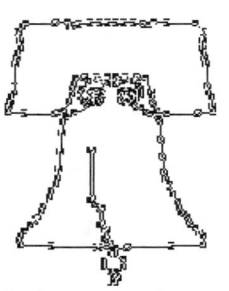

Figure 45d. *A **Traced** image is created with all its points selected.*

74

POINTS AND PATHS 7

Every object in FreeHand is really an arrangement of points connected along a path, so it is important to know how to work with points and paths. In this chapter, you will learn how to select single points, multiple points, an entire object, or multiple objects. You will learn how paths can be grouped or ungrouped. You will learn how to follow the rules for effective placement of points. You will learn the difference between the types of points: corner, curve, and connector. You will also learn how to convert points from one type to another. You will learn how to add and delete points on a path. You will learn the difference between open and closed paths and how to convert one to the other. And you will learn how to change the positions and dimensions of objects.

Figure 1. *When you stop drawing a path, the path is displayed with its **anchor points** selected.*

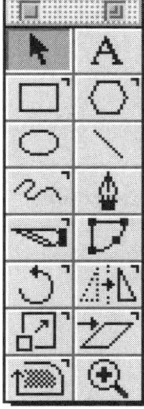

Figure 2. *The **Selection** tool in the toolbox.*

Figure 3. *When a point on a path is selected, it is displayed as a **white dot**.*

To select points by clicking:

1. Draw a wavy line with the Freehand tool *(see page 66)*. As soon as you let go of the mouse, you will see your path. There will be black squares along the path. These are the anchor points that define the path (**Figure 1**).

2. Click on the Selection tool in the toolbox or press the number 0 on your keyboard (**Figure 2**). This will switch you to the Selection tool.

3. Select the point by taking the tip of the arrow and placing it on one of the points. Click. The point will turn into a white dot with two levers coming out of it (**Figure 3**).

(Continued on the following page)

75

Chapter 7

4. To change the shape of the path, move the point you have selected (**Figure 4**).

5. To select additional points, hold the Shift key and click on those points.

Tips

- Hold the Command key while in any tool to temporarily go to the Selection tool. Let go of the Command key to go back to the tool you were originally in.

- Once you have a point or points selected, you can deselect those points by clicking anywhere off the object.

- If you have several points selected and you wish to deselect one, hold the Shift key and click on the point you want deselected.

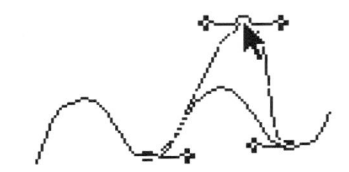

Figure 4. *One way to* ***change the shape of a path*** *is to drag a point on that path.*

Another way to select points is by dragging with the Selection tool. This will create a selection marquee.

To select points or objects with a selection marquee:

1. With the Selection tool chosen, place the arrow outside the point or points you want to select.

2. Press and drag along the diagonal of the rectangle that would surround the points you want selected (**Figure 5a**).

3. Let go of the mouse. Any points that were inside the rectangle that you created with the marquee will be selected (**Figure 5b**).

Tip

- To select the points within more than one area, do your first selection marquee as usual. Then hold the Shift key and do your next selection marquee.

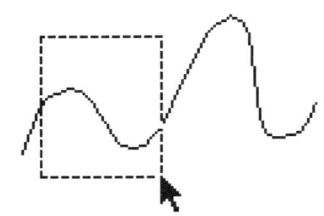

Figure 5a. *Dragging a* ***marquee*** *with the Selection tool.*

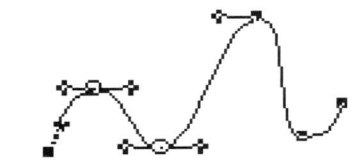

Figure 5b. *The* ***points*** *that were within the rectangle created by the marquee will be selected.*

Points and Paths

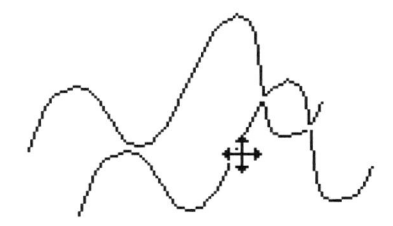

Figure 6a. *A line dragged with a preview.*

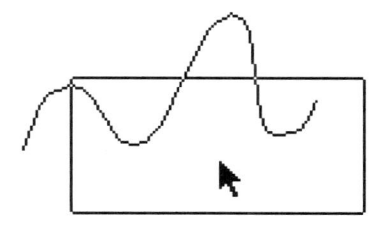

Figure 6b. *A line dragged with a bounding box.*

To select and move an entire object:

1. Use the Selection tool to press on a line segment of an object. Your object is now selected with its points as black dots.

2. If you hold for a moment, you will see a four-headed cross. If you drag with that cross, you will see a preview as you drag your object (**Figure 6a**).

3. If you start your drag quickly, you will see a box and a single arrow as you drag. This is the bounding box that will contain the object that you are dragging. Position the bounding box where you want your object, then let go of the mouse. You will then see your object (**Figure 6b**).

Tips

- If you want to select more than one object, hold the Shift key and click on any additional objects.

- If you have multiple objects selected and wish to deselect one without losing your other selections, hold the Shift key and click on the object you wish to deselect.

- If you drag multiple objects, you may not see the preview drag. The Preferences setting for Redraw controls this *(see page 272)*.

- If you have your Preferences set so that you do not see a preview of the objects, tap the Option key after you start your drag to see a preview of the objects you are moving.

Chapter 7

As you have seen, dragging on a point will change the shape of an object. In order to protect the shape of your object, or to make it easier to select many objects at once, you can group the points on the paths or the objects.

To group paths:
1. Select the path or paths that you want to have grouped.
2. Choose Group from the Arrange menu or press Command-G. Instead of the individual points selected, there will be four group anchor points arranged in a rectangle around the path or paths (**Figure 7**).

Figure 7. *A **grouped object** displays **four group anchor points**.*

To work with grouped objects:
1. To select a grouped object, click with the Selection tool on the object.
2. To reshape a grouped object, drag on one of the four group anchor points that surround the object (**Figure 8a**).
3. To resize the object without distorting its shape, hold the Shift key as you drag on one of the group anchor points (**Figure 8b**).

Figure 8a. *Drag on one of the **group anchor points** to resize a grouped object.*

Figure 8b. *Hold the **Shift** key while dragging to resize without distorting the shape of the object.*

Points and Paths

Figure 9a. *When a group is selected, you cannot see its individual anchor points.*

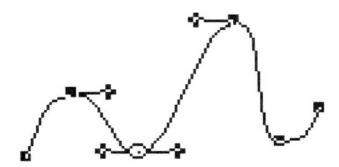

Figure 9b. *Holding the **Option** key allows you to select the individual points of a grouped object.*

Once you have grouped an object, you may want to select and reshape an individual point on that object. Because the object is grouped, you will need to follow some special steps (**Figure 9a**).

To select individual points within a group:

1. With the object selected, hold the Option key and click with the Selection tool on the object. You should see the individual points of the object (**Figure 9b**).

2. Still holding the Option key, click on the point you wish to select.

3. If you wish to select additional points, hold the Shift key and click on those points.

Tips

- Rectangles and ellipses are automatically grouped when you draw them.

- Holding the Option key does not work to select the individual points of a rectangle or ellipse. First, choose Reverse Direction from the Path Operations submenu of the Arrange menu. This will both change the way the object is drawn and ungroup the object. Regroup the object. You will then be able to select individual points using the Option key.

79

Chapter 7

When you are working with grouped objects, you may want to create levels of groups to make it easier for you to select certain objects. This is called "nesting."

To nest objects:

1. Select and group the first object (**Figure 10a**). After the object is grouped, deselect it.
2. Select the next object and group it (**Figure 10b**). After that object is grouped, deselect it. If you have additional objects that you want to nest, repeat this step.
3. Select all the groups and group them (**Figure 10c**).

Tips

- There is a limit of 8 levels for nested objects.
- Numerous nesting levels can cause problems when it comes to printing your file.

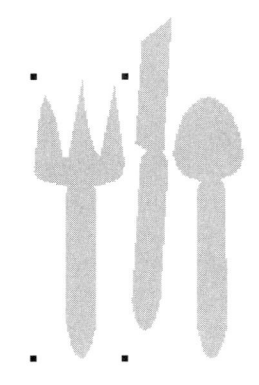

Figure 10a. *To nest objects, select and **group** the first object.*

Figure 10b. *Continue to select and group each object. Each grouped object will display its own **group anchor points**.*

Figure 10c. *Select all the individual groups and group them. There will now be another set of **group anchor points** for the larger group.*

Points and Paths

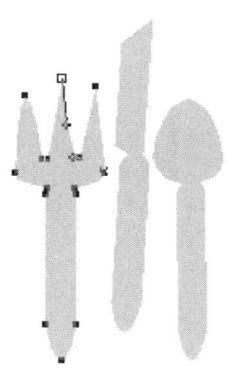

Figure 11a. *To select an individual object or point in a nested group, hold the* **Option** *key as you click on the group. You will then see the individual anchor points of the object.*

To work with nested groups:

1. Hold the Option key to select an individual object or point in a nested group (**Figure 11a**).
2. Press the Tilde key (~) on your keyboard to select the next level of the nest (**Figure 11b**).
3. Continue to press the Tilde key until you have all the levels you want selected (**Figure 11c**).

Once you have an object grouped, you may want to ungroup it.

To ungroup an object:

1. Select the grouped object.
2. Choose Ungroup from the Arrange menu or press Command-U. Your object will be ungrouped and its individual anchor points will be visible.

Tip

■ If you have nested objects in a group, you will have to ungroup them for each level of the nest.

Figure 11b. *To select the next level of the nest, press the* **Tilde** *key.*

Figure 11c. *Continue to press the* **Tilde** *key until you see the* **group anchor points** *for the final level of the nest.*

Chapter 7

The basics of points

Once you start working with points, you will discover there are levers or handles that extend out of points. These are called point handles or Bézier (pronounced Bay-zee-ay) handles, named after the French mathematician Pierre Bézier. Point handles are nonprinting lines that control the direction that any path curves along Changing the direction of the point handles will change the shape of a path (**Figures 12a–b**).

There are three different types of points that make up FreeHand objects. In order to have a complete understanding of the program, it is vital to understand how points work.

Corner points

Corner points are anchor points that allow paths to have an abrupt change in direction. Depending on how they were created, there are three different types of corner points: points with straight lines on both sides, points with a straight line on one side and a curved line on the other, and points with curved lines on both sides (**Figure 13**).

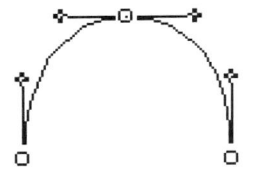

Figure 12a. *An object with its **point handles** visible.*

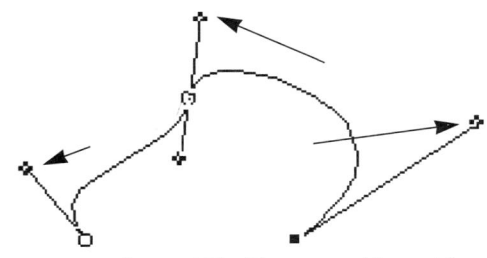

Figure 12b. *The same object with the **point handles** manipulated in the directions indicated.*

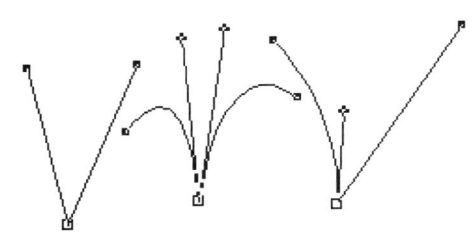

Figure 13. *The three different types of **corner points** with their **point handles** visible: corner points with **no handles** (left), corner points with **two handles** (middle), and corner points with **one handle** (right).*

Curve points

Curve points are anchor points that make a smooth, curved transition along the direction of the path. The length of the point handles governs how great the curved transition is (**Figure 14**).

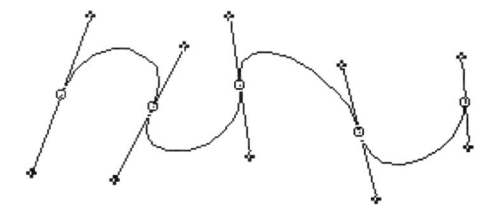

Figure 14. *Different* **curve points** *with their* **point handles** *visible. The length of the point handle will change the shape of the curve.*

Connector points

The purpose of connector points is to constrain the transition between segments so that they cannot be moved out of a special alignment. There are two types of connector points: those that control the transition between a straight-line segment and a curved segment, and those that control the transition between two curved segments.

When a connector point is between a straight-line segment and a curved segment, the point handle runs along the same direction as the straight line. When a connector point is between two curved segments, the point handles are constrained by the position of the points on either side of the connector point (**Figure 15**).

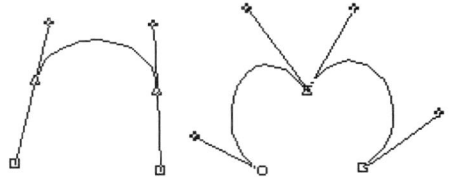

Figure 15. *Two different types of* **connector points** *with their* **point handles** *visible: connector points between a straight line and a curved segment (left) and connector points between two curved segments (right).*

The one-third rule

As a general rule, you need only two curve points to create a curve on a path. If your curve is too steep, however, you will find that the point handles start to break the one-third rule. This rule states that the point handles for any segment should not extend more than one-third of the length of that segment (**Figure 16**).

What happens if you break the one-third rule? Well, no one will come to arrest you, but you will find it difficult to edit your curves with huge handles that pivot all over the place.

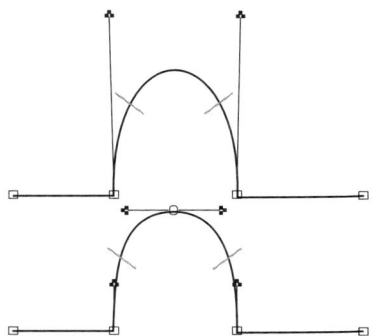

Figure 16. *You are breaking the* **One-Third Rule** *if the point handles for any segment extend more than one-third of the length (gray lines) of that segment (top). Add another point to reduce the length of the handles (bottom).*

Chapter 7

The best way to learn about points is to convert them from one type to another. Fortunately, FreeHand provides a very simple way of doing this.

To manipulate and convert points using the Inspector palette:

1. Use the Freehand tool to create a wavy line with at least three anchor points.
2. Use the Selection tool to select one of the anchor points on the inside of the path. Notice that if you rotate the point handle on one side of the point, the other handle on the opposite side also moves. It is this "lever" action that makes the curve transition smooth (**Figure 17**).
3. Open the Document Inspector palette and choose the Object icon. Under Point type, you will see the Curve Point icon selected (**Figure 18**).

Figure 17. *A **curve point** with its **point handles** selected. Rotating one handle will also move the handle on the other side.*

Object icon

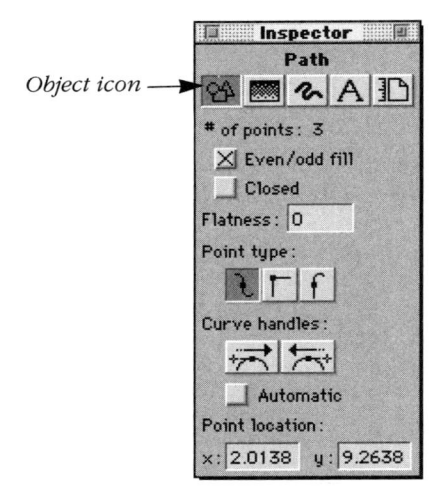

Figure 18. *The **Document Inspector** palette with the **Object** icon selected and the **Curve Point** icon selected as the **Point type**.*

Convert Points

84

Points and Paths

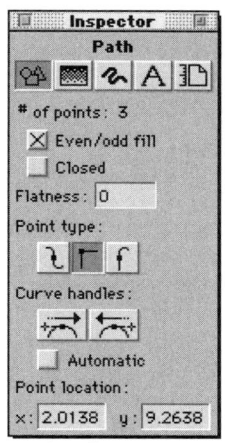

Figure 19. *To change a point to a corner point, click on the **Corner Point** icon in the **Inspector** palette.*

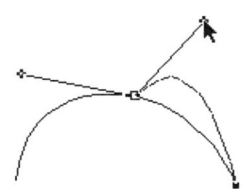

Figure 20. *Moving the **point handles** of a **corner point** will change its shape.*

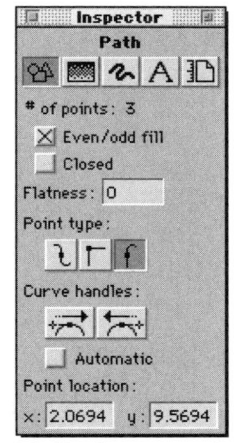

Figure 21. *To change a point to a connector point, click on the **Connector Point** icon in the **Inspector** palette.*

4. Under Point type, click on the Corner Point icon (**Figure 19**). The point and the handles will not change shape, but the anchor point will change from a white circle to a white square. Use the Selection tool to drag one of the handles that extends from this point. You will see that you can create different looks depending on how you move the handles (**Figure 20**).

5. To convert this point into a connector point, click on the Connector point icon in the Document Inspector palette (**Figure 21**). You will notice that the white square has been changed to a triangle (**Figure 22**). The two point handles that extend from the connector point will now be fixed to a specific angle.

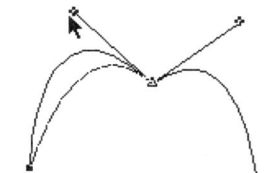

Figure 22. *A **connector point** is displayed as a white triangle. Its **point handles** cannot be moved side to side, only lengthened.*

Chapter 7

As explained earlier in this chapter, there are three types of corner points. When you convert a curve point into a corner point as in the above steps, the corner point still has point handles extending from it. To create a corner point with straight lines extending from it, you will need to retract the handle into the point.

To retract corner point handles using the Inspector palette:

1. Select a corner point with two point handles that extend out from it.
2. Click on one of the Curve handles icons in the Inspector palette (**Figure 23**). One of the point handles on the corner point will retract (**Figure 24**).
3. Click on the other Curve handles icon to retract the other handle.
4. If the points on either side are curve points, your line segment will not be straight. To make it straight, you need to retract the point handles for those curve points.

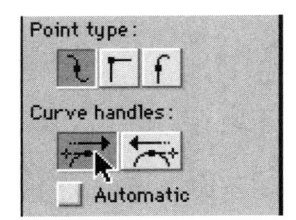

Figure 23. *To retract Point Handles click on the **Curve handle** icons in the **Inspector** palette.*

Figure 24. *When you click on the Curve handles icons in the Inspector palette, the **point handles** will retract into the point.*

Once you've retracted point handles, you can use the Inspector palette to extend them from the point.

To extend handles using the Inspector palette:

1. Click on the point that you want to extend the point handles from.
2. If it is a corner point, use the Point type icons to convert it to a curve point or a connector point.
3. Click on the Automatic checkbox under the Curve handles icons (**Figure 25**). If the point is a curve point, there will be two handles. If the point is a connector point, there will be one or two handles depending on the shape of the path.

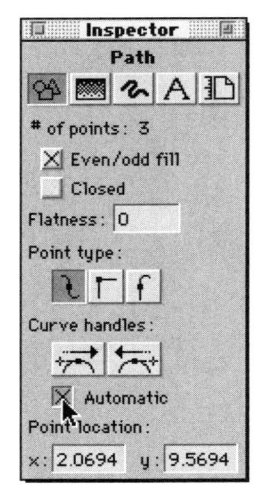

Figure 25. *Clicking on the **Automatic** checkbox will restore point handles to a curve or connector point.*

86

Points and Paths

Figure 26. *You can **manually drag a point handle** back into its anchor point.*

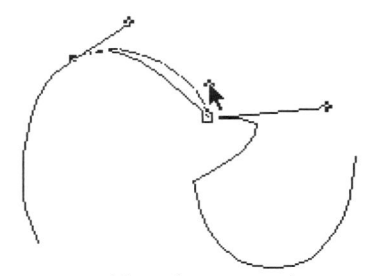

Figure 27. *Holding the **Option** key and then **dragging from a point** allows you to **manually extend point handles** from that point.*

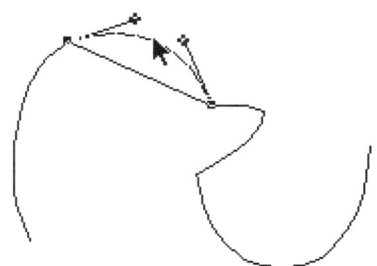

Figure 28. *Holding the **Option** key and then **dragging on a line segment** allows you to **manually extend point handles** from both ends of the segment.*

You can also use the Selection tool to retract or extend handles from a point.

To retract handles manually:

1. Make a wavy line and select one of the points so its point handles are visible.

2. Place your Selection tool on the four dots at the end of the handle.

3. Drag the handle back into the point (**Figure 26**).

To extend handles manually:

1. Click with the Selection tool to select the point you want to extend the handles from. (The selected point must be a white point, not a black point.)

2. Press on the Option key, then drag out from the point. You should see the handle extend from the point. (**Figure 27**).

3. If you hold the Option key, then drag along the line segment, you will extend the point handles from both points of the segment. (**Figure 28**).

Chapter 7

Once you create points or paths, you may find that you want to eliminate them. Though the procedure is the same for deleting both points and paths, the results are different.

To delete an object:
1. Choose the object so that all its anchor points are visible or its four group anchor points are visible.
2. Press the Delete key on your keyboard or choose Clear from the Edit menu. The object will be deleted.

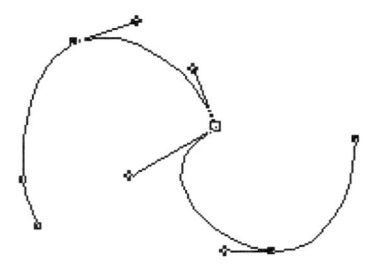

Figure 29a. *To delete a point from a path, select the point.*

To delete a point from a path:
1. Choose the point that you want to delete so that the selected point is white and the other points are black.
2. Press the Delete key on your keyboard. (Do not choose Clear from the Edit menu or you will eliminate the entire object.) The point will be deleted and the path will be reshaped (**Figures 29a–b**).

Figure 29b. *Pressing the **Delete** key on the keyboard will delete the selected point and reshape the path.*

Points and Paths

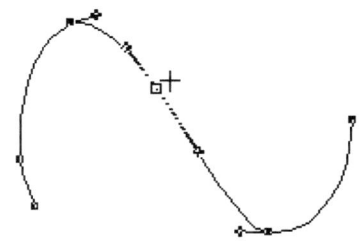

Figure 30. To **add** a point, click with the **Pen** or the **Bézigon** tool on the path. A new point will appear at the spot where you clicked.

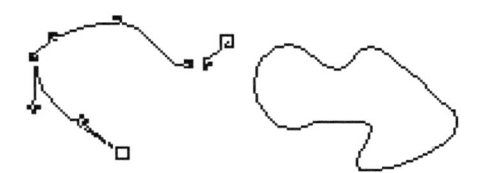

Figure 31. An **open path** (left) has two end points. A **closed path** (right) has no end points.

Figure 32. To close a path as you are drawing, simply bring your cursor over the first point you drew. The path will be closed.

Adding a point to a path is a little more sophisticated. You will need to use either the Pen or the Bézigon tool.

To add a point to a path:

1. With the path selected, click on either the Pen or the Bézigon tool in the toolbox. *(For a complete explanation of the differences between these two tools, see Chapter 8, "Pen and Bézigon Tools.")*

2. Click with the plus sign (+) cursor on the path. A point will appear at the spot where you clicked (**Figure 30**).

3. You may now move or manipulate the point as you wish.

Tip

- If you click too far off the path, you will create a new point that is not part of the original path.

There are two types of paths you can create, open and closed. Open paths are paths that start on one point and end on another. Closed paths are paths that go round and round with no start or end. A piece of string is an open path. A rubber band is a closed path (**Figure 31**).

To close a path as you are drawing:

If you are drawing with the Freehand, or the Pen, or the Bézigon tool, you can close a path by bringing your cursor over the first point that you drew (**Figure 32**).

89

Chapter 7

To close a path previously drawn:

If you have already created an open path and decide you want it closed, you can close it by dragging one of the end points onto the other. As soon as the points touch each other, FreeHand will close the path (**Figure 33**).

Figure 33. *To close a previously drawn path, drag one of the **end points** over the other.*

To determine if a path is open or closed:

If you have a path selected, you can determine if it is open or closed by clicking on the Object icon in the Document Inspector palette. Closed objects have the Closed checkbox filled. Open objects do not (**Figure 34**).

To open or close a path using the Inspector palette:

1. Click on the object you wish to change.

2. Choose the Object icon from the Inspector palette.

3. If you want to close the path, click on the blank Closed checkbox. (An "X" will appear, indicating the path is closed.) The path will automatically be closed with a straight line that extends between the two end points (**Figure 35**).

4. If you want to open the path, click on the "X" in the Closed checkbox. The path will automatically be opened by deleting the segment between the two end points.

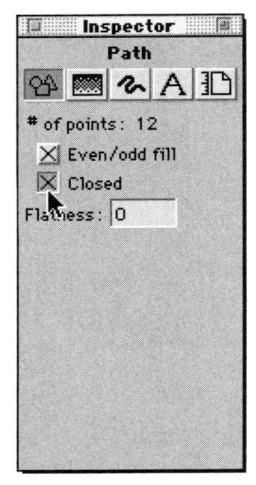

Figure 34. *To determine if an object is open or closed, click on the **Object** icon in the Document Inspector palette. The **Closed** checkbox indicates the status.*

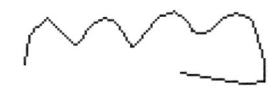

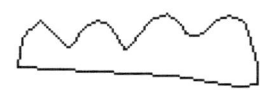

Figure 35. *Closing an open path (top) will automatically draw a straight line between the two end points (bottom).*

Points and Paths

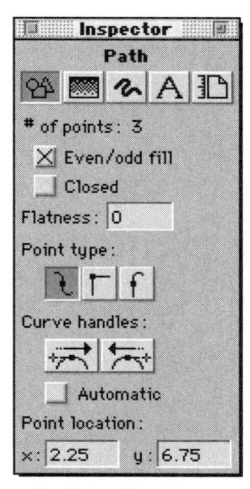

Figure 36. *If you have a single point selected, its **x and y coordinates** are listed at the bottom of the **Path** palette of the **Document Inspector**.*

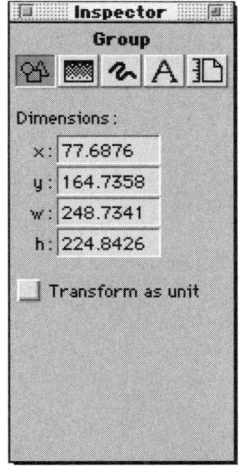

Figure 37. *If you have a grouped object selected, the **x and y coordinates** of its lower-left group anchor point are listed in the **Group** palette of the **Document Inspector**.*

Once you have created an object, you may wish to reposition it or resize it. Though it is rather easy to just drag with the Selection tool to manually move a point or reshape an object, there may come a time when you want to move or resize numerically.

To move a point or a grouped object numerically:

1. Click on the point or grouped object.
2. Choose the Document icon from the Inspector palette.
3. If you have chosen a point, you will see the information for that point on the path. At the bottom of the palette, you will see the x and y coordinates for your point location (**Figure 36**).
4. If you have chosen a grouped object, you will see the dimensions for the group. At the top of these dimensions, you will see the x and y coordinates for the lower-left group anchor point (**Figure 37**).
5. Double-click on the x and y fields and enter the coordinates of the position where you would like your point or grouped object to be moved. Unless you have changed your zero point, the x coordinates start at the lower-left point of the page and increase as you move horizontally to the right. The y coordinates start at the lower-left point of the page and increase as you move up vertically.
6. Press the Return or Enter key to set the new coordinates.

Tip

■ If you wish to move an object numerically without grouping it, you can use the Move distance settings in the Transform palette *(see page 112)*.

Chapter 7

To change the size of a grouped object numerically:

1. Select the grouped object.
2. Choose the Document icon from the Inspector palette.
3. You will see the Dimensions for the Group. In the middle of the palette you will see the width (w) and height (h) dimensions. (**Figure 38**).
4. Double-click on the fields and enter the dimensions you would like the grouped object to be.
5. Press the Return or Enter key to set the new coordinates.

Tips

- All rectangles and ellipses are automatically grouped. However, they do not show the label "Group" in the Document Inspector.
- The dimensions for the x and y coordinates and the object width and height are listed in the same unit of measurement as the document. *(To change the unit of measurement for your document, see page 21.)*

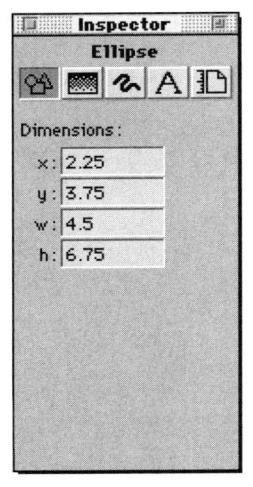

Figure 38. *The **width (w)** and **height (h)** dimensions are listed in the **Group** palette of the **Document Inspector**.*

PEN AND BÉZIGON TOOLS 8

As mentioned in Chapter 6, the Pen and the Bézigon tools allow you to draw much more precisely. In this chapter, you will learn the differences between the Pen and the Bézigon. You will learn how to make the different types of points with each tool. You will also learn the most efficient way to place points on different types of paths.

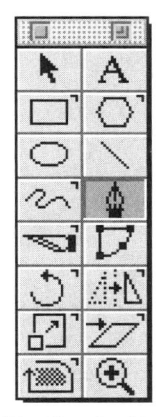

Figure 1. *The **Pen** tool in the toolbox.*

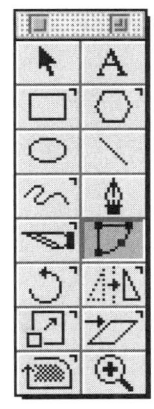

Figure 2. *The **Bézigon** tool in the toolbox.*

The difference between the Pen and the Bézigon tools:

As you saw in Chapter 6, both the Pen (**Figure 1**) and the Bézigon (**Figure 2**) allow you to draw much more precisely than the Freehand tool. But the question is what is the difference between the two tools? At first glance, there is very little difference. In fact, once a path is created, there is no way to tell which tool created it. The main difference is that the Pen tool allows you to place points and manipulate their point handles at the same time. The Bézigon tool allows you to quickly click to place points, but all the points created with the Bézigon tool have their point handles set at the automatic settings. After you place points with the Bézigon tool, you must then go back to adjust their point handles.

Because so many beginners to FreeHand find the Pen tool daunting, the Bézigon is an excellent way to learn how to create precise paths. But if you wish to truly master FreeHand, you will need to become proficient with the Pen.

93

Chapter 8

The exercises in this chapter are listed first for the Bézigon and then for the Pen. If there is no difference between the steps for both tools, then the exercise is listed only once.

To create an object with straight sides:

1. Choose either the Pen or the Bézigon from the toolbox.
2. Position the plus sign (+) cursor where you would like the object path to start. Click. You will see a corner point that appears as a white square.(**Figure 3a**).
3. Position the plus sign (+) cursor where you would like the next point of the object to be. Click. You will see a line extending from the first point to the second corner point you have just created.
4. Continue clicking until you have created all the sides of your object (**Figure 3b**).
5. If you want to create a closed path, click again on the first point that you created. FreeHand will close your path.

Tips

- If you have created an open path and wish to start a second path, you will need to deselect the first path. Press the Tab key on your keyboard. This will deselect your path and allow you to continue drawing.
- Hold the Shift key while clicking to constrain your lines to a vertical or horizontal axis, or a specific constrain angle. The default constrain angle is set in the Document Inspector as 0°. If you change the constrain setting, holding the Shift key will constrain your artwork to the new angle (**Figure 4**).

Figure 3a. *Clicking with either the* **Pen** *or the* **Bézigon** *tool creates a* ***corner point***.

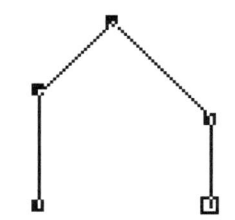

Figure 3b. *As you create more corner points, straight lines extend between them.*

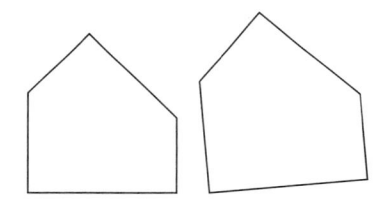

Figure 4. *An object drawn with a* ***constrain angle of 0°*** *(left) and the same object drawn with a* ***constrain angle of 15°*** *(right).*

Pen and Bézigon Tools

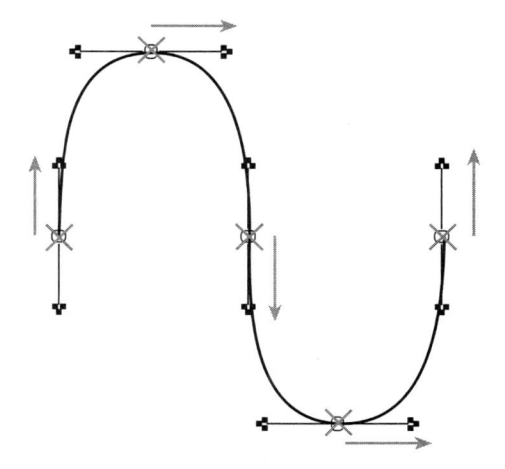

Figure 5. *A smooth curved path with its point handles visible. The point handles control how the curve is shaped. The arrows show how the path is dragged with the **Pen**. The "X's" show where the **Bézigon** is clicked while holding the **Option** key.*

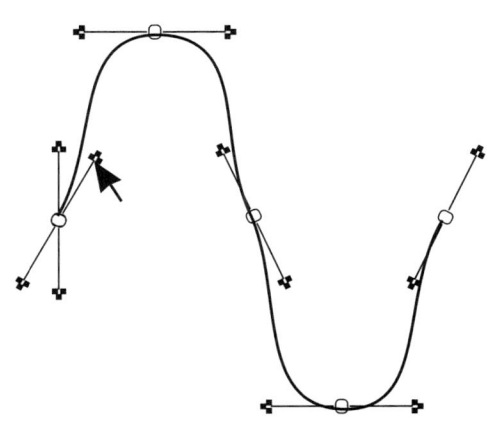

Figure 6. *The **point handles** created by the **Bézigon** tool need to be manually adjusted after they are formed.*

One of the benefits of drawing with the Pen and Bézigon tools is that you can draw perfectly smooth curves. A smooth curve is one where the transition from one direction to another is smooth, without any abrupt changes. Think of a smooth curve as the type of curve created by a rollercoaster. There are no abrupt changes as the track moves up and down. Though the process to create the points differs between the Pen and the Bézigon, both tools position their points at the same spots to create a smooth curved path (**Figure 5**).

To create a smooth curved path using the Bézigon:

1. Choose the Bézigon and hold the Option key until you have finished drawing the path.

2. Start with the left point and, while holding the Option key, click on each of the spots where the anchor points need to be (**Figure 5**)

3. Continue clicking until you have completed laying down the points.

4. Adjust the point handles so that the curve is the proper shape (**Figure 6**).

Chapter 8

To create a smooth curved path using the Pen:

1. Choose the Pen.
2. Start with the left point and drag up (do not click) until you have created a point handle that extends about a third of the way up the curve you want to create (**Figure 7a**).
3. Continue dragging until you have completed laying down the points (**Figure 7b**). If you want to start a new path, press the Tab key to deselect the first path.

Tip

- Start your drag and then hold the Shift key to constrain your point handles to horizontal or vertical lines.

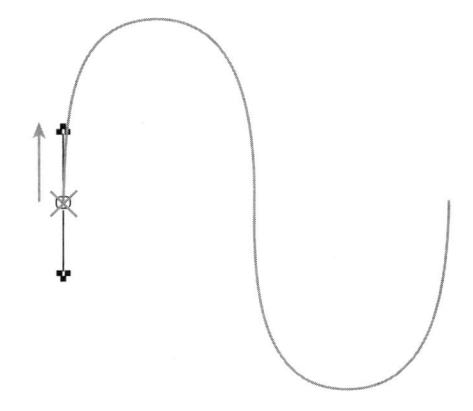

Figure 7a. *To draw a **smooth curved path** with the **Pen** tool, drag up until you have created a point handle that extends a third of the way up the curve you want to create (indicated in gray).*

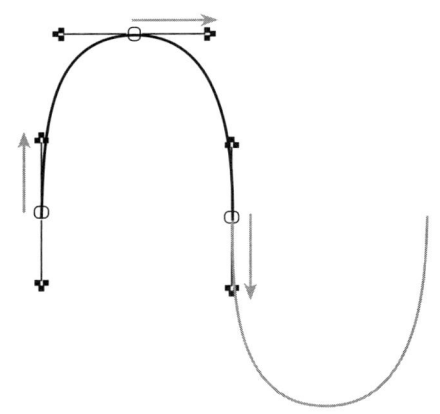

Figure 7b. *The **point handles** created by the **Pen** tool can be positioned correctly by dragging in the proper direction.*

Smooth Curved Path with Pen

96

Pen and Bézigon Tools

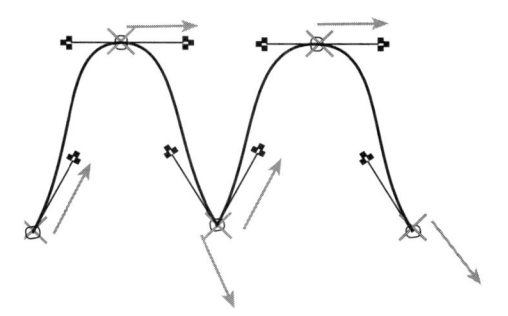

Figure 8. *A **bumpy curved path** is one where the curve abruptly changes direction.*

Life is not all smooth, and neither are most curved paths. Much of the time you will want to create a bumpy curved path instead of a smooth curve. Think of a bumpy curve as the path a bouncing ball would make. The abrupt change is where the ball hits the ground and then bounces back up (**Figure 8**).

To draw a bumpy curved path with the Bézigon tool:

1. The first point is a corner point, so click with the Bézigon tool where you would like the first point to be (**Figure 9a**).

2. The next point is a curve point, so Option-click with the Bézigon tool (**Figure 9b**).

3. The third point is a corner point, so click with the Bézigon tool (**Figure 9c**). At this step, notice that there are point handles from the corner points. This is because FreeHand automatically extends handles out from corner points that are connected to curve points.

4. The fourth point is a curve point, so Option-click with the Bézigon tool.

5. The last point is a corner point, so click with the Bézigon tool.

6. Manually adjust the point handles until the curved path is the shape you want.

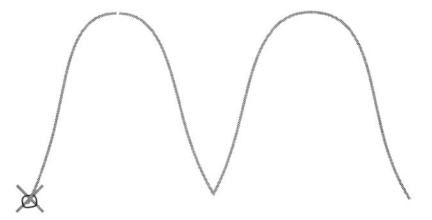

Figure 9a. *To start the bumpy curved path, click with the **Bézigon** tool. This creates a **corner point**.*

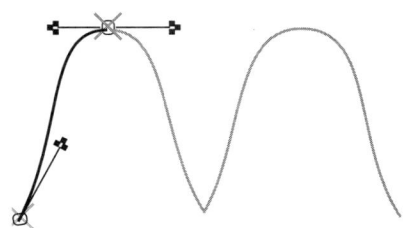

Figure 9b. *To continue the bumpy curved path, **Option-click** with the **Bézigon** tool. This creates a **curve point**.*

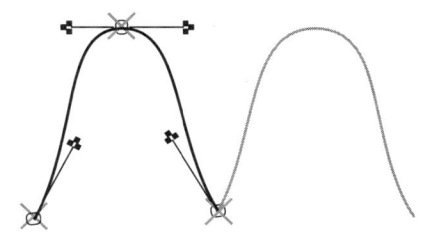

Figure 9c. *To continue the bumpy curved path, click with the **Bézigon** tool. This creates a **corner point**. Notice that FreeHand automatically fills in handles when a corner point is connected to a curve point.*

Bumpy Curved Path with Bézigon

97

Chapter 8

To draw a bumpy curved path with the Pen tool:

1. Hold the Option key and drag with the Pen to create the first corner point with a handle (**Figure 10a**).
2. Drag to create the second point, a curve point (**Figure 10b**).
3. Drag down at the third point. You will see the point handle extend from the point. Do not let go of the mouse.
4. When this point handle has been extended backward enough, press on the Option key. Rotate the second point handle so that it is aligned in the proper direction (**Figure 10c**).
5. Drag to create the fourth point, a curve point.
6. Drag to create the final point. You will see the point handle extend from the point. Do not let go of the mouse.
7. When this point handle has been extended backward enough, release the mouse.
8. Hold the Option key and click on the final point. This will retract the point handle extending from it.

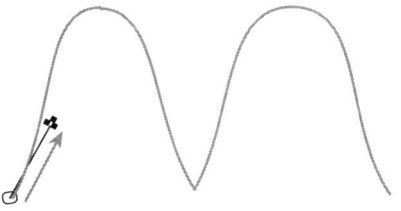

Figure 10a. *To start the bumpy curved path, hold the **Option** key and drag with the **Pen** tool. This creates a **corner point** with a handle extending up.*

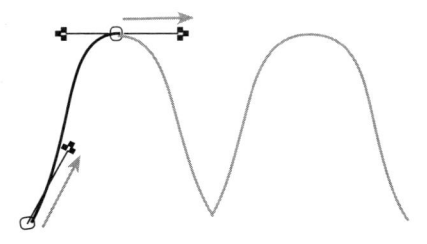

Figure 10b. *To continue the bumpy curved path, drag with the **Pen** tool. This creates a **curve point**.*

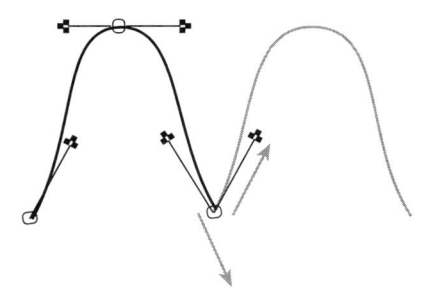

Figure 10c. *To continue the bumpy curved path, drag with the **Pen** tool. When the handle extends back enough, hold the **Option** key and then drag in the direction of the second arrow. This creates a **corner point** with two handles.*

Pen and Bézigon Tools

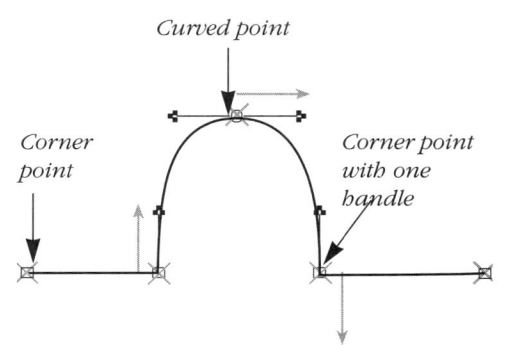

*Figure 11. A **straight-to-bumpy** path with its point handles visible. The arrows indicate the direction of the drags with the **Pen**. The "X's" indicate where the **Bézigon** is clicked.*

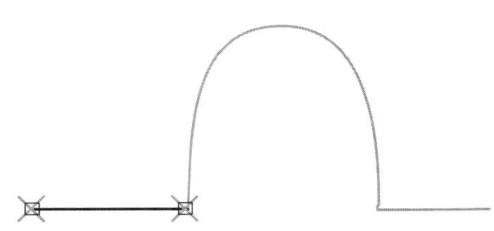

*Figure 12a. To start the straight-to-bumpy path, click with the **Bézigon** tool at the first two positions. This creates two **corner points**.*

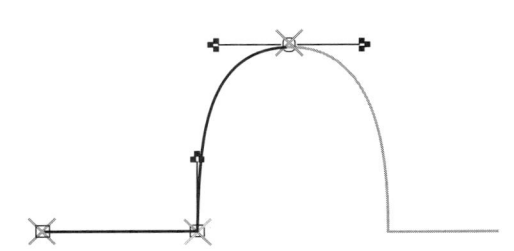

*Figure 12b. To continue the straight-to-bumpy path, **Option-click** with the **Bézigon** tool. This creates a **curve point** at the top of the curve.*

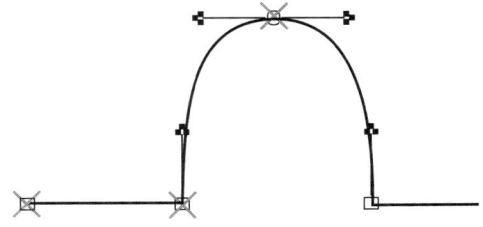

*Figure 12c. To continue the straight-to-bumpy path, click with the **Bézigon** tool at the last two positions. This creates two **corner points**.*

Imagine you were riding along a road, and there was suddenly a bump in the road, and then the road continued straight. That's the shape of a straight-to-bumpy path (**Figure 11**).

To draw a straight-to-bumpy path with the Bézigon tool:

1. The first point is a corner point, so click with the Bézigon tool where the first point should be.

2. The next point is a corner point, so click with the Bézigon tool. If you want your line to be constrained, hold the Shift key as you click (**Figure 12a**).

3. The third point is a curve point, so Option-click with the Bézigon tool where you want the top of the bump to be (**Figure 12b**).

4. The fourth point is a corner point, so click with the Bézigon tool.

5. The last point is a corner point, so click with the Bézigon tool (**Figure 12c**).

6. Manually adjust the point handles to the shape you want. Notice that point handles were automatically added to the points created in Steps 2 and 4.

Chapter 8

To draw a straight-to-bumpy path with the Pen tool:

1. The first point is a corner point, so click with the Pen tool where the first point should be (**Figure 13a**).

2. The next point is a corner point with one handle extending from it, so hold the Option key first, then drag with the Pen tool (**Figure 13b**).

3. The third point is a curve point, so drag with the Pen tool where you want the top of the bump to be.

4. The next point has a handle extending up, so drag with the Pen tool to create a curve point with two handles. Release your mouse when you are satisfied with the length of the handle extending into the curve.

5. You need to convert the curve point you just created into a corner point with one handle. Hold the Option key and click on the point you created in Step 4. This will convert the point into a corner point and retract the second handle coming out of the point (**Figure 13c**).

6. The last point is a corner point, so click where you want that point located.

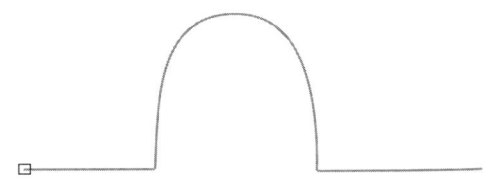

Figure 13a. *To start the straight-to-bumpy path, click with the **Pen** tool at the first position. This creates a **corner point**.*

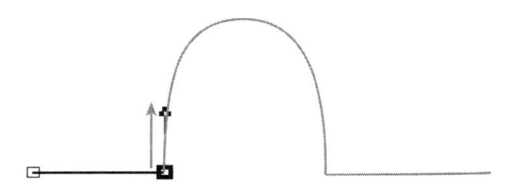

Figure 13b. *To make a **corner point with only one handle** with the **Pen** tool, hold the **Option** key and then start your drag on the point indicated (bold outline).*

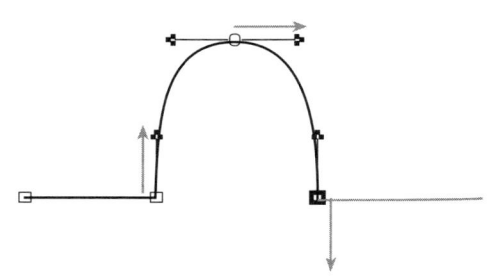

Figure 13c. *To convert a curve point into a corner point with only one handle, hold the **Option** key and click again on the point indicated (bold outline). This will retract the first handle coming out of the point, leaving just the*

Pen and Bézigon Tools

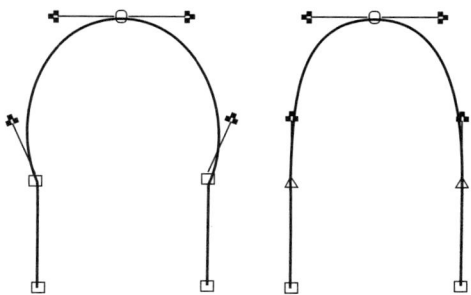

Figure 14. *The difference between using **corner points** as the transition between segments (left) and using **connector points** (right).*

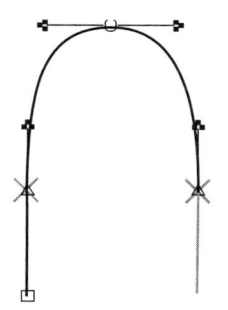

Figure 15. *To create connector points with the **Bézigon** tool, hold the **Control** key as you click (connector points are indicated by "X's").*

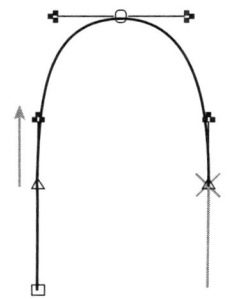

Figure 16. *To create connector points with the **Pen** tool, **Control-drag** to create handles that extend out from the point (indicated by an arrow) and **Control-click** to create handles that extend backward from the point (indicated by an "X").*

In FreeHand, connector points are used to create a smooth transition between a straight-line segment and a curved segment. Connector points are indicated by a triangle. (**Figure 14**).

To create connector points using the Bézigon or Pen:

1. With the Bézigon tool, hold the Control key and click. This will create a connector point. The handle will be automatically created and aligned when you create the segment that follows (**Figure 15**).

2. With the Pen, hold the Control key and drag to create a connector point with a handle that extends out from the point. The handle will automatically be aligned with the straight-line segment that precedes it.

3. With the Pen, hold the Control key and click to create a connector point with a handle that extends backward from the point. The handle will automatically be aligned when you create the straight-line segment that follows it (**Figure 16**).

Chapter 8

You may finish creating a path and then realize that you want to add more segments to it. You then need to add points to the end of the path. (This only works with open paths. Closed paths have no end points to add onto.)

To add points to the end of a path:

1. Select the path you want to add to.

2. Select one of the path's end points so that it is white.

3. Click or drag with the Pen or the Bézigon tool on the spot where you want the next point to occur (**Figure 17**). FreeHand will fill in the line segment. You can then continue adding segments as needed.

Tip

■ Other path operations, such as joining two open paths together, splitting paths, and cutting paths, are covered in Chapter 18, "Path Operations."

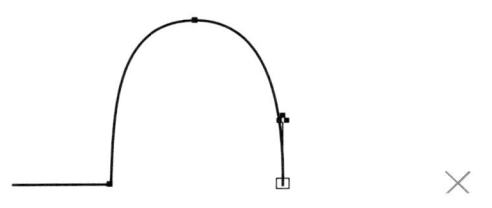

Figure 17. *To continue a path, select one of the end points. Then click or drag with the **Pen** or **Bézigon** tool where you would like the next point to be (indicated by an "X").*

MOVE AND TRANSFORM 9

Just because you've created an object doesn't mean you can't change it. In fact, it is in moving and transforming your objects that you can create some very sophisticated effects. In this chapter, you will learn: how to move objects; how to copy as you move; and how to move, scale, rotate, skew, and reflect objects both by eye and numerically. You will learn what the settings on the Info Bar mean. You will learn how to cut, copy and paste objects. You will learn the difference between the Cut, Copy, and Paste commands and the Clone and Duplicate commands. You will also learn the technique called "Power Duplicating."

As discussed on page 77, you can move an object by simply selecting it and dragging it anywhere on your page. If you would like to know the distance and the position of the object you are dragging, you can see that information in the Info Bar ar the top of your document window.

To read the Info Bar:

1. Choose Info Bar from the View menu or press Command-Shift-R to show the Info Bar (**Figure 1a**).

(Continued on the following page)

Figure 1a. *The **Info Bar** is shown at the top of the document window.*

Chapter 9

2. The Info Bar readings change depending on the position of your cursor, the tool chosen, or the action taken (**Figure 1b**). The following are explanations of the various readings on the Info Bar.

units: indicates the current unit of measurement

x: position of cursor along the horizontal axis.

y: position of cursor along the vertical axis.

dx: horizontal distance you have moved an object.

dy: vertical distance you have moved an object.

dist: total distance along any angle you have moved an object.

angle: angle that any object is being moved, created, or transformed along.

cx: horizontal location of the center point that any object is being created or transformed around.

cy: vertical location of the center point that any object is being created or transformed around.

sx: horizontal scale or skew of an object expressed as a ratio to object's original size (e.g., 1.00 = 100%).

sy: vertical scale or skew of an object expressed as a ratio to object's original size (e.g., 1.00 = 100%).

width: width of rectangle or ellipse.

height: height of rectangle or ellipse.

radius: size of radius of polygon.

sides: number of sides of polygon.

padlock: indicates the selected object or objects are locked.

Note: The Info Bar does not allow you to enter numbers directly into it.

x:5.699732   y:7.111112

dx:1.843908   dy:4.555556

dist:0.58195   angle:83

cx:4.010576   cy:8.621686

sx:0.33 sy:0.46

width:2.13360 height:3.42195

radius:1.343478   sides:5

🔒   units: inches

Figure 1b. *Other displays which are seen on the Info Bar.*

Move and Transform

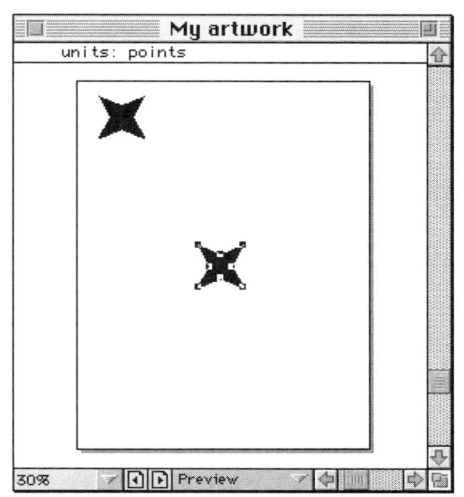

Figure 2. *An **object that is cut or copied** from one position (upper left) will be pasted in the **center of the window**.*

Figure 3a. *To make an Option-copy of an object, hold the **Option** key as you move the object. You will see an **arrow with a plus sign (+)** as you drag.*

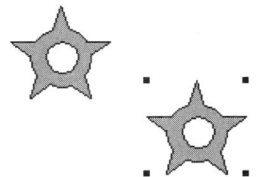

Figure 3b. *When you let go of the **Option** key after you move an object, you will have an exact duplicate of the object.*

To cut, copy, or paste objects:

Once you have an object selected, you can choose Cut (Command-X) or Copy (Command-C) from the File menu. You can then choose Paste (Command-V) from the File menu to paste the object onto the same page, a different page, or a different document. The object will be pasted in the center of the window (**Figure 2**).

To move and copy an object:

1. Select the object you want to copy.
2. Start dragging the object. Press the Option key as you drag. You will see an arrow with a plus sign (+) (**Figure 3a**). This indicates that you are creating a copy of the object.
3. When the object is in the position you want, release the mouse first, then the Option key. The original object will be in its position and a copy will be at the point where you stopped dragging (**Figure 3b**).
4. If you choose Duplicate from the Edit menu or press Command-D, you will continue to make copies of the original object, each positioned the same distance away from the previous copy (**Figure 3c**).

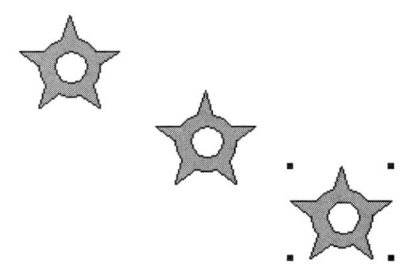

Figure 3c. *If you choose **Duplicate** from the **Edit** menu or press **Command-D** after you have made an Option-copy of an object, you will continue to create additional copies of the object.*

Chapter 9

To rotate an object by eye:

1. Select the object and click the Rotating tool in the toolbox (**Figure 4a**).
2. Move your cursor over the work page. Your cursor will turn into a star.
3. Position the star on the spot you would like the object to rotate around. For instance, if you want to rotate an object around its lower-left corner, place the star on the lower-left corner of the object (**Figure 4b**).
4. Press down on the point you have chosen. Do not let go of the mouse. You will see a line extend out. This is the rotation axis (**Figure 4c**).
5. Still pressing down, drag your cursor away from the original transformation point. Then move the rotation axis. You will see your object rotate as you change the rotation axis (**Figure 4d**).
6. Hold the Shift key to constrain your rotation to 45° increments.
7. Release the mouse when you are satisfied with the position of the rotated object. Your object will now be rotated into position (**Figure 4e**).

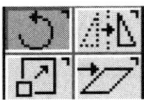

Figure 4a. *To rotate an object by eye, click on the **Rotating** tool in the toolbox.*

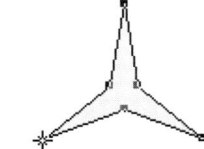

Figure 4b. *When you choose the Rotating tool, your cursor turns into a **star**. Position the star on the point you want the object to rotate around.*

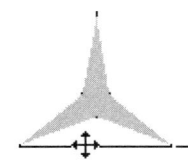

Figure 4c. *Pressing down with the Rotating tool shows the **rotation axis**, the line that the object will be rotated around.*

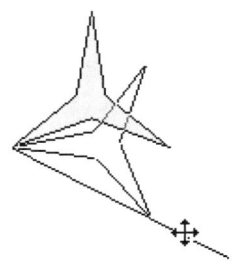

Figure 4d. *As you drag the object to be rotated, the **rotation axis** and the **preview** shows the position to which the object will be rotated.*

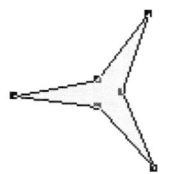

Figure 4e. *The original object rotated by eye.*

Move and Transform

Figure 5. *When you perform a rotation or a reflection, move your cursor along the line to a point away from the transformation point. This will make it easier to control the transformation.*

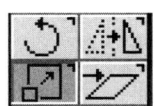

Figure 6a. *To scale an object by eye, click on the **Scaling** tool in the toolbox.*

Figure 6b. *When you choose the Scaling tool, your cursor turns into a **star**. Position the star on the point from which you want the object to scale.*

Figure 6c. *As you press down with the Scaling tool and then drag, you will see an **outline** of the object that indicates the scaling of the object.*

Figure 6d. *The original object scaled by eye.*

Tip

- The farther you drag your cursor away from the transformation point during rotation or reflection, the easier it will be to control the transformation. Keeping your cursor near the transformation point will cause the object to transform quickly. Farther away, the transformation will occur more slowly (**Figure 5**).

To scale an object by eye:

1. Choose the object you want to scale and click on the Scaling tool in the toolbox (**Figure 6a**).

2. Move your cursor over to the work page. Your cursor will turn into a star (**Figure 6b**).

3. Position the star on the spot from which you would like the object to scale. For instance, if you want to have an object grow from the bottom up, you would place the star on the bottom edge of the object.

4. Press down on the point you have chosen. Do not let go of the mouse.

5. Still pressing down, drag your cursor away from the original transformation point. You will see an outline of your object change its size as you move the cursor (**Figure 6c**).

6. Hold the Shift key to constrain the scale to a proportional change.

7. Release the mouse when you are satisfied with the size of the scaled object. Your object will now be scaled into position (**Figure 6d**).

Scale an Object by Eye

107

Chapter 9

To reflect an object by eye:

1. Choose the object you want to reflect and click on the Reflecting tool in the toolbox (**Figure 7a**).
2. Move your cursor over to the work page. Your cursor will turn into a star.
3. Position the star on the point you want the object to reflect around (**Figure 7b**). For instance, if you want to reflect an object around a spot to the right of the object, place the star to the right of the object.
4. Press down on the point you have chosen. Do not let go of the mouse. You will see a line extend out from the star. This line is the reflection axis (**Figure 7c**). Think of the reflection axis as the mirror in which your object is being reflected.
5. Still pressing down, drag your cursor away from the original transformation point. Move your cursor so that the object takes the position you want it to (**Figure 7d**).
6. Hold the Shift key to constrain your reflection to 45° increments.
7. Release the mouse when you are satisfied with the position of the reflected object. Your object will now be reflected into position (**Figure 7e**).

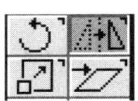

Figure 7a. *To reflect an object by eye, click on the **Reflecting** tool in the toolbox.*

Figure 7b. *When you choose the Reflecting tool, your cursor turns into a **star**. Position the star on the point you want the object to reflect around.*

Figure 7c. *Pressing down with the Reflecting tool shows the **reflection axis**, the line that the object will be reflected around.*

Figure 7d. *As you drag the object to be reflected, the **reflection axis** and **preview** show the position to which the object will be reflected.*

Figure 7e. *The original object reflected by eye.*

Move and Transform

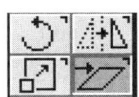

Figure 8a. *To skew an object by eye, click on the **Skewing** tool in the toolbox.*

Figure 8b. *When you choose the Skewing tool, your cursor turns into a **star**. Position the star on the point from which you want the object to skew.*

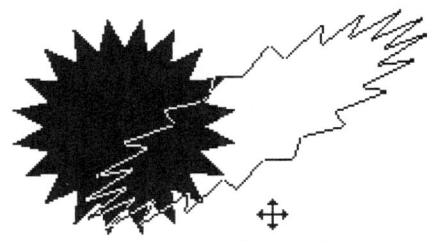

Figure 8c. *As you press down with the Skewing tool and then drag, you will see an **outline** of the object that indicates the skewing of the object.*

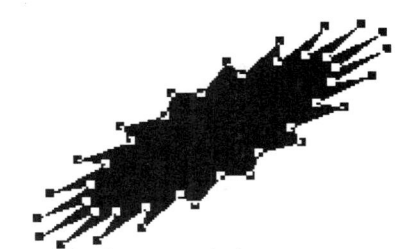

Figure 8d. *The original object skewed by eye.*

To skew an object by eye:

1. Choose the object you want to skew and click on the Skewing tool in the toolbox (**Figure 8a**).

2. Move your cursor over to the work page. Your cursor will turn into a star.

3. Position the star on the spot from which you would like the object to skew (**Figure 8b**). For instance, if you want to skew an object around its lower-left corner, you would place the star on the lower-left corner of the object.

4. Press down on the point you have chosen. Do not let go of the mouse.

5. Still pressing down, drag your cursor away from the original transformation point. You will see an outline of your object change its shape as you move the cursor (**Figure 8c**).

6. Hold the Shift key to constrain the skew. If you drag in a general horizontal direction, the skew will be constrained exactly horizontal. If you drag in a general vertical direction, the skew will be constrained exactly vertical.

7. Release the mouse when you are satisfied with the position of the object. Your object will be skewed into position (**Figure 8d**).

109

To make a copy as you transform an object:

If you hold the Option key as you drag to transform, you will see a plus sign (+) next to the star. Let go of the mouse first, then the Option key, to create a copy of the original object transformed to the position you chose (**Figure 9a**). If you do not see the plus sign (+), check the Preferences settings for Object Editing *(see page 267)*. Choose Duplicate from the Edit menu or press Command-D (**Figure 9b**) to create additional transformed copies.

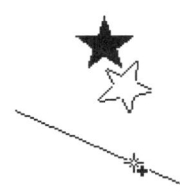

Figure 9a. *If you hold the Option key as you perform a transformation, you will see a **plus sign (+)** next to your cursor. When you let go of the mouse, you will have a copy of the original object transformed into position.*

To use Power Duplicating:

Making a copy as you transform an object allows you to create very sophisticated effects. But FreeHand offers you an even more sophisticated technique called "Power Duplicating." This allows you to "store" up to five different transformations and then apply them all together as you make copies.

To use the transformation tools for Power Duplicating:

1. Choose the object that you want to transform.

2. Choose Clone from the Edit menu or press Command-=. You have just created a clone (copy) of your object that is on top of the original (**Figure 10a**).

3. Move this clone with your arrow, or use any of the transformation tools to change the clone (**Figure 10b**).

4. If you wish, you can apply any of the other transformations (**Figure 10c**). You cannot apply a transformation function more than once.

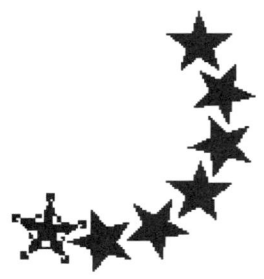

Figure 9b. *Once you have made a copy by holding the Option key, choosing **Duplicate** from the **Edit** menu or pressing **Command-D** will create additional transformed copies of the object.*

Figure 10a. *To do a **Power Duplication**, you need to clone your object. Choose **Clone** from the **Edit** menu or press **Command**-=.*

Figure 10b. *Perform the **first transformation** on the clone. In this case, the object was rotated.*

Move and Transform

Figure 10c. *Perform any **additional transformations**. In this case, the object was scaled.*

5. Each of the transformations you have performed is now stored. There is a limit of five transformations that can be stored.

6. Choose Duplicate from the Edit menu or press Command-D. The object you created will be copied according to the transformations you stored.

7. Choose Duplicate again and again. Each command will create a new object transformed according to the stored transformation settings (**Figure 10d**).

8. If you deselect the object before choosing Duplicate, you will not be able to make the Power Duplication.

Figure 10d. *Choose **Duplicate** from the **Edit** menu or press **Command-D**. You will create additional copies of the object, each one with all transformations applied. In this case, both rotation and scale transformations result in an object that moves around in a circle and grows bigger as it moves.*

Chapter 9

So far we've done our transformations by eye. If you've got a steady hand, and a keen eye on the Info Bar, you can be pretty precise. To work more precisely, you need the Transform palette.

To view the Transform palette:

Choose Transform from the Window menu or press Command-M. The Transform palette will appear.

To move an object using the Transform palette:

1. Choose the object you want to move. Click on the Move icon in the Transform palette (**Figure 11**).
2. Enter the amount that you want to move the object in the x and y fields.
3. Check the Contents setting to have any contents pasted inside the path moved along with the path *(see Chapter 18, "Path Operations")*.
4. Check the Fills setting to have any Graduated, Radial, or Tiled fills moved along with the path *(see Chapter 11, "Fills")*.
5. Click the Apply button or press the Return or Enter key to apply the move.

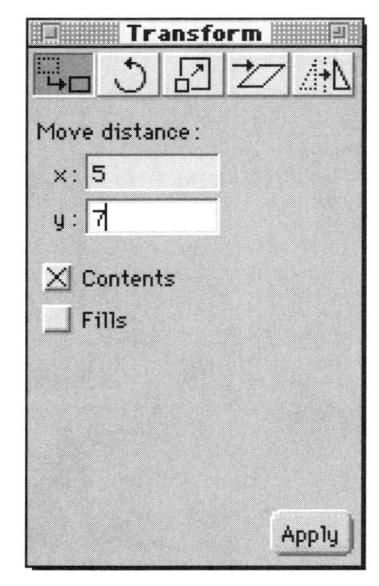

Figure 11. *The* **Move** *settings in the* **Transform** *palette let you move objects numerically. Click on the* **Move** *icon in the Transform palette to see the Move settings.*

Move and Transform

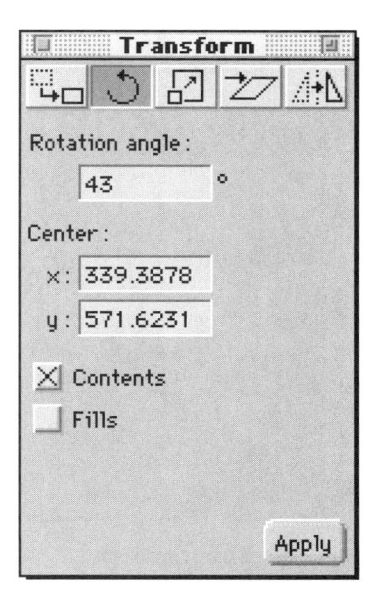

Figure 12a. *The **Rotation** settings of the **Transform** palette.*

Figure 12b. *The top whale was rotated to the bottom two positions. The left position had the **Contents box checked** so the pasted-in lines rotated with the object. The right position had the **Contents box unchecked** so the pasted-in lines did not rotate with the object.*

To rotate an object using the Transform palette:

1. Choose the object you want to rotate. Click on the Rotation icon in the Transform palette (**Figure 12a**).

2. Enter the amount that you want to rotate the object in the Rotation angle field.

3. The point of transformation will automatically be the center point of the object. To change this point, enter the coordinates you want in the x and y fields. (If you need to know the coordinates for a certain point, position your cursor over that point and look at the listing in the Info Bar.)

4. Check the Contents setting to have any contents that are pasted inside the path rotated along with the path (**Figure 12b**).

5. Check the Fills setting to have any Graduated, Radial, or Tiled fills rotated along with the path.

6. Click the Apply button or press the Return or Enter key to apply the rotation.

Chapter 9

To scale an object using the Transform palette:

1. Choose the object you want to scale. Click on the Scale icon in the Transform palette (**Figure 13a**).

2. Enter the scale amount that you want to change the object. For a proportional scale, keep the Uniform box checked. To scale the object nonproportionally, deselect the Uniform box and fill in the settings for the x (horizontal) and y (vertical) fields.

3. The point of transformation will automatically be the center point of the object. To change this point, enter the coordinates in the x and y fields.

4. Check the Contents setting to have any contents that are pasted inside the path scaled along with the path.

5. Check the Fills setting to have any Graduated, Radial, or Tiled fills scaled along with the path (**Figure 13b**).

6. Click the Apply button or press the Return or Enter key to apply the scale.

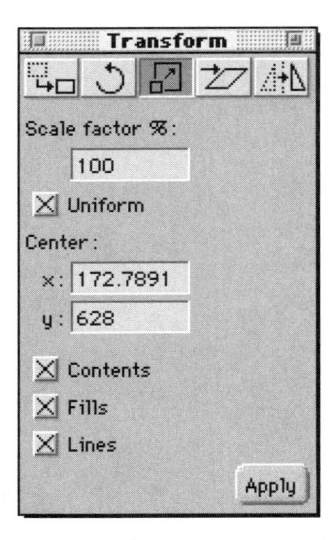

Figure 13a. *The **Scale** settings of the **Transform** palette.*

Figure 13b. *The top cookie jar was scaled to the bottom three jars. The left jar had the **Fills box checked** so the pattern tile scaled with the object. The middle jar had the **Fills box unchecked** so the pattern tile did not scale with the object. The right jar was scaled with the **Uniform setting unchecked**.*

Move and Transform

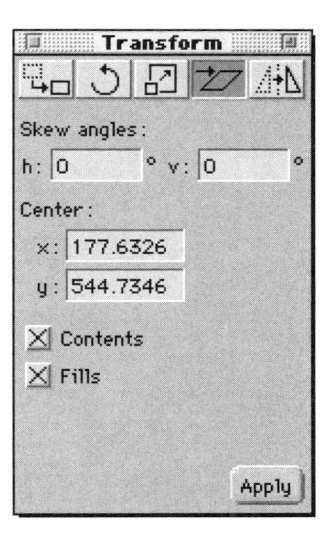

Figure 14. *The **Skew** settings of the **Transform** palette.*

To skew an object using the Transform palette:

1. Choose the object. Click on the Skew icon in the Transform palette (**Figure 14**).
2. Enter the horizontal amount that you want to skew the object in the h field.
3. Enter the vertical amount that you want to skew the object in the the v field.
4. The point of transformation will automatically be the center point of the object. If you want to change this point, enter the coordinates you want in the x and y fields.
5. Check the Contents setting to have any contents that are pasted inside the path skewed along with the path.
6. Check the Fills setting to have any Graduated, Radial, or Tiled fills skewed along with the path.
7. Click the Apply button or press the Return or Enter key to apply the skew.

Chapter 9

To reflect an object using the Transform palette:

1. Choose the object you want to reflect. Click on the Reflection icon in the Transform palette (**Figure 15**).

2. Enter the angle that you want the object to reflect around in the Reflect axis field.

3. The point of transformation will automatically be the center point of the object. If you want to change this point, enter the coordinates you want in the x and y fields.

4. Check the Contents setting to have any contents that are pasted inside the path reflected along with the path.

5. Check the Fills setting to have any Graduated, Radial, or Tiled fills reflected along with the path.

6. Click the Apply button or press the Return or Enter key to apply the skew.

Tips

- Once you have made a Clone of an object (choose Clone from the Edit menu or press Command-=), you can use the Transform palette to create Power Duplication effects.

- For Power Duplicating, you can mix numerical transformations and transformations done by eye.

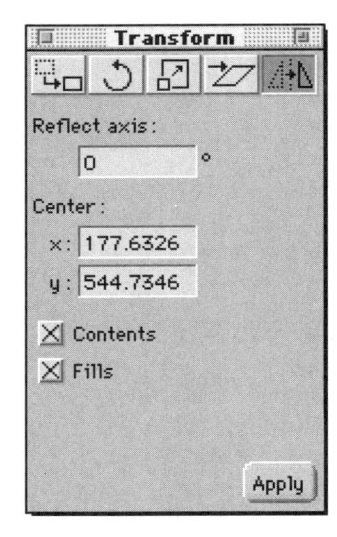

Figure 15. *The **Reflection** settings of the **Transform** palette.*

COLOR 10

One of the most versatile parts of FreeHand is the way it works with color. In this chapter, you will learn how to define colors in the Color Mixer using FreeHand's color systems: CMYK, RGB, HLS, Tint, and the Macintosh color settings and wheel. You will learn how to use FreeHand's Color List to: add a color; rename a color; convert process and spot colors; move, duplicate, or remove colors; make a tint; and add multiple colors. You will also learn how to work with color-matching libraries and how to create a custom color library.

There are two different palettes that control most of the color functions in FreeHand. The Color List is where all the colors in your FreeHand document are stored. The Color Mixer is where you can define new colors. We'll start with the various ways to define colors using the Color Mixer and then learn how to add them to the Color List.

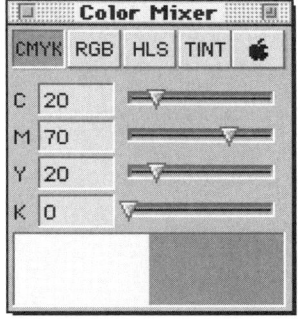

Figure 1. *The **Color Mixer** in the **CMYK** mode.*

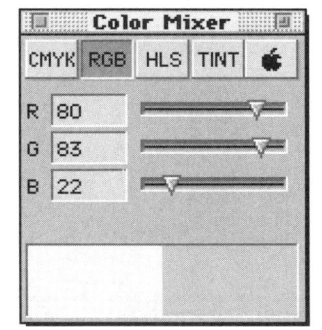

Figure 2. *The **Color Mixer** in the **RGB** mode.*

Five ways to define colors in the Color Mixer:

1. CMYK: Defines the color according to the four process colors used by most commercial printers—Cyan, Magenta, Yellow, and Black. This is the most common and best-known color system used by graphic artists (**Figure 1**).

2. RGB: Defines the color according to the Red, Green, and Blue components. This is primarily a video color system, and many people who design for multimedia and the World Wide Web use RGB to define their colors (**Figure 2**).

(Continued on the following page)

Color Mixer

117

Chapter 10

3. **HLS**: Defines the color according to Hue, Lightness, and Saturation components (**Figure 3**). This system lets you pick different colors with similar values. Pastel colors are examples of colors with similar lightness and saturation but different hues.
4. **Tint**: Takes a previously defined color and displays the different tints available for that color (**Figure 4**).
5. : Shows the Macintosh color settings and wheel (**Figure 5**).

To decide which color system to use:

If you are defining a color for use in a four-color printing process, you will most likely want to use the CMYK color system to define your colors. But if you are trying to match colors that are defined by other systems, you should use those systems when defining your colors.

Figure 3. *The Color Mixer in the HLS mode.*

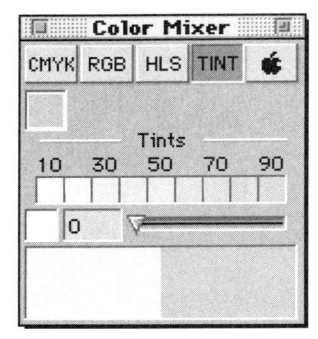

Figure 4. *The Color Mixer in the Tint mode.*

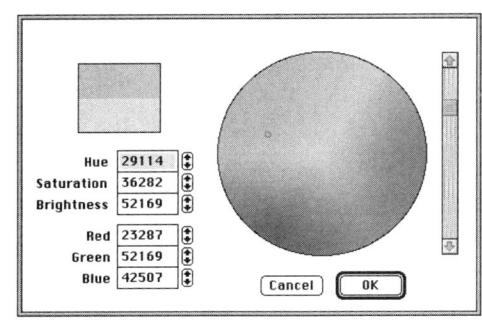

Figure 5. *The Macintosh color settings and wheel, shown when the is chosen.*

Color

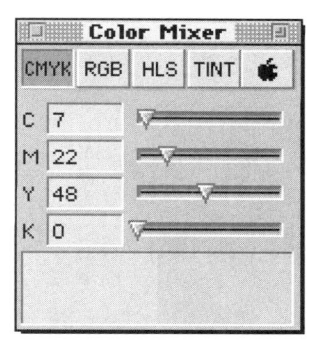

Figure 6a. *Double-click on the **CMYK** fields to enter exact values for your color.*

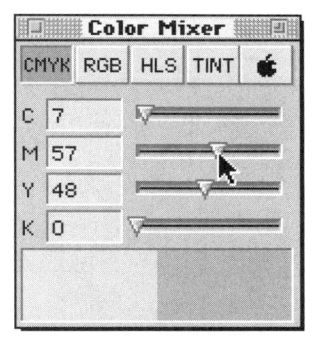

Figure 6b. *Use the **sliders** to change the CMYK values of your color.*

Figure 6c. *In HLS, click on the **color wheel** to define the hue and saturation. Use the slider to adjust the lightness.*

To define a color:

1. Choose the Color Mixer from the Window menu or press Command-Shift-C.

2. Click on the mode you want to use in the Color Mixer.

3. In the CMYK mode, double-click in the CMYK fields to enter the color values (**Figure 6a**). Once a field is highlighted, use the Tab key to move from one field to another.

or

In the CMYK mode, drag the sliders to change the values of the colors (**Figure 6b**).

or

In the HLS or modes, click on the desired portion of the color wheel (**Figure 6c**).

Tips

■ If the Color Mixer is not displayed, double-clicking on any color swatch will display the Color Mixer.

■ If the Color Mixer is displayed, double-clicking on any color swatch will hide the Color Mixer.

Chapter 10

Once you've defined a color, you will want to store it in your document. To do this, you need to use the Color List.

To add a color to the Color List:

1. Choose Color List (Command-9) from the Window menu.
   or
   Double-click in the Color Well of the Color Mixer to open the Color List.
2. Place your arrow on the color square created in the Color Mixer. Drag that color off the Color Mixer (**Figure 7**).
3. Once you have dragged the color off the Color Mixer, you can drop it onto the color drop box (**Figure 8a**).
   or
   Choose New from the Options pop-up menu (**Figure 8b**). Whichever color is defined in the Color Mixer will be added to the Color List.
   or
   Drop the color onto the Color List itself (**Figure 8c**). This allows you to position new colors exactly where you would like them in the list.

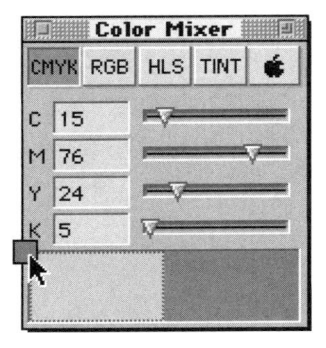

Figure 7. *To store a color, drag the color off the Color Well, the bottom area of the **Color Mixer**.*

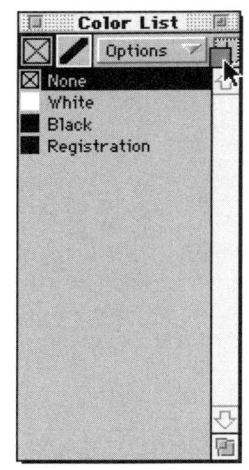

Figure 8a. *To add colors to the Color List, you can drop them onto the **color drop box**.*

Color

Tips

- Once you have added a new color to the Color List, you will see that the color is named according to its CMYK values. Even if you define the color using one of the other systems, such as RGB, the color will be displayed in the Color List according to CMYK values.

- If you would like to see your colors in RGB values, change the Color preferences *(see page 263)*.

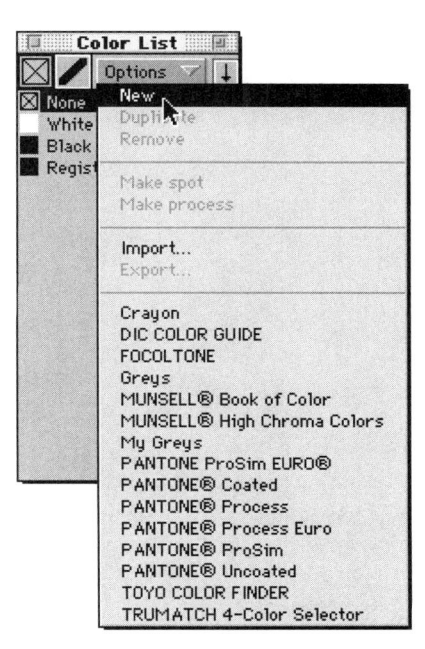

Figure 8b. *To add colors to the Color List, you can choose **New** from the Color List **Options** pop-up menu.*

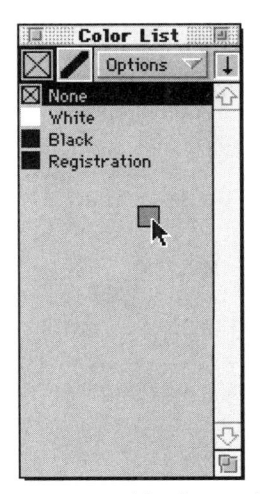

Figure 8c. *To add colors to the Color List, you can drop them onto the **Color List** in the spot you would like them to appear.*

Chapter 10

To rename a color:

1. Double-click on the name of the color in the Color List. The name will appear highlighted, indicating that it is selected (**Figure 9a**).
2. Type the new name for the color (**Figure 9b**).
3. Press Return or click on another color in the Color List. The color will now be renamed (**Figure 9c**).

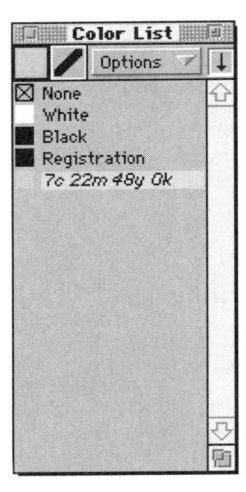

Figure 9a. *To rename a color in the Color List, double-click on the name of a color. This will highlight the*

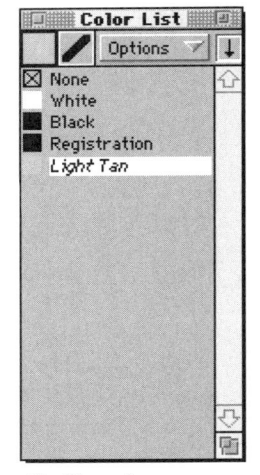

Figure 9b. *Type the new name for the color.*

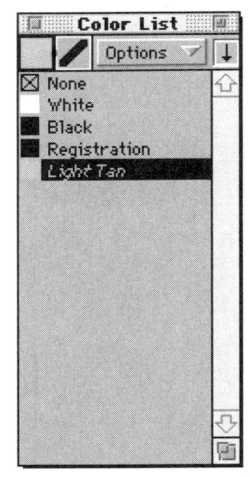

Figure 9c. *Press* **Return** *or click on another color.*

Color

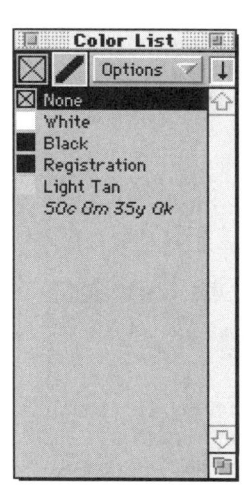

Figure 10a. *Process colors are listed in an **italic** typeface in the Color List. **Spot** colors are listed in a **roman** typeface.*

All colors that you define in the Color Mixer come as process colors, which means they will be separated into CMYK color plates during the separation process. If you want, you can change colors from process to spot. Spot colors will not be broken down into their CMYK values; they will be separated onto their own plates.

To convert process and spot colors:

1. Click on the name of the color in the Color List. Process colors are written in italic type, and spot colors are written in roman type (**Figure 10a**).
2. If the color is process, choose Make spot from the Options pop-up menu of the Color List (**Figure 10b**).
3. If the color is spot, choose Make process from the Options pop-up menu of the Color List (**Figure 10c**).

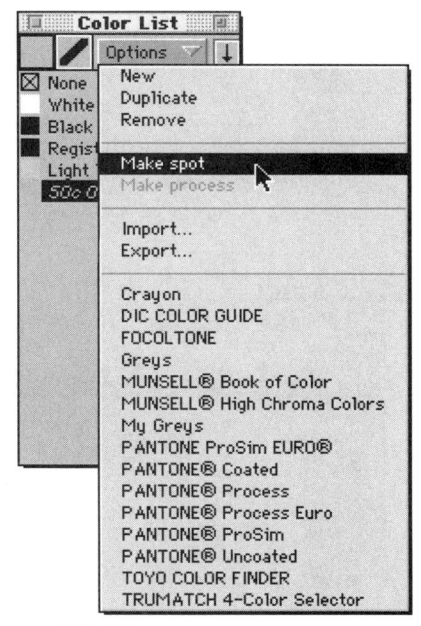

Figure 10b. *To convert a process color to spot, choose **Make spot** from the **Options** pop-up menu.*

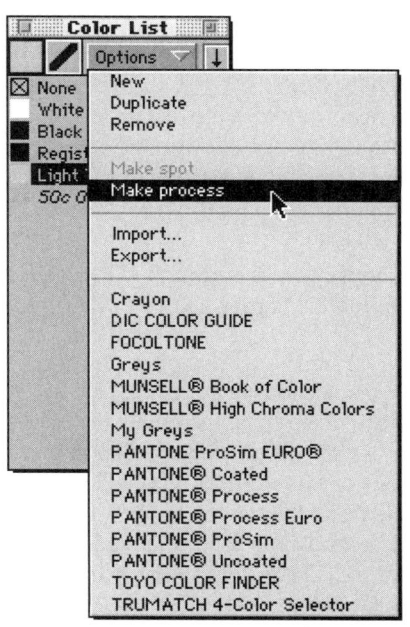

Figure 10c. *To convert a spot color to process, choose **Make process** from the **Options** pop-up menu.*

Chapter 10

If you're working with a lot of colors, you're going to want to have your favorite colors at the top of the Color List. Or you may want to group certain colors together. To do so, you can move the names of the colors in the Color List.

To move color names:
1. Press on the name of the color you want to move.
2. Drag it to the new position and then release the mouse (**Figure 11**).

To duplicate a color:
1. Click on the name of the color you wish to duplicate.
2. Choose Duplicate from the Options pop-up menu (**Figure 12**). The new color will be listed as "Copy of Color Name."

To remove a color:
1. Click on the name of the color you wish to remove. The name will be highlighted.
2. If you want to remove a group of colors listed together, click on the top name, hold the Shift key, and click on the bottom name. All the names should be highlighted.
3. Choose Remove from the Options pop-up menu (**Figure 13**).

Tip
- If you try to remove a color that is being used by an object, is the base of a tint, is part of a placed EPS file, or is part of a style sheet, you will get an alert box telling you the color is being used and cannot be removed. You need to find all uses of the color and change them before you can remove the color.

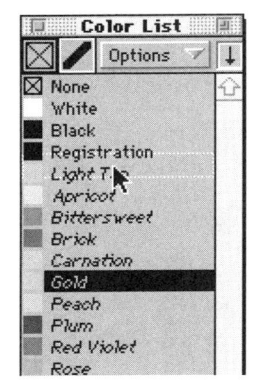

Figure 11. *To move a color to a new position in the Color List, drag the color and then release the mouse.*

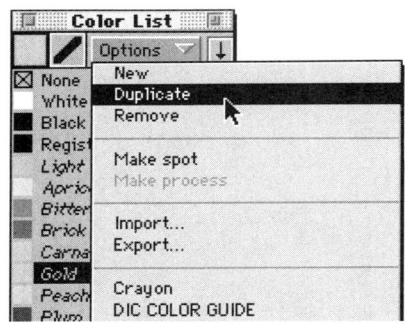

Figure 12. *Choosing* **Duplicate** *from the* **Options** *pop-up menu will make a copy of the selected color.*

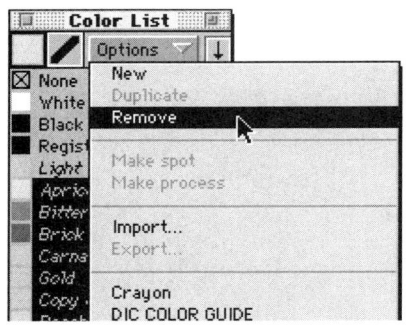

Figure 13. *Choosing* **Remove** *from the* **Options** *pop-up menu will remove all selected colors from the Color List.*

Move, Duplicate, or Remove Color in Color List

124

Color

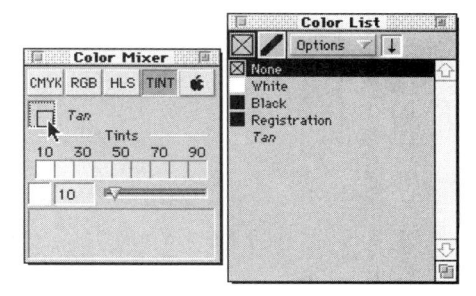

Figure 14a. *To create a tint of a base color, drag the swatch of that color from the **Color List** onto the drop box of the **Tint Color Mixer**.*

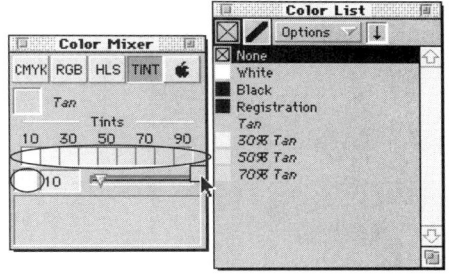

Figure 14b. *To store a tint in the Color List, drag one of the tint swatch boxes (circled) from the **Color Mixer**. Do not drag from the Color Well, the bottom area of the Color Mixer.*

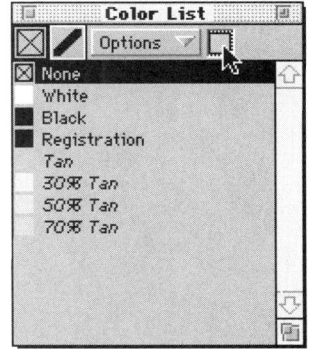

Figure 14c. *To put a tint swatch in the Color List, drop the swatch on the **Color List** drop box or on the list itself.*

If you have a color defined, you can then use that color as the basis for a tint. This is useful if you are working with spot colors and wish to apply tints of those colors.

To make a tint of a color:

1. Make sure both the Color List and the Tint mode of the Color Mixer are displayed.

2. Place your arrow on the color swatch—not the name—of the color you want to create a tint of. Drag the color swatch from the Color List and drop it onto the drop box at the top left of the Color Mixer Tint area (**Figure 14a**).

3. You should now see the name of the color to the right of the drop box. Drag one of the tint swatch boxes from the Color Mixer back over to the Color List (**Figure 14b**).

4. Drop the tint swatch onto the Color List drop box or onto the list itself (**Figure 14c**).

5. The tint will be listed as a percentage of the color's name (**Figure 14d**).

Tip

- If you change a base color from process to spot (and vice versa), any tints defined from that base color will change from process to spot.

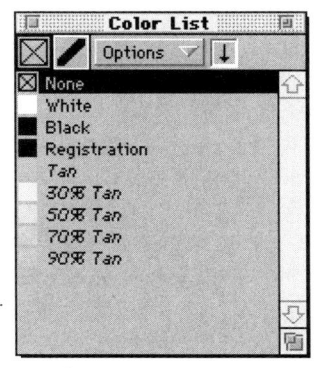

Figure 14d. *Tints will be named as percentages of their original color name.*

125

Chapter 10

So far you have added colors to the Color List one at a time. Though this is fine for one or two colors, it could be laborious if you need many colors. FreeHand has other ways of adding colors to the Color List.

To add colors from copied objects:

If you have created an object with a named color in one FreeHand file, and you copy and paste that object into another file, the color will be added to the Color List.

To add colors from imported EPS files:

If you place an EPS file that uses named colors, those named colors will be added to the Color List *(for more information about placing images, see pages 239–240)*.

To add colors from custom color libraries:

Once you have created a Color List, you can export those colors as a custom color library. You can export a custom color library to the Color List of other documents.

To add colors from color-matching system libraries:

FreeHand supplies you with various premade color libraries that are used by many commercial printers, artists and designers. These color libraries may be process or spot. They are customarily used with printed swatches that allow you to pick a color from the library and compare it to a specific color. This is a better way to match colors than relying on the output of typical desktop printers.

Some of the color-matching systems that ship with FreeHand include Pantone (both process and spot), Trumatch (process), and Toyo (process).

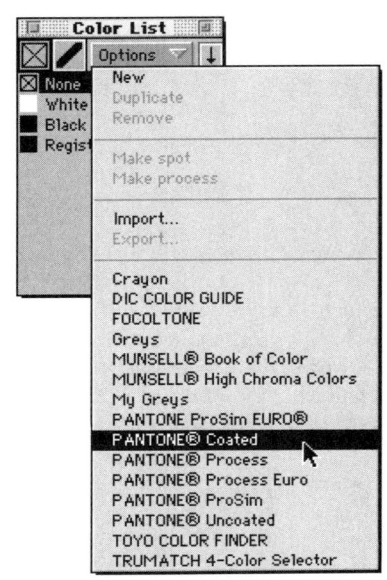

Figure 15a. *Under the* **Options** *pop-up menu of the* **Color List***, choose the name of the color-matching system that you want to add colors from.*

Color

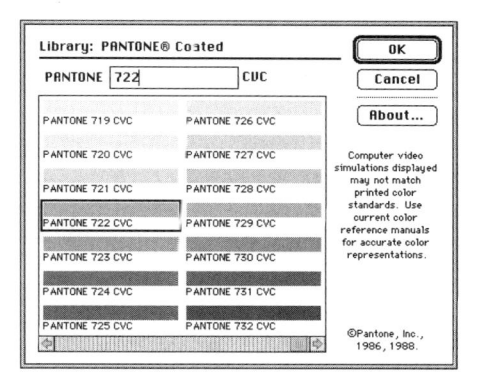

Figure 15b. *In the **Library** dialog box, type in the code of the color or click on the name of the color you want to add to your Color List.*

In addition, FreeHand supplies a library of colors called Crayon. These are colors defined to look like the colors in a typical box of coloring crayons. Also, FreeHand supplies a library of colors called "Greys." These are both spot and process gray colors broken down in 1% increments. Neither the Crayon nor the Greys library is part of any color-matching system. If you need more information on which color-matching system to use, consult with the print shop that will be printing your work.

If you want to work with certain colors from one of the color-matching systems, you will need to add those colors to your Color List.

1. Choose the name of the color-matching system from the Options pop-up menu of the Color List (**Figure 15a**).

2. In the Library dialog box, type in the number or code of the color you want to add to your Color List (**Figure 15b**).

3. Click OK to add the color to your Color List.

4. If you want to add more than one color, hold the Shift key and click on any additional colors. Click OK when you have all the colors you want.

Tip

- To add many colors at once from a library, hold the Shift key and click on the first name you want to add. Still holding the Shift key down, click on the names of the other colors you want to add. Each of the colors will be selected. Click OK when you have all your colors selected.

Chapter 10

To export your own custom color library:

1. Choose Export from the Options pop-up menu of the Color List (**Figure 16a**).

2. The Export Colors dialog box will appear. Use the Shift key to select as many colors as you want (**Figure 16b**). Click OK.

3. In the Create color library dialog box, enter the Library name and the File name (**Figure 16c**). The Colors per column and Colors per row fields control how the library will be displayed.

4. Choose Save to place your custom color library in the Color folder located in the FreeHand application folder. Choose Save as... to specify a different folder or disk.

Tips

- To delete custom color libraries from the Options pop-up menu, delete them from the Color folder in the FreeHand application folder.

- Colors you add to one document will not automatically appear in the next document you create. To have a list of colors always appear in new documents, you need to add colors to the FreeHand Defaults file. *(To create a new defaults file, see page 278.)*

- The FreeHand Xtras commands let you name all unamed colors; adjust the values of colors in differently colored objects; and saturate, desaturate, lighten, and darken the colors in different objects. *(For more information on changing colors using the Xtras commands, see Chapter 19, "Xtras.")*

Figure 16a. *To create your own custom color library, choose* **Export** *from the* **Options** *pop-up menu.*

Figure 16b. *In the* **Export Colors** *dialog box, use the* **Shift** *key to select as many colors as you want from the Color List.*

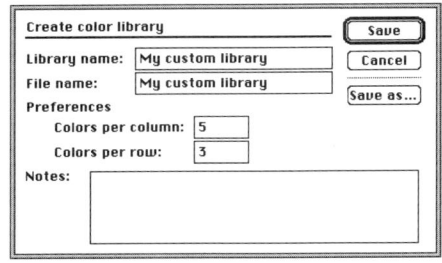

Figure 16c. *In the* **Create color library** *dialog box, the* **Library name** *is how the library will be listed in the Color List. The* **File name** *is how the file will be named. The* **Colors per column** *and* **Colors per row** *fields govern how the colors are arranged.*

Export a Custom Color Library

128

FILLS 11

Once you've got an object on your page, you're going to want to fill it various ways. In this chapter, you will learn which objects can be filled. You will learn the different types of fills: Basic, Graduated, Radial, Tiled, Custom, Textured, Pattern, PostScript, and Multi-Colored. You will also learn how to apply the different types of fills to objects, as well as special techniques for making the fills look their best. You will learn the use of None as a fill. Finally, you will learn the basics of the Overprint option.

You can apply a fill to any object, but only closed paths will display the fill that you apply. If you close an open path that has a fill applied to it, you will then see the fill. To see if an object is open or closed, choose the Object icon of the Inspector palette and see if the Closed box is checked or unchecked. *(For more information on open and closed paths, see pages 89–90.)*

To fill an object:

All the fills in FreeHand are chosen through the Fill icon of the Document Inspector palette (**Figure 1**). Once you have chosen the Fill icon in the Inspector palette, you access the fills through the pop-up menu.

Figure 1. *To fill an object, choose the* **Fill** *icon of the* **Document Inspector** *palette.*

129

Chapter 11

To apply a Basic fill using the Document Inspector:

1. Select the object you wish to apply the fill to.
2. Click on the Fill Icon of the Document Inspector palette.
3. Choose Basic from the pop-up menu (**Figure 2**).

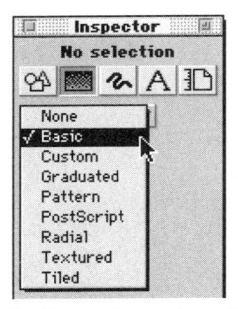

Figure 2. *To see the various fill choices, press on the **Fill** icon **pop-up** menu of the **Inspector** palette.*

Once you have a Basic fill applied to any object, there are many ways to change the fill color. Choose whichever method is most convenient for you.

To change the color of a Basic fill:

1. With the object selected, click on the name of the color in the Color List (**Figure 3a**). Notice that the Fill drop box in the upper left has a black line around it (**Figure 3b**). That indicates that whichever color is clicked will become the color of the Fill of the object. The box next to the Fill drop box indicates the color of the stroke of the object *(see Chapter 12, "Strokes")*.

   or

   Drag a color swatch from the Color Mixer or the Color List onto the drop box in the Inspector palette (**Figure 4**).

   or

   Drag a color swatch from the Color Mixer onto the Fill drop box in the Color List (**Figure 5**).

   or

   Drag a color swatch from the Color Mixer or the Color List onto the middle of the object (**Figure 6**).

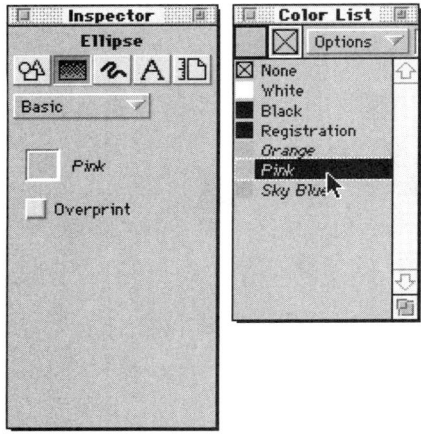

Figure 3a. *Clicking on the **name** of the color in the **Color List** will apply that color to whichever object is selected.*

Figure 3b. *If the **Fill drop box** has a black line around it, clicking on a color will apply that color to the fill of the object. If the Stroke drop box has a black line around it, clicking on a color will apply that color to the stroke of the object.*

130

Fills

Tip

■ If you have no object selected, any changes you make to the Fill icon of the Inspector palette or the Fill drop box of the Color List will be applied to the next object created.

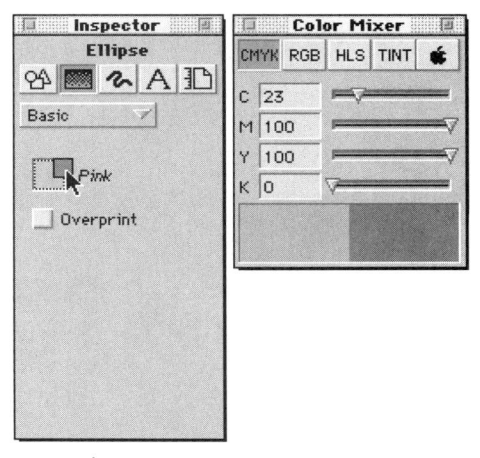

Figure 4. *To change the color of a Basic fill, drag a swatch from the **Color Mixer** or **Color List** onto the **drop box** of the **Inspector** palette.*

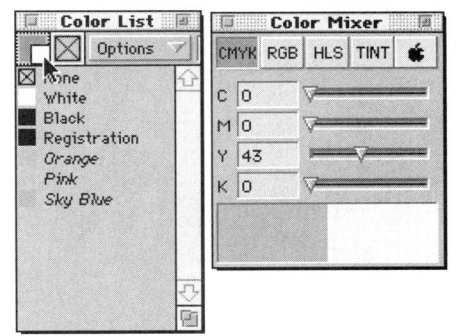

Figure 5. *To change the color of a Basic fill, drag a swatch from the **Color Mixer** onto the **Fill drop box** in the **Color List**.*

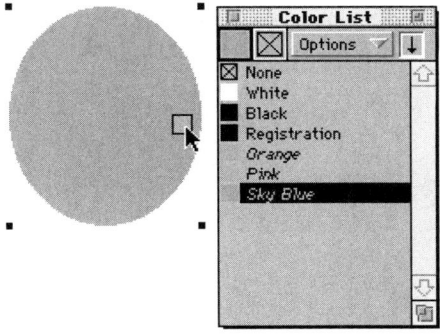

Figure 6. *To change the color of a Basic fill, drag a swatch from the **Color Mixer** or the **Color List** onto the **middle of the object**.*

Basic Fills

131

Chapter 11

FreeHand lets you create special fills that start with one color and change into another. There are two types of these fills: Graduated and Radial. In a Graduated fill, the colors change along a line that can be angled in any direction. *(For information on Radial fills, see page 134.)*

To apply a Graduated fill using the Document Inspector:

1. With the object selected, choose Graduated from the pop-up menu in the Inspector palette. The settings for a Graduated fill will appear (**Figure 7**).
2. Drag a color swatch onto the From drop box to hold whichever color you want to start the Graduated fill.
3. Drag a color swatch onto the To drop box to hold whichever color you want to end the Graduated fill.
4. Choose Linear or Logarithmic from the Taper pop-up menu. A linear taper changes in uniform increments from one color to another. A logarithmic taper changes in increasing increments from one color to another (**Figure 8**).
5. Enter the angle you want the fill to change along by entering the angle in the Angle field or rotating the wheel.

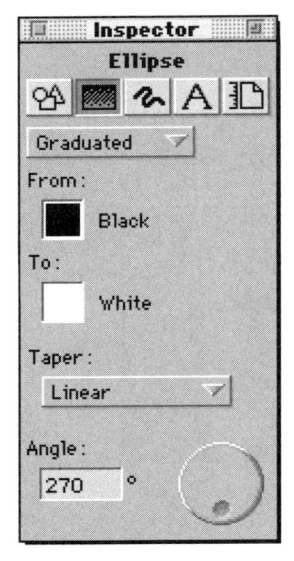

Figure 7. *The **Graduated** fill settings in the **Inspector** palette.*

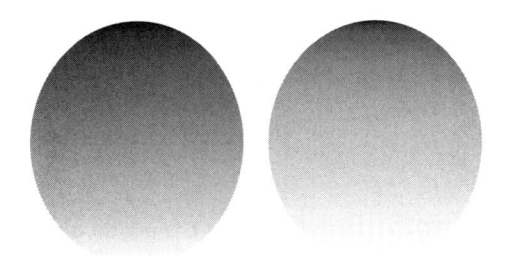

Figure 8. *The difference between a **Linear** fill (left) and a **Logarithmic** fill (right).*

Fills

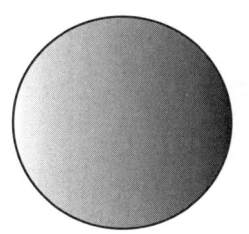

Figure 9a. *To **start** the 3-D button, fill a circle with a **Graduated** fill.*

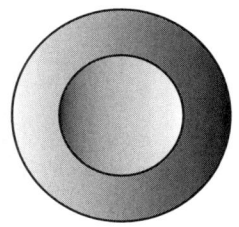

Figure 9b. *To **finish** the button, create a smaller circle and fill it with another **Graduated** fill.*

Once you understand the Graduated fill, you can use it to create various effects.

To create a 3-D button using Graduated fills:

1. Create a circle. Fill it with a Graduated fill that changes from black to white along a 180° angle and has a Linear taper (**Figure 9a**).

2. Create a smaller circle and place it inside the larger one. Fill this circle with a Graduated fill that changes from black to white along a 0° angle and has a Logarithmic taper (**Figure 9b**).

Tip

- Vary the angle and taper for other looks.

To apply a Graduated fill by dragging a color:

1. Select an object.

2. Drag a color swatch onto the object while holding the Control key (**Figure 10a**). The object will take on a Graduated fill with the color that you dragged as the To color. The angle of the fill will be determined by the spot where you dropped the color swatch (**Figure 10b**).

Tip

- Once you have a Graduated fill applied to an object, you can change the To and From colors by dragging color swatches directly onto the object. Where you drop the swatch sets the angle of the color change.

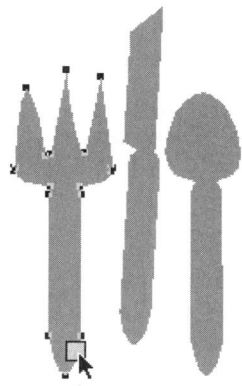

Figure 10a. *If you hold the **Control** key as you drag a color swatch onto an object...*

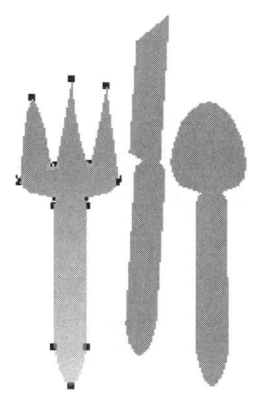

Figure 10b. *...you will apply a **Graduated** fill to that object.*

133

Chapter 11

In a Radial fill, the color starts at a center point and moves outward in a circle to the other color. A Radial fill is like a sun radiating colors outward.

To apply a Radial fill using the Document Inspector:

1. With the object selected, choose Radial from the pop-up menu in the Inspector palette. The settings for the Radial fill will appear (**Figure 11**).
2. Onto the Outside drop box, drag a color swatch of whichever color you want to be at the outside of the fill.
3. Onto the Inside drop box, drag a color swatch of whichever color you want to be at the center of the fill.
4. Move the center point in the Locate center box to change the position of the Inside color (**Figures 12a–b**).

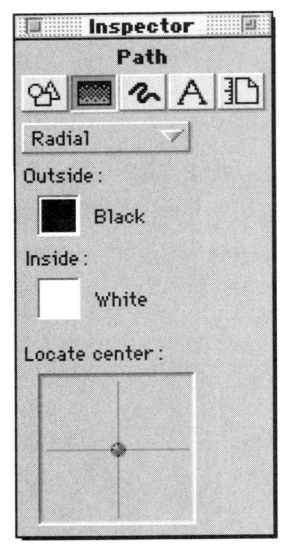

Figure 11. *The **Radial** fill settings in the **Inspector** palette.*

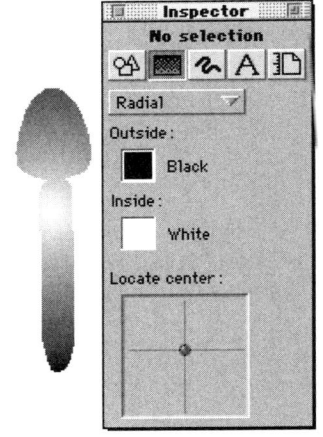

Figure 12a. *A **Radial** fill with the **center location** in the center of the object.*

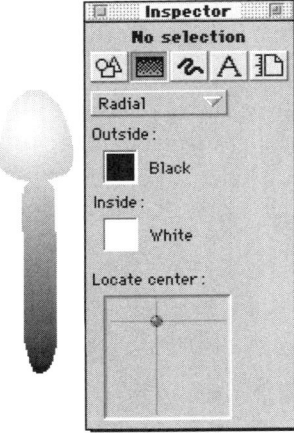

Figure 12b. *The same **Radial** fill with the **center location moved** by dragging the **Locate center** point in the **Radial** fill settings of the **Inspector** palette.*

134

Fills

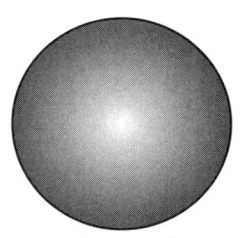

Figure 13a. *To **start** the spherical 3-D button, fill a circle with a **Radial** fill.*

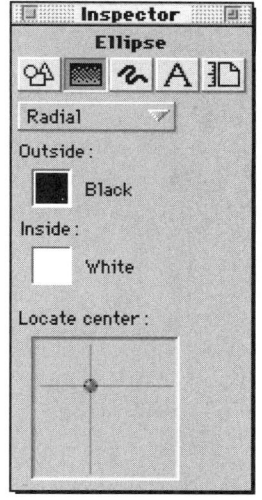

Figure 13b. *To **finish** the button, create a smaller circle and fill it with a **Radial** fill. Change the center to the upper-left quadrant of the circle.*

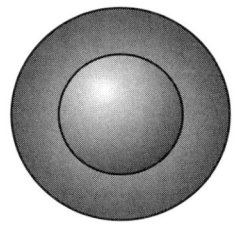

Figure 13c. *The finished spherical 3-D button.*

Like the Graduated fill, the Radial fill can be used to create 3-D effects.

To create a spherical 3-D button using Radial fills:

1. Create a circle. Fill it with a Radial fill that goes from black outside to white inside with the center left in the middle of the object.(**Figure 13a**).

2. Create a smaller circle and place it inside the larger one. Fill this circle with a Radial fill that goes from black to white but position the center of the fill in the upper-left quadrant of the object (**Figure 13b**). The button will take on a 3-D appearance (**Figure 13c**).

To apply a Radial fill by dragging a color:

1. Select an object.

2. Drag a color swatch onto the object while holding the Option key. The object will take on a Radial fill with the color that you dragged as the Inside color. The center of the fill will be determined by the spot where you dropped the color swatch.

Radial Fills

135

Chapter 11

Tips

- Once you have a Radial fill applied to an object, you can change the Inside and Outside colors by dragging color swatches directly onto the object. Where you drop the swatch sets the angle of the color change.
- You cannot mix spot and process colors as the two colors in Graduated or Radial fills.
- You cannot mix two different spot colors as the two colors in Graduated or Radial fills.
- You cannot combine the default black color in Graduated or Radial fills with any other color except tints of itself or white.
- If you want to combine black with a process color in Graduated or Radial fills, you must create a process color that consists of 100% black (**Figure 14**). This color can be mixed with any other process color. *(For information on how to create process colors, see page 123.)*
- If you want to create Graduated or Radial fills with more than one color change, choose Multi-Color Fill from the Colors submenu of the Xtras menu *(see page 145)*. The Multi-Color Fill dialog box will appear.

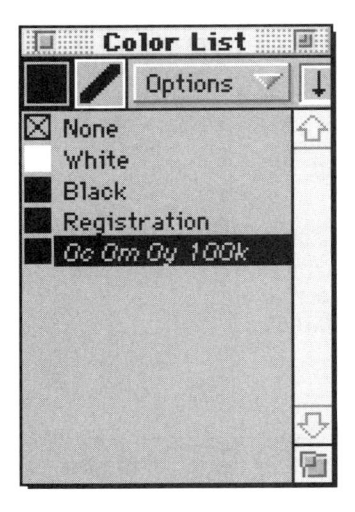

Figure 14. *In order to use black with other colors in a Graduated or Radial fill, you must create a new* **process color black** *(in italic typeface) to use instead of the default black (in roman typeface).*

Fills

Figure 15a. *To create a **Tiled** fill start by creating the artwork that you would like to repeat. Copy it.*

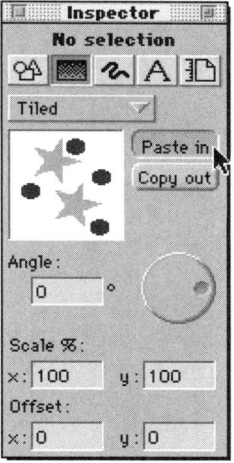

Figure 15b. *Click the **Paste in** button to paste the copied artwork into the **Tiled** fill settings box.*

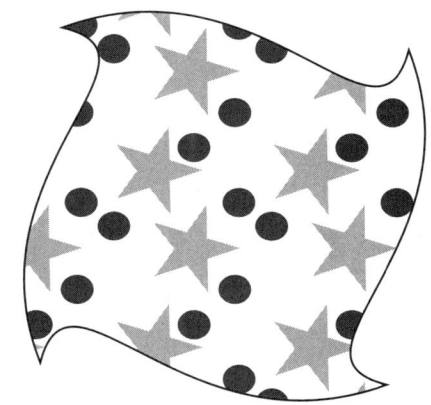

Figure 15c. *The object selected will have that **Tiled** fill applied to it.*

The next kind of fill you have to create yourself. It is called a Tiled fill. Another way to think of a Tiled fill is as a repeating pattern.

To create and apply a Tiled fill:

1. Create the pattern that you would like to repeat and copy it (**Figure 15a**). Deselect your artwork.

2. Select the object that you would like to be filled with the Tiled fill.

3. Choose Tiled from the Fill icon choices of the Inspector palette.

4. Click the Paste in button. The artwork you copied will appear in the Tiled preview box (**Figure 15b**). Your object will be filled with the Tiled fill (**Figure 15c**).

Tips

- If you want your Tiled fill to have a white or colored background, place your artwork on a rectangle filled with white or the color. Select both the artwork and the rectangle to copy and paste into the Tiled fill box.
- If you want your Tiled fill to be transparent, leave your artwork on an empty area or on a rectangle with no fill.
- The more complex the artwork, the longer it takes for your screen to redraw and for the artwork to print.
- Any object that can be copied can be used as a Tiled fill except EPS and bitmapped graphics, and objects that already have Tiled fills applied to them.

Tiled Fills

Chapter 11

To adjust a Tiled fill within an object:

1. Select the Tiled fill object and choose the Fill icon in the Inspector palette.
2. To change the the size of the Tiled fill, use the Scale % x and y fields (**Figures 16a–b**). Use the same amounts for both x and y to scale the fill uniformly.
3. To move a Tiled fill within the object, enter positive or negative values in the Offset x and y fields (**Figures 17a–b**).
4. To angle a Tiled fill within the object, move the angle wheel or enter the exact angle in the Angle field (**Figures 18a–b**).

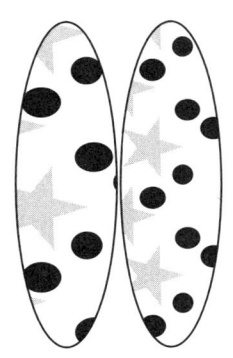

Figure 16a. *A **Tiled** fill object with **no scaling** applied (left) and with a **75% scaling** applied (right).*

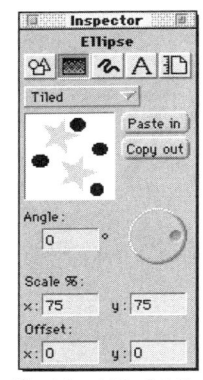

Figure 16b. *The **Tiled** fill settings box with **75% scale** amounts entered.*

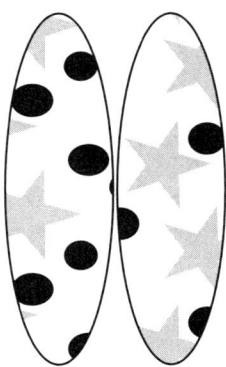

Figure 17a. *A **Tiled** fill object with **no offset** applied (left) and with a **half-inch offset** applied (right).*

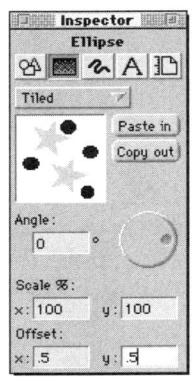

Figure 17b. *The **Tiled** fill settings box with **half-inch offset** amounts entered.*

138

Fills

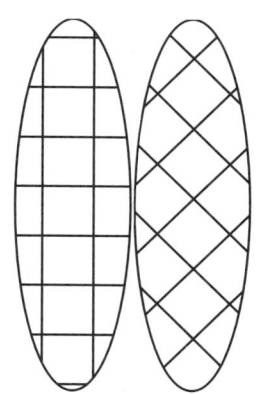

Figure 18a. *A **Tiled** fill object with **no angle** applied (left) and with a **45° angle** applied (right).*

Tips

- Positive x values in the Offset field move the fill to the right.
- Positive y values in the Offset field move the fill up.
- Negative x values in the Offset field move the fill to the left.
- Negative y values in the Offset field move the fill down.

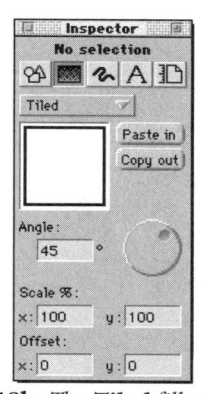

Figure 18b. *The **Tiled** fill settings box with a **45° angle** entered.*

Chapter 11

Custom fills are premade patterns that simulate the look of various textures. After you choose a Custom fill, you can still make refinements to the basic texture.

To apply a Custom fill:

1. Select the object and choose Custom from the Fill icon pop-up menu in the Inspector palette.
2. Choose one of the Custom fills from the second pop-up menu that appears (**Figure 19**).
3. Where applicable, make whatever changes you want to the settings of the fill.
4. Instead of seeing a preview of the fill in the object, you will see a series of "C's" that fill the object. You will only be able to see the fill by printing your object (**Figures 20a–b**).

Tips

- For a complete printout of all the Custom fills, see Appendix B.
- Six of the Custom fills have transparent backgrounds. Any objects behind these fills will be visible through the empty spaces of the fills *(see Appendix B for illustrations of this effect)*.
- All of the Custom fills, except Black & white noise, are editable using the settings in the Fill icon section of the Inspector palette.
- Some of the Custom fills will let you apply a color to the fill. The color will be applied to the solid-color portion of the Custom fill. Any white area of the Custom fill will remain white *(see Appendix B for illustrations of this effect)*.
- Custom fills cannot be scaled with an object and do not print to non-PostScript printers.

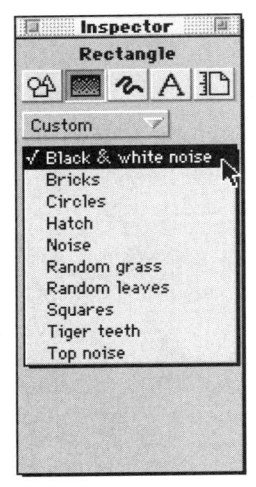

Figure 19. *The pop-up menu for the* **Custom** *fills.*

Figure 20a. *How an object filled with a* **Custom** *fill appears* **onscreen**.

Figure 20b. *How an object filled with a* **Custom** *fill* **prints**.

Fills

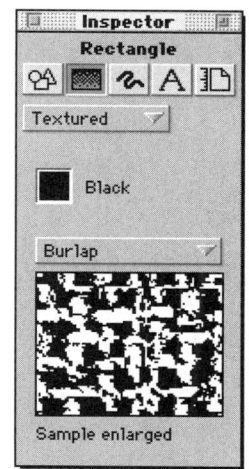

Figure 21. The **Textured** fills settings in the **Inspector** palette.

Textured fills are very similar to Custom fills.

To apply a Textured fill to an object:

1. Select an object and choose Textured from the Fill icon pop-up menu in the Inspector palette.

2. Choose one of the Textured fills from the second pop-up menu that appears (**Figure 21**).

3. The Sample enlarged box will show you a preview of the Textured fill. In the object, however, you will see a series of "C's". You will only be able to see the actual fill by printing your object (**Figure 22**).

Tips

- For a complete printout of all the Textured fills, see Appendix B.

- All of the Textured fills have opaque backgrounds. Any objects behind these fills will not be visible through the empty spaces of the fills (*see Appendix B for illustrations of this effect*).

- Textured fills are not editable in the Fill icon section of the Inspector palette.

- All of the Textured fills let you apply any color to the fill. The color will be applied to the solid-color portion of the fill. Any white area of the Textured fill will remain white (*see Appendix B for illustrations of this effect*).

- Textured fills cannot be scaled with an object and do not print to non-PostScript printers.

Figure 22. *How an object filled with a **Textured** fill prints.*

Chapter 11

Pattern fills are bitmapped patterns that can be edited pixel by pixel. They are familiar to anyone who has used programs such as MacPaint.

To apply a Pattern fill to an object:

1. Select an object and choose Pattern from the Fill icon pop-up menu in the Inspector palette.
2. Use the slider bar at the bottom of the Inspector palette to choose one of the Pattern fills from the series of small boxes (**Figure 23**).
3. Use the large preview box on the left to edit the pattern by clicking on each of the pixels. The large preview box on the right shows what your pattern will look like when applied to the object.
4. Use the Clear button to clear all the pixels from the large preview boxes so you can start on a fresh edit.
5. Use the Invert button to change the black pixels into white and vice versa.
6. Use the color drop box to apply any color to the dark pixels of a pattern. (*See the Tips below for important information on how colored patterns will print.*)
7. The Pattern fills appear onscreen as they will print (**Figure 24**).

Tips

- For a complete printout of the default Pattern fills, see Appendix B.
- All of the Pattern fills have opaque backgrounds. Any objects behind these fills will not be visible through the empty spaces of the fills.
- Pattern fills cannot be transformed with an object.

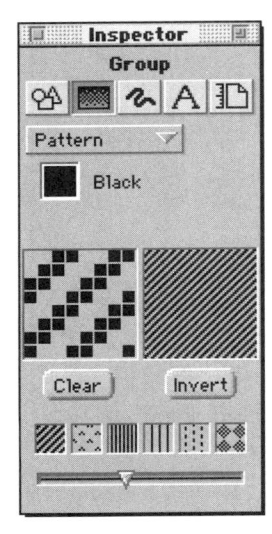

Figure 23. *The **Pattern** fill settings in the **Inspector** palette.*

Figure 24. *An object filled with a **Pattern** fill displays and prints that pattern.*

Fills

Figure 25. *The **PostScript** fill settings in the **Inspector** palette.*

- Pattern fills are designed for use on low-resolution printers (including non-PostScript devices), not high-resolution imagesetters and film recorders.
- All of the Pattern fills let you apply any color to the fill. This color will be applied to the solid-color portion of the fill. Any white area of the Pattern fill will remain white.
- On PostScript Level 1 printers, Pattern fills print correctly only if the spot colors are not tints and the process colors use inks at 100%.
- On PostScript Level 2 printers, Pattern fills print correctly using any spot or process colors.

To apply a PostScript fill to an object:

When you choose a PostScript fill from the Fill icon pop-up menu, you will see a large box with the word "fill" in it (**Figure 25**). The purpose of this box is to allow you to type in specific PostScript code that will create a pattern. Learning and working with PostScript code is much too advanced to cover here. If you are interested in learning the language of PostScript, consult a book such as *Learning PostScript: A Visual Approach* by Ross Smith (Peachpit Press, 1990).

Chapter 11

One of the drawbacks of the Graduated and Radial fills is that they only allow you one color change. Freehand, however, has provided Multi-Color fills in the Xtras tools that allow you to create Graduated or Radial fills with up to 64 different colors.

To create a Multi-Color fill and apply it to an object:

1. Select the object that you want to be filled with the Multi-Color fill.

2. Choose Operations from the Other submenu of the Window menu. Click on the Multi-Color Fill icon in the Operations palette (**Figure 26a**).
   or
   Choose Multi-Color Fill from the Colors submenu of the Xtras menu (**Figure 26b**).

3. The Multi-Color Fill dialog box will appear (**Figure 27**).

4. To change the colors in the Multi-Color fill, drag color swatches from the Color List or the Color Mixer onto the three existing drop boxes in the dialog box.

5. To add additional colors to the fill, drag color swatches from the Color List or the Color Mixer onto the color ramp that displays the preview of the fill.

6. To change the position of any colors in the fill, drag the color swatches to new positions.

7. To delete any colors from the fill, drag the color swatch box off the color ramp.

8. The pop-up menu lets you choose between a Graduated fill or a Radial fill. (*See the following steps on how to apply these choices.*)

9. Click Apply to see a preview of the fill on the selected object. If you are satisfied with your fill, click OK (**Figure 28**).

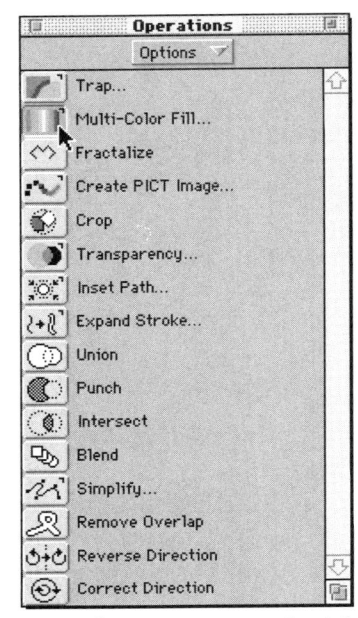

Figure 26a. *To create a Multi-Color fill, click on the **Multi-Color Fill** icon of the **Operations** palette.*

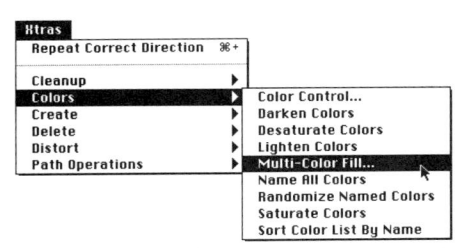

Figure 26b. *To create a Multi-Color fill, choose **Multi-Color Fill** from the **Colors** submenu of the **Xtras** menu.*

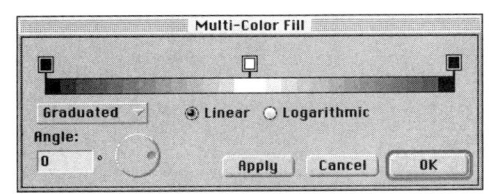

Figure 27. *The **Multi-Color Fill** dialog box lets you create different multi-color fills.*

144

Fills

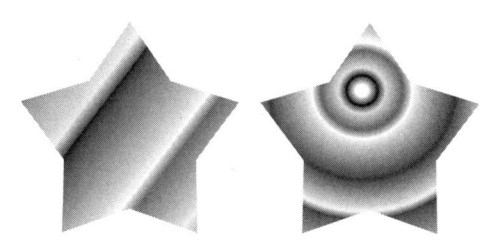

Figure 28. *A **Graduated Multi-Color** fill (left) and a **Radial Multi-Color** fill (right).*

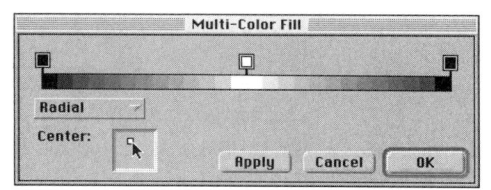

Figure 29. *The **Multi-Color Fill** dialog box set for a **Radial** fill. The **Center** box controls the position of the center of the fill.*

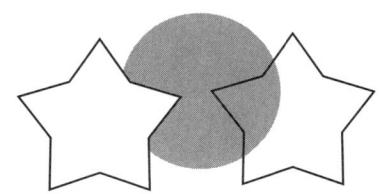

Figure 30. *Applying a **None** fill to an object lets you see through that object to any other objects behind it.*

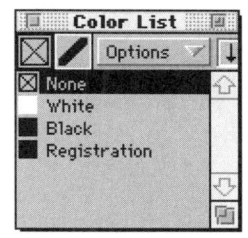

Figure 31. *The **Fill drop box** with a **None** fill applied.*

To create a Graduated Multi-Color fill:

1. In the Multi-Color Fill dialog box, choose Graduated from the pop-up menu.
2. Choose Linear or Logarithmic for the type of taper.
3. Drag the Angle wheel or enter the exact angle in the Angle field for the direction of the fill.

To create a Radial Multi-Color fill:

1. In the Multi-Color Fill dialog box, choose Radial from the pop-up menu.
2. The color swatch on the left controls the inside color. The color swatch on the right controls the outside color. The color swatches in between move from inside to outside along the ramp.
3. Drag the white square in the Center box to the position where you want the inside of the fill to start (**Figure 29**).

When you apply a None fill, your object becomes see-through. Any objects behind your object will show through the front (**Figure 30**). If you apply a None fill to an object, you will probably want to add a stroke so that you can see the edges of the object *(see Chapter 12, "Strokes")*.

To apply a None fill to an object:

1. Choose the object that you wish to fill with "None."
2. Make sure the Fill drop box is selected in the Color List.
3. Click on the None name. An "X" will appear in the Fill drop box indicating that None has been applied as a fill (**Figure 31**).

Chapter 11

To use the Overprint feature:

Ordinarily, when you place one colored object over another, the top object will knock out the bottom one. This means that if you have a portion of a yellow star that is touching a blue circle, the yellow star will erase the part of the circle it touches.

Overprinting cancels that knockout. If you set an object to Overprint (**Figure 32**), that object will not knock out any colors below it, but will mix the colors. You cannot see the results of overprinting on your screen. Any objects that have an overprint applied to them will be displayed in their color with a pattern of white "O's" on top (**Figure 33**). You will not see overprinting in the output of most color printers. You need to make separations of your colors to see where the colors will overprint.

If you are working with process colors, you can simulate the effect of overprinting by applying the Transparency command (*see page 224*).

Tips

- If you do not want to see the "O's" in an overprinting object, you can change the Peferences settings (*see page 271*).
- If you do not understand how to use overprinting, talk to the print shop that will be printing your artwork. They will be able to explain where you may or may not want to overprint.

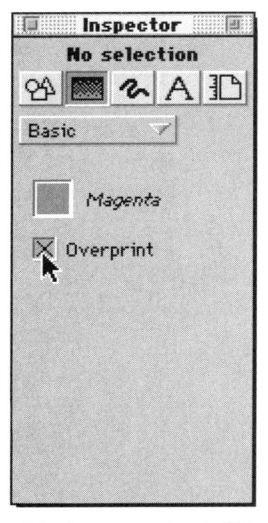

Figure 32. *Setting a Basic fill to* ***Overprint***.

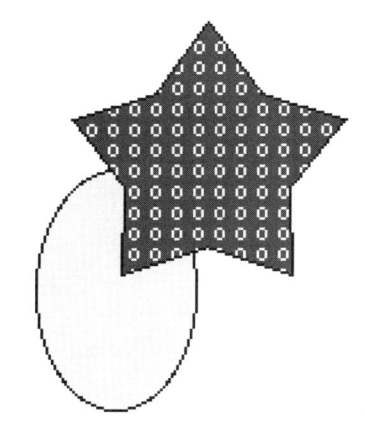

Figure 33. *How an overprinting object appears onscreen.*

STROKES 12

If fills are what fill up the inside of objects, strokes are what surround the outside of objects. While there aren't as many choices for strokes as there are for fills, there are still quite a few types of effects you can create using strokes. In this chapter you will learn how to set the attributes of a Basic stroke: Color, Width, Cap, Join, Miter limit, Dash, and Arrowheads. You will learn how to create your own Dash patterns using the Dash Editor and how to create your own arrowheads using the Arrowhead Editor. You will learn how to create special stroke effects such as multi-colored dashes and a "string of pearls." You will also learn about the three other stroke settings: Custom, Pattern, and PostScript.

Figure 1. *The **Stroke** icon of the **Inspector** palette.*

Unlike fills, strokes can be applied to both open and closed paths. In fact, if you have an open path with no stroke applied to it, then the object will be invisible, since an open path does not display a fill. All the strokes in FreeHand are chosen through the Stroke icon of the Document Inspector palette (**Figure 1**). Once you have chosen the Stroke icon in the Inspector palette, you can access the different types of strokes through the pop-up menu.

To apply a Basic stroke using the Inspector palette:

1. Select the object you want to apply the stroke to.

2. Click on the **Stroke icon** of the Inspector palette.

3. Choose **Basic** from the pop-up menu (**Figure 2**).

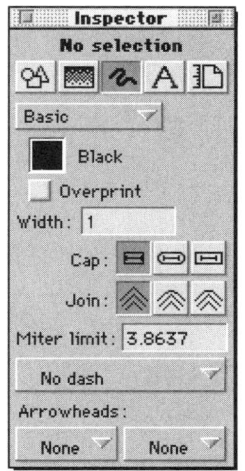

Figure 2. *The **Basic** stroke choices of the **Inspector** palette.*

Basic Strokes

147

Chapter 12

Once you have applied a Basic stroke, there are more choices that you must make for your stroke. The first is color. Like the choices for fills, there are many different ways to change the color of a stroke.

To change the color of a stroke:

1. With the object selected, click on the name of the color in the Color List. If the Stroke drop box has a black line around it, then the color will be applied to the stroke of the object (**Figure 3**).

or

Drag a color swatch from the Color Mixer or the Color List onto the Stroke color drop box in the Inspector palette.

or

Drag a color swatch from the Color Mixer onto the drop box in the Color List.

or

Drag a color swatch from the Color Mixer or the Color List onto the edge of the object (**Figure 4**).

Tip

■ If you have no object selected, any changes you make to the Stroke icon of the Inspector palette or the Stroke drop box of the Color List will be applied to the next object created.

The Stroke drop box

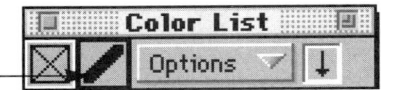

Figure 3. *The black line around the* **Stroke drop box** *indicates that it is selected. Any changes to the color selected in the Color List will apply to the stroke.*

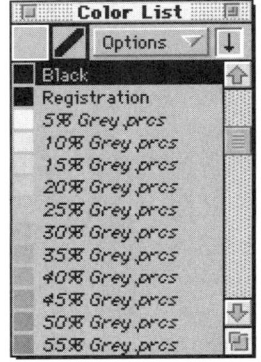

Figure 4. *Dragging a* **color swatch** *onto the* **edge of an object** *will change its stroke color.*

Once you've got a Basic stroke, you've still got quite a few looks to choose from. The first is the thickness or the width of the stroke.

To change the width of a stroke:

1. Select the object that you want to change. There should be a Basic stroke applied to it.

148

Strokes

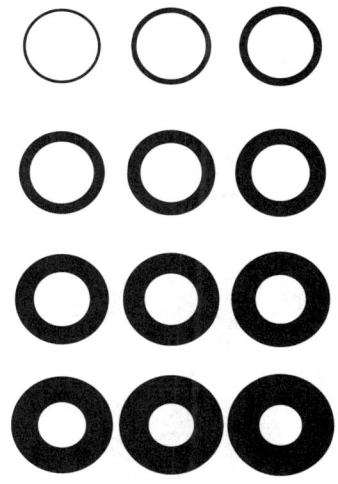

Figure 5. *Changing the* **Width** *amount changes the thickness of the stroke. These circles are all the same size but have different stroke widths that range from 1 point to 12 points.*

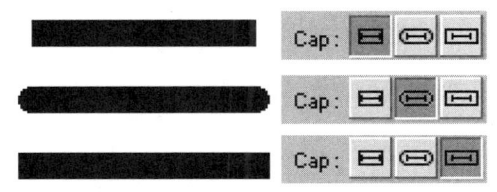

Figure 6. *The three different* **Cap** *choices:* **Butt** *(top),* **Round** *(middle), and* **Square** *(bottom). The difference between the Butt and Square is that the Square extends out beyond the anchor points.*

2. In the Width field box, type the thickness that you would like your stroke to be (**Figure 5**).

3. Press the Return key on your keyboard or click anywhere on the Inspector palette.

Tip

- Even if your document is in inches, you can enter the width of your stroke in points by typing "p" and then the number.

The next choice you have is how the ends of the stroke will be treated. This is called the "cap" of the stroke. Changing the cap of a stroked object only affects open paths, since they are the only ones with end points.

To apply a cap to a stroke:

1. Select an open path. In order to see the effects of changing the cap, choose a rather thick width such as 24 points (**Figure 6**).

2. The default cap is the Butt cap. This cap means that the stroke stops exactly on the end point of the path.

3. Click on the Round cap icon. This choice means that the stroke extends past the end points in a curved shape.

4. Click on the Square cap icon. This choice means that the stroke extends past the end points in a square shape.

Tip

- Use the Round cap to "soften" the computer-like look of your drawings.

Stroke Caps

149

Chapter 12

The next choice you have is how the joints of the stroke will be treated. This is called the "join" of the stroke. Any path that has a corner or connector point inside the path will be affected by changing the join.

To apply a join to a stroke:

1. Select a path. In order to see the effects of changing the join, choose a rather thick width such as 24 points. Make sure at least one point inside the path is a corner or connector point (**Figure 7**).

2. Click on the Miter join icon. This join means that the stroke of the path extends out into a "V" where the two line segments change directions. The sharper the angle between the two segments, the longer the extension of the stroke.

3. Click on the Round join icon. This join means that the stroke of the path makes a curve between the two line segments.

4. Click on the Bevel join icon. This prevents the "V" extension between the two line segments and cuts the stroke in a straight line between the two segments.

Tip

■ Use the Round join together with the Round cap for a look similar to that of a marker pen.

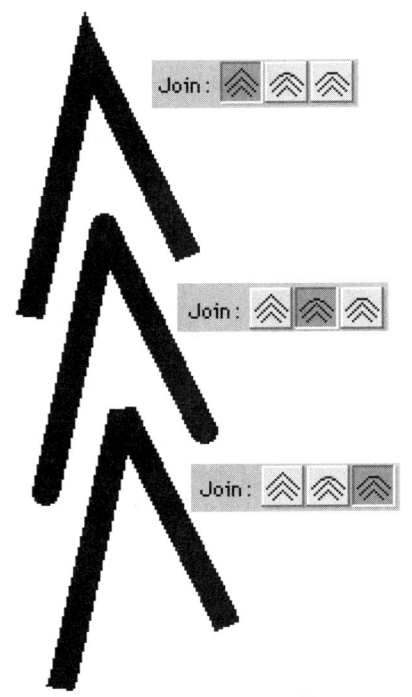

Figure 7. *The three different* **Join** *choices:* **Miter** *(top),* **Round** *(middle), and* **Bevel** *(bottom).*

150

Strokes

The next choice you have is the Miter limit. Changing the Miter limit of a stroked object prevents joins with very steep angles from becoming too spikey.

To change the Miter limit:

1. Select a path with a Miter join. In order to see the effects of changing the Miter limit, choose a rather thick width such as 24 points and create two line segments with a very acute angle between them. This should look like a spike.

2. Lower the Miter limit to 1 or 2 and notice how you have eliminated the spike between the two segments (**Figure 8**).

Figure 8. *A higher* **Miter limit** *(left) will allow spikes between line segments. A lower Miter limit (right) cuts the spikes off into a Bevel join.*

The next choice you have is the dash pattern of the stroke. Both open and closed paths, with any kinds of points, can have dash patterns applied to them.

To apply a dash pattern:

1. Select a path. In order to see the effects of changing the dash, choose a rather thick width such as 24 points. Choose a Butt cap.

2. Press on the Dash pop-up menu and choose from the default list of premade dash patterns. Each of these choices will create a new dash pattern for your stroke (**Figure 9**).

Tip

- The spaces between the dashes of a stroke are transparent, not white. If you lay your dashed stroke over another object, you will see through the spaces to that other object.

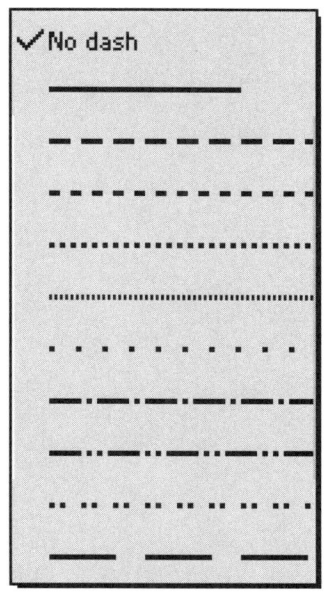

Figure 9. *The default pop-up list of* **Dash** *patterns.*

151

You may find that you want to create your own dash patterns for strokes. That is done using the Dash Editor dialog box.

To edit a dash pattern:

1. With the Stroke section of the Inspector palette displayed, hold the Option key as you select one of the dash patterns from the Basic stroke settings. The Dash Editor will appear (**Figure 10**).
2. The lengths of the visible portion of the dash is set by entering numbers in the On fields.
3. The lengths of the spaces between the dashes is set by entering numbers in the Off fields.
4. Up to four different sets of On and Off values can be entered.
5. When you have finished entering the pattern, click OK. The dash pattern that you created will be displayed at the bottom of the dash list. You will not have eliminated the original pattern.

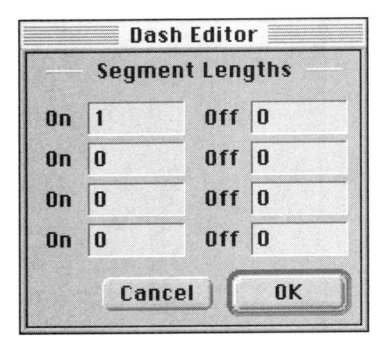

Figure 10. *The **Dash Editor** dialog box lets you enter your own dash patterns. Choose up to four sets of On and Off patterns.*

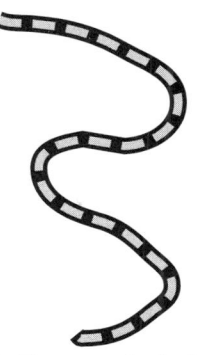

Figure 11. *To create the look of multi-colored dashed lines, use two or more lines on top of each other. This effect uses both a bottom thick black line and a top dashed line that's lighter and thinner.*

Figure 12a. *The settings for the "string of pearls."*

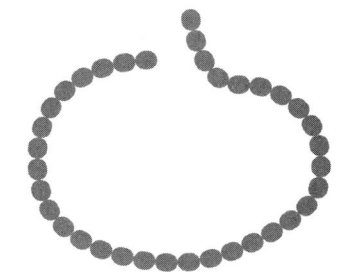

Figure 12b. *The finished string of pearls.*

Dashes don't have to be plain. In fact, with just a little experience you can create some very sophisticated effects.

To create a multi-colored dash:

1. Create a line with the Basic stroke you want. Use a fairly thick stroke, such as 12 points, with no dash.
2. Choose Clone (Command-=) from the Edit menu. You now have a copy sitting on top of your line.
3. Choose a smaller width and add a contrasting color for this copy. Choose a dash pattern that creates large spaces in this second line. You will now have a dashed line with two colors (**Figure 11**).

To create a "string of pearls":

1. Use the Freehand tool to draw a wavy line on your work page.
2. Set the Width to 24 points.
3. Set the Cap to Round. (This makes the dashes a round shape.)
4. Hold the Option key and choose any of the dash patterns. (This gives you the Dash Editor.)
5. Set your dash pattern to On 1, Off 24. Click OK.
6. Your wavy line will now look like a string of pearls (**Figures 12a–b**).

Tip

■ If you have two or more objects on top of each other, hold the Control key as you click on the top object. This will allow you to select objects beneath the top object.

Chapter 12

The last choice for Basic strokes is arrowheads. You can only see arrowheads on open paths.

To apply arrowheads:

1. Select a path. In order to see the different arrowheads, choose a rather thick stroke such as 24 points.
2. To add an arrowhead to the start of your path, press on the left Arrowheads pop-up menu and choose from the default list of premade arrowheads.
3. To add an arrowhead to the end of your path, press on the right Arrowheads pop-up menu and choose from the default list of premade arrowheads (**Figure 13**).

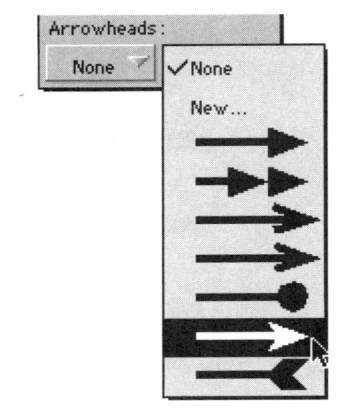

Figure 13. *The **Arrowheads** pop-up menu lets you add arrowheads to open paths with Basic strokes.*

Tips

- The arrowheads take their size from the point size of the stroke.
- Even if your path started on the right, the left pop-up menu controls the arrowheads at the start of the path.
- Even if your path ends on the left, the right pop-up menu controls the arrowheads at the end of the path.

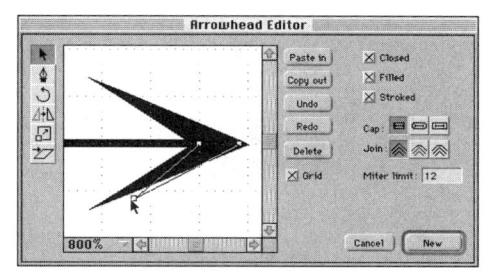

Figure 14. *The **Arrowhead Editor** dialog box lets you modify the premade arrowheads or create your own custom arrowheads.*

FreeHand gives you the Arrowhead Editor dialog box where you can create your own arrowheads.

To edit the premade arrowheads:

1. Hold the Option key as you select one of the arrowheads from the either the left or right Arrowheads pop-up menu of the Basic stroke Inspector palette. The Arrowhead Editor dialog box will appear with the arrowhead that you chose in the window (**Figure 14**).

2. Use any of the Arrowhead Editor tools to modify the arrowhead in the Arrowhead Editor window.

3. When you are satisfied with the results of your work, click the New button. The arrowhead you modified will appear at the end of the left and right lists of arrowheads. The original arrowhead will be unchanged in the arrowhead lists.

To create your own arrowheads:

1. Press on either the left or right Arrowheads pop-up menu and choose New. You will now see the Arrowhead Editor dialog box.

2. Use any of the Arrowhead Editor tools to create an arrowhead.

3. When you are satisfied with the results of your work, click the New button. The arrowhead you created will appear at the end of the left and right lists of arrowheads.

Tip

■ Use the Paste in and Copy out buttons to transfer arrowheads between the Arrowhead Editor and the work page. This allows you to use all the FreeHand tools to create arrowheads.

Chapter 12

Just as there are Custom fills, FreeHand provides you with Custom stroke patterns.

To apply a Custom stroke pattern:

1. Choose Custom from the Stroke pop-up menu of the Inspector palette (**Figure 15**).

2. Choose the color you want for your stroke.

3. Choose the width for the stroke.

4. Choose the Custom stroke Effect from the pop-up menu. Use the Sample enlarged window to judge the look of the Custom stroke.

5. Set the Length field to control the size of the repeating element in the stroke.

6. Set the Spacing field to control the space between each repeating element in the stroke (**Figure 16**).

Tips

- For a complete printout of the default Custom strokes, see Appendix B.
- Custom stroke patterns appear solid on the screen.
- The white areas of the Custom stroke patterns (except Arrow, Braid, and Neon) are transparent when printed. This means that any objects behind the stroked object will show through the spaces of the Custom stroke.
- The Custom stroke patterns do not transform with the object.
- The Custom stroke patterns print to any PostScript device.

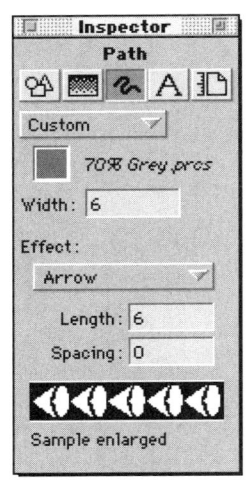

Figure 15. *Choose* **Custom** *from the* **Stroke** *icon section of the* **Inspector** *palette to see the settings for the Custom strokes.*

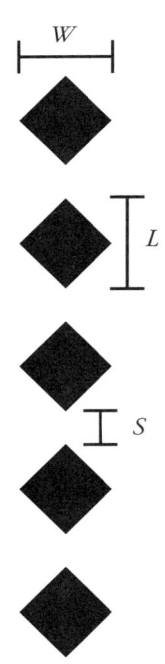

Figure 16. *The* **Width** *(W),* **Length** *(L), and* **Spacing** *(S) settings control the look of a* **Custom** *stroke.*

156

Strokes

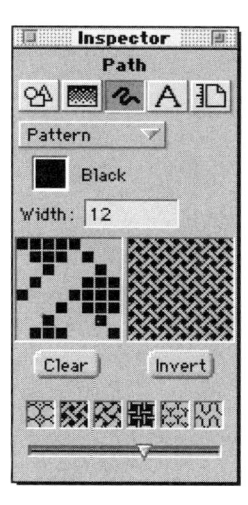

Figure 17. The **Pattern** stroke settings in the **Inspector** palette.

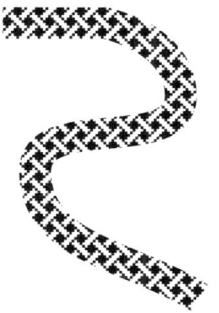

Figure 18. An object with a **Pattern** stroke displays and prints that pattern.

The next set of strokes are the Pattern strokes. Like the Pattern fills, these are bitmapped patterns that can be edited pixel by pixel.

To apply a Pattern stroke:

1. Select the object and choose Pattern from the Stroke icon pop-up menu in the Inspector palette.

2. Use the slider bar at the bottom of the palette to choose one of the Pattern strokes from the series of small boxes above it (**Figure 17**).

3. Use the large preview box on the left to edit the pattern by clicking on each of the pixels in the pattern. The large preview box on the right shows what your pattern will look like when applied to the object.

4. Use the Clear button to clear all the pixels from the large preview boxes so you can start on a fresh edit.

5. Use the Invert button to change the black pixels into white and vice versa.

6. Use the color drop box to apply any color to the dark pixels of a pattern. (*See the Tips below for important information on how colored Pattern strokes will print.*)

7. The Pattern strokes appear onscreen as they will print (**Figure 18**).

Tips

- For a complete printout of the default Pattern strokes, see Appendix B.
- All of the Pattern strokes have opaque backgrounds. Any objects behind these strokes will not be visible through the empty spaces of the strokes.
- Pattern strokes cannot be transformed with an object.

(*Continued on the following page*)

Chapter 12

- Pattern strokes are designed for use on low-resolution printers (including non-PostScript devices), not high-resolution imagesetters and film recorders.
- All of the Pattern strokes let you apply any color to the stroke. This color will be applied to the solid-color portion of the stroke. Any white area of the Pattern stroke will remain white.
- On PostScript Level 1 printers, Pattern strokes print correctly only if the spot colors are not tints and the process colors use inks at 100%.
- On PostScript Level 2 printers, Pattern strokes print correctly using any spot or process colors.

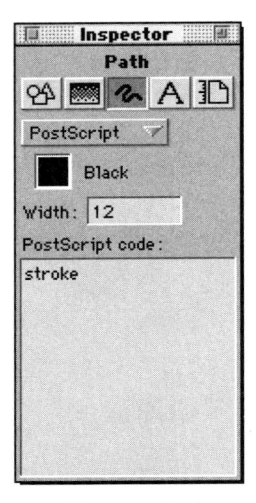

Figure 19. *The **PostScript** stroke settings in the **Inspector** palette.*

To apply a PostScript stroke to an object:

When you choose a PostScript stroke from the Stroke icon pop-up menu, you will see a large box with the word "stroke" in it (**Figure 19**). The purpose of this box is to allow you to type in specific PostScript code that will create a pattern. Learning and working with PostScript code is much too advanced to cover here. If you are interested in learning the language of PostScript, consult a book such as *Learning PostScript: A Visual Approach* by Ross Smith (Peachpit Press, 1990).

BLENDS 13

Figure 1a. *Blends give the effect of one object turning into another.*

Figure 1b. *The same blend with only some of the intermediate steps displayed to show the **progression of the blend**.*

Figure 2a. *Two shapes with **Graduated** or **Radial fills**.*

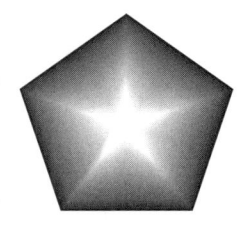

Figure 2b. *The same shapes with **Blends**.*

Blends are one of the most sophisticated features of FreeHand. With blends, you can create subtle shadings and contours, dramatic changes of shape, 3-D looks, and many other effects. In this chapter, you will learn some of the uses of blends and how blends differ from Graduated and Radial fills. You will learn how to create your own blends and how to set the number of steps in your blends. You will also learn how to use FreeHand's Live Blends feature to modify existing blends. You will learn which objects can be blended and how to optimally view your blends onscreen. Finally, you will learn some of the basic steps to making sure your blends print correctly.

Blends give the effect of one object turning into another. When you see an object such as an oval that seems to turn into another object such as a star, what you are actually seeing is hundreds of intermediate steps in which the object has been reshaped ever so slightly in each step (**Figures 1a–b**).

If all you want to do is make an object change from one color to another, then all you need is a Graduated or Radial fill (**Figure 2a**). But if you would like the object to transform into another shape during the color change, then you need to use blends (**Figure 2b**).

159

Chapter 13

Blends don't have to be just for color or shape changes. They can be used to create intermediate steps where both the stroke width and stroke shape change (**Figure 3**).

To create a simple blend:

1. Start with a simple shape. If you create a rectangle or oval, make sure the object is ungrouped. Make your object a dark color.
2. Create a second shape such as a star or a triangle. Color this object with a lighter color or white (**Figure 4a**).
3. Select one point on the first object and another point on the second object (**Figure 4b**). (If you are blending between two open paths, these points must be end points on the paths.)
4. Choose Blend (Command-Shift-B) from the Path Operations submenu of the Arrange menu (**Figure 4c**). You will see the blend from one object to another (**Figure 4d**).

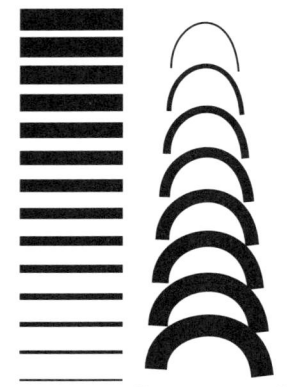

Figure 3. *Two different ways of using* **blends** *to change the shape and width of* **strokes***.*

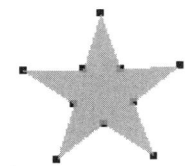

Figure 4a. *To create a simple blend, start with two ungrouped objects.*

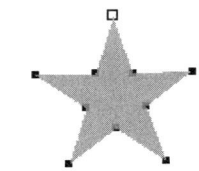

Figure 4b. *Select one point on each object.*

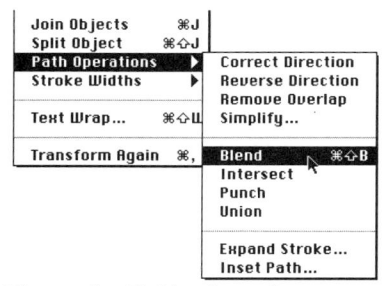

Figure 4c. *To blend an object, choose* **Blend** *from the* **Path Operations** *submenu of the* **Arrange** *menu.*

Create a blend

160

Blends

Figure 4d. *The results of blending the two shapes.*

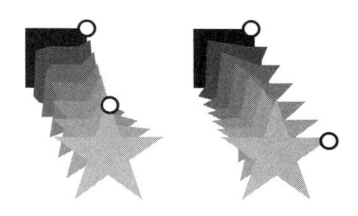

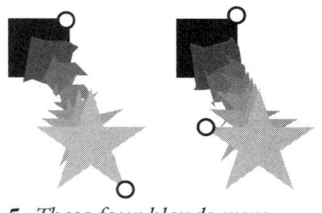

Figure 5. *These four blends were made by choosing different points (indicated by circles).*

Figure 6. *To change the number of steps in a blend, choose the **Object** icon of the **Inspector** palette.*

Tip
- If you are trying to make your blends as smooth as possible, try to pick points on each object that are in equivalent positions. Choosing nonequivalent points can result in unwanted blending (**Figure 5**).

Once you have a blend, you may want to change the number of steps. This may be to make the blend as smooth as possible or it may be to see each of the steps.

To change the number of steps in a blend:

1. With the blend selected, click on the Object icon of the Inspector palette (**Figure 6**).

2. Enter how many steps you want in the Number of steps field.

3. Press the Return key or click anywhere on the Inspector palette. The blend will reform with the correct number of steps (**Figure 7**).

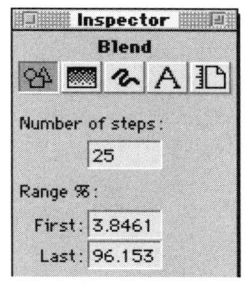

Figure 7. *In the **Number of Steps** field, type in the number of steps you want.*

161

Chapter 13

To change the number of steps in your document:

When you create a blend, FreeHand calculates the number of steps by using the Printer resolution that is set in the Document Setup section of the Inspector palette *(see page 21)*. Higher resolutions will give you greater numbers of steps for your blends. If you change the Printer resolution, you will change the number of steps that are automatically created for any new blends. But changing the Printer resolution will only change the number of steps for those blends made after you changed the Printer resolution. Any blends made before you changed the Printer resolution will still have their original number of steps.

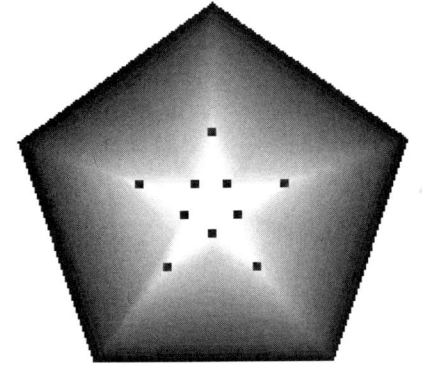

Figure 8a. *To make a **Live Blend**, hold the **Option** key as you click on either of the original objects of the blend.*

Once you have created a blend, you can still make changes to either of the end objects of the blend. FreeHand calls this Live Blends.

To create a Live Blend:

1. Hold the Option key and use the Selection tool to select one of the two end objects of the blend (**Figure 8a**). (If you do not hold the Option key, you will select the entire blend.)

2. Make any changes you want to the object, such as shape, fill color, or stroke width (**Figure 8b**).

3. The blend will automatically reform when you make the changes (**Figure 8c**).

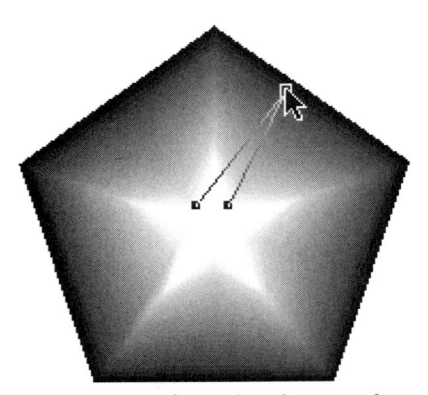

Figure 8b. *Make whatever changes you want to size, shape, color, etc.*

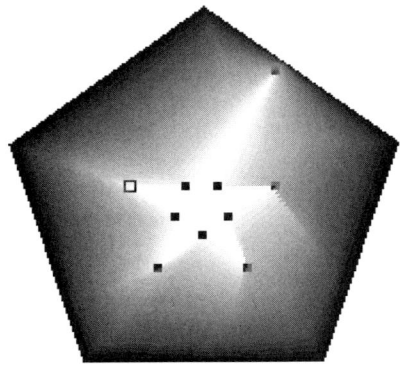

Figure 8c. *The blend will automatically redraw.*

Blends

The rules of blends

You may find that you are unable to do certain things when working with blends. This is because there are limitations to which objects you can blend between.

1. You cannot blend an open path to a closed path.

2. You cannot blend between interior points of open paths.

3. You cannot blend a grouped path.

4. You cannot blend a composite path.

5. You cannot blend between paths that have different stroke or fill types.

6. Blends between two spot colors will be filled with process colors.

To view blends:

Once you have created a blend, you may find that you do not like the way the blend looks onscreen. The blend may look "chunky," with bands across each color change. This is simply a function of the screen display. If you want to see your blend with a smoother display, you will need to change your Preferences settings (*see page 271*).

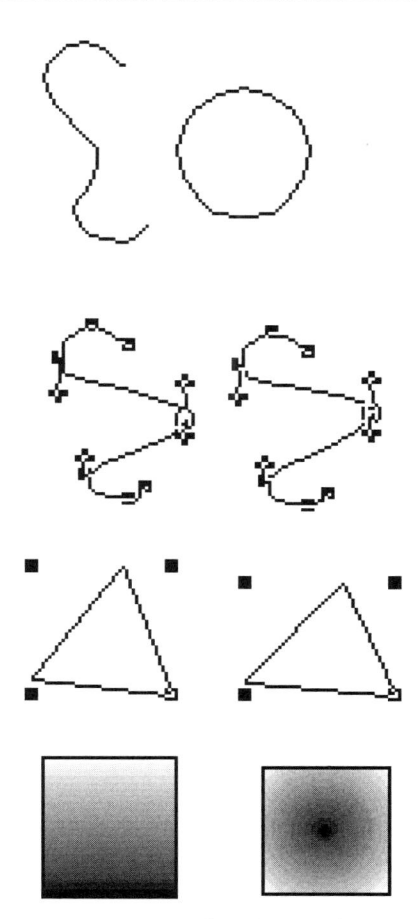

Figure 9. *Four examples of types of objects you cannot blend. From top to bottom: open path to closed path, interior points of an open path, grouped objects, and objects with different fill types.*

163

Chapter 13

To print blends:

If you are printing your file to a low-resolution output device such as a laser printer, you may not be satisfied with the results. This is because those printers cannot reproduce all the intermediate tones necessary to create a smooth blend.

If you are printing your file on a high-resolution device such as an imagesetter, your blend should print smoothly. However, there are some situations where blends produce an effect called "banding." Banding makes the blend seem to jump from one color to another, rather than smoothly changing from one to another (**Figure 10**). The following is information for printing your file on PostScript devices. *(For more information on printing, see Chapter 21, "Printing.")*

1. Print at high resolutions. For most work, this is a minimum of 2400 dpi.

2. Lower the halftone screen. If you have banding, try a lower screen line count. This is especially helpful when printing to laser printers.

3. Avoid blends over 7 inches long. This is especially true if you are outputting to a PostScript Level 1 device. If you are sending to a PostScript Level 2 device, you may not need to limit the length of your blends.

4. Make large differences between colors. Examine the difference between the tint values of colors. If you are getting banding, try increasing the difference between the tints.

5. Increase the number of steps. If you are getting banding, try increasing the number of steps of the blend. However, if you are outputting to a PostScript Level 1 device, you do not need any more than 256 steps.

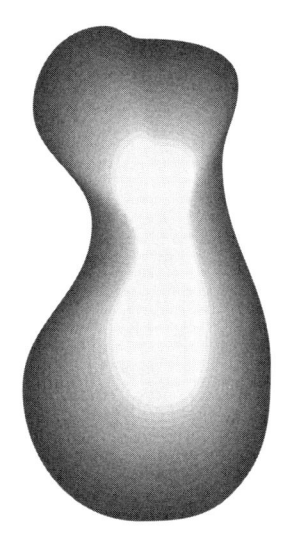

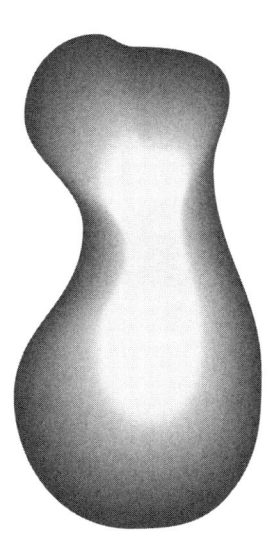

Figure 10. *A blend with* **banding** *(top) and the same blend with more steps used to decrease the banding (bottom).*

TEXT 14

Most people think of FreeHand as a program to create illustrations—graphics, drawings, and artwork. FreeHand also provides a wealth of features to create different text effects. In this chapter, you will learn how to: create text in text blocks; change the size of text blocks; apply borders to text blocks; inset text from the borders of text blocks; and precisely place text blocks. You will learn how to import text from word processing programs and format text characters and paragraphs. You will also learn how to use indents, tabs, rules, columns, and rows to create different paragraph effects. You will learn how to turn on and control hyphenation. Finally, you will learn how to link text so that it flows from one column or page to another.

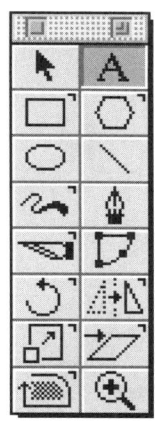

Figure 1. *To create a text block, choose the* **Text** *tool in the toolbox.*

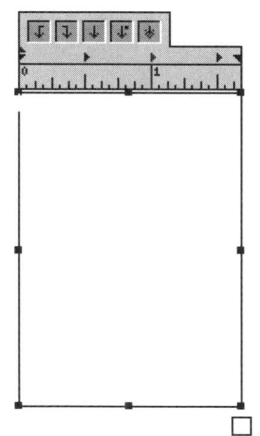

Figure 2. *A* **text block** *with a* **text ruler**.

To create a text block by dragging:

1. Select the Text tool (**Figure 1**) from the toolbox and drag on your page. The size of your drag determines the size of the text block you create.

2. As soon as you let go, you will see the text block and text block ruler (**Figure 2**).

3. Start typing. Your text will fill the text block. You do not have to hit the return at the end of a line. The text will automatically wrap within the text block.

Tip
■ If you do not see the text ruler, choose Text Rulers from the View menu.

165

Chapter 14

To create a text block by clicking:

1. Select the Text tool from the toolbox and click anywhere on your page. You will see a blinking insertion point and a text ruler.

2. Start typing and you will see your text. Your text will not automatically wrap within the text block. If you want the text to shift to the next line, you will need to type a Return or a Shift-Return. If your text does wrap within the box, check your Preferences settings *(see page 268)*.

Figure 3. *To change the size of a text block, drag on one of the corner points of the block.*

Once you have created a text block, you may want to change its size. There are different techniques to do this depending on how you created the text block.

To change the size of a dragged text block:

Use the Selection tool and drag on one of the corner points of the text block (**Figure 3**).

or

With the text block selected, click on the Document icon of the Inspector palette Then click on the Dimensions-and-Inset icon. Under Dimensions, change the measurements in the w (width) or h (height) fields (**Figure 4**).

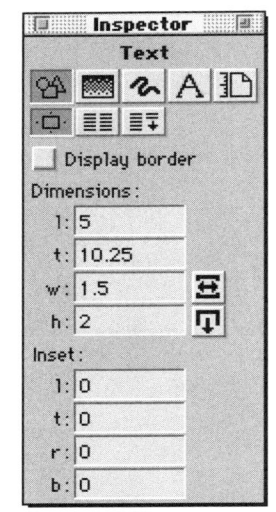

Figure 4. *The **Document** icon of the **Inspector** palette with the **Dimensions-and-Inset** icon selected.*

166

Text

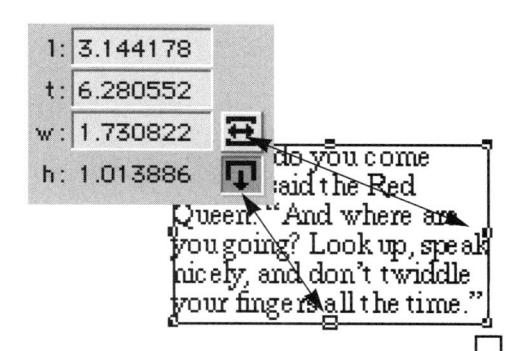

Figure 5. *When the icons next to the width and height fields are dark, or the side handles are white, it means that the fields are **unlocked** and will **auto-expand**. Clicking on the icons, so they turn light or clicking on the handles so they turn black, will **lock** the field so that it does **not** auto-expand.*

If you created the text block by clicking, the width and height fields will be set to auto-expand. This means that the text block will automatically change its size as you type. However, you cannot drag to change the size of the text block, nor can you enter new measurements in the fields (**Figure 5**).

To change the auto-expansion settings of a text block:

1. With the text block selected, click on the Document icon of the Inspector palette. Then choose the Dimensions-and-Inset icon.
2. Click on the icons next to the w (width) and h (height) fields. If the icon is dark, the field set to auto-expand as new text is entered. If the icon is light, the field is not set to auto-expand.
3. When auto-expansion is off, you can drag to resize the text block or you can enter new measurements in the width and height fields.

Tips

- You can also change the auto-expansion of a text block by double-clicking on the bottom handle or either of the side handles.
- Set the height of a text block to auto-expand but keep the auto-expansion of the width turned off. This is very useful for creating a column of text.
- If you hold the Control key as you drag horizontally to create a text block, the text block width will be fixed, but the height will auto-expand.
- If you hold the Control key as you drag vertically to create a text block, the text block height will be fixed, but the width will auto-expand.

Chapter 14

Another way to resize a text block is to have the block automatically shrink to fit the size of the text.

To automatically shrink a text block:

1. Select a text block that has extra space not filled by text.
2. Using the Selection tool, double-click on the Link box of the block (**Figure 6**). The text block will automatically shrink to fit.

Tip

- If there is no text in a text block, double-clicking on the Link box will delete the text block.

Figure 6. *Double-clicking on the* **Link box** *will shrink a text box with extra space (top) to the exact size of the text (bottom).*

To apply a border to a text block:

1. Select the text block you want to have a border.
2. Click on the Object icon and then the Dimensions-and-Inset icon of the Inspector palette.
3. Click the Display border checkbox (**Figure 7a**). (This allows you to see the border; however, it does not create the border.)
4. Choose the Stroke icon from the Inspector palette.
5. Apply a stroke using any of the stroke styles (**Figure 7b**).

Figure 7a. *The* **Display border** *checkbox will allow you to set a stroke or border around a text block.*

Figure 7b. *The* **Stroke** *icon lets you set the size, width, color, and style of the text box border.*

**Shrink a Text Block;
Apply a Border to Text Block**

168

Text

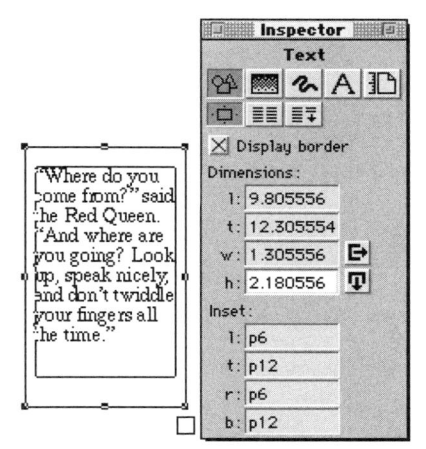

Figure 8. *Under **Inset**, the **l** (left), **t** (top), **r** (right), and **b** (bottom) fields let you move text away from the edges of a text block.*

Once you have given a text block a border, you will probably want to move your text away from the edge of the stroke.

To inset text away from a stroked text block:

1. Select the text block.

2. Choose the Object icon of the Inspector palette. Click on the Dimensions-and-Inset icon.

3. Under Inset, enter the amount that you would like to move the text away from the stroke in the l (left), t (top), r (right), and b (bottom) fields. Press Return or Enter to set the amounts (**Figure 8**).

Tip

■ Negative amounts will position the text outside the border of the text block.

A text block can be moved by dragging, or you can move the text block to a precise position.

To position a text block precisely on the page:

1. Select the text block.

2. Choose the Object icon of the Inspector palette. Click on the Dimensions-and-Inset icon.

3. Under Dimensions, enter the coordinate you want for the left edge of the text block in the l field.

4. Under Dimensions, enter the coordinate you want for the top edge of the text block in the t field. Press the Return or Enter key (**Figure 9**).

Tip

■ Unless you have changed the 0 point of the rulers, your page starts at the bottom-left corner.

Figure 9. *Under **Dimensions**, the **l** (left) and **t** (top) fields let you move a text block to a specific position.*

Chapter 14

Once you have a text block on your page, you can type directly into it. However, if you are working on a document that has a lot of text, you may want to import the text directly from a word processing program. FreeHand lets you import two types of text (**Figure 10**).

RTF Text (Rich Text Format): This is the preferred format. RTF text will allow you to import the text with its formatting intact. This includes font, size, style, margins, tabs, indents, alignment, baseline shift, letterspacing, and color.

ASCII (pronounced "as-kee"): Use this format only if you cannot get RTF text. ASCII text does not allow you to import with the formatting intact. Only the keystrokes (characters) are imported. If you import ASCII text, you will need to reformat it.

Figure 10. *RTF text (top) imports with all its formatting and styling.* **ASCII** *text imports its characters only.*

To import text:

1. Choose Place from the File menu. Your cursor will change into a corner.

2. Position the corner where you would like your text to start.

3. If you want your text block to be a certain size on the page, drag the cursor to create a rectangle the size you want the text block to be.

4. If you just want the text on the page, click. You will now have a text block filled with text.

Text

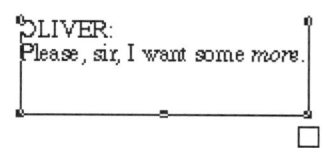

Figure 11a. *A **white Link box** indicates all the text is visible within the text block.*

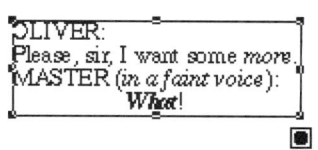

Figure 11b. *A **black circle** in the **Link box** indicates an overflow—additional text not visible in the block.*

At the bottom of the text block is a little square. This is the Link box. There are several different ways this box appears.

To work with the Link box:

1. If the Link box is white, then all the text in the block is visible (**Figure 11a**).

2. If the Link box has a black circle in it, it means there is more text than can fit inside the text block (**Figure 11b**). This is called an overflow.

3. If the Link box has left and right arrows in it, it means the text block has been linked to another object *(see page 180)*.

FreeHand gives you several places to change character attributes. The first two are the Type menu and the Type palette, where you can change the typeface, type size, or type style.

To change typeface, type size, or style:

1. Select the text by dragging across it. If you are about to type, you can format without any text selected. Any text you type afterwards will be styled correctly.

2. To change the Font, Size, or Type Style, choose those items from the Type menu (**Figure 12a**).
or
Choose Type from the Window menu. The Type palette will appear (**Figure 12b**). Use the pop-up menus to select the font, style, or size.

Tip

■ Type size will always be measured in points regardless of which unit of measurement you have selected.

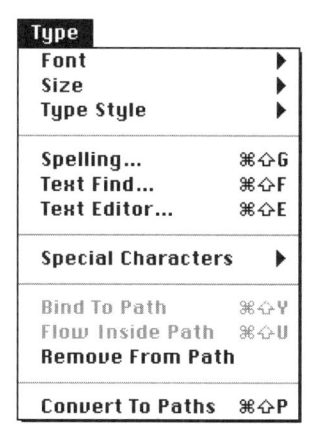

Figure 12a. *The various choices for styling text via the **Type** menu.*

Figure 12b. *The various choices for styling text via the **Type** palette.*

171

Chapter 14

Change Character Inspector Attributes

The third place to change character attributes is the Character Inspector. This is where you can change the leading, Horizontal scale, Kerning, Range kerning, and Baseline shift. It is also where you can turn off hyphenation and line breaks for a word.

To use the Character Inspector:

1. With the text selected, choose the Character icon of the Text Inspector (**Figure 13**).
2. To set the spacing between the lines of text, choose one of the three leading options: Extra, Fixed, or Percentage. (**Figure 14**). Extra sets extra space between the lines in addition to the space used by the characters. Fixed sets an amount of space that is fixed and does not change if the text size changes. Percentage adds an amount of space that is a percentage of the point size of the text.
3. To change the width of the characters, enter a percentage in the Horizontal scale field (**Figure 15**).
4. If your insertion point is blinking between two letters, you can enter a value in the Kerning field. Positive values increase the space between the letters. Negative values decrease the space between the letters (**Figure 16**).

Figure 13. *The* **Character** *icon of the* **Text Inspector**.

Figure 14. *The three choices for* **text leading** *are* **Extra**, **Fixed**, *and* **Percentage**.

Figure 15. *The* **Horizontal scale** *stretches the width of the characters. Here, a Horizontal scale of 150% has been applied to the bottom initials.*

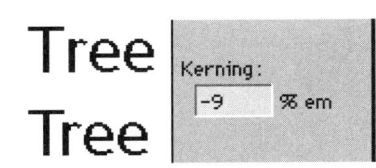

Figure 16. **Kerning** *adjusts the space between two letters. Here, a Kerning of -9 has been applied to the letters "T" and "r" in the bottom word.*

172

Text

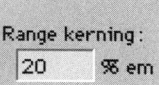

Figure 17. ***Range kerning*** *changes the letterspacing over a range of letters. Here, a Range kerning of 20 has been applied to the bottom text.*

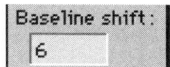

Figure 18. ***Baseline shift*** *raises or lowers text from its baseline. Here, the text has been shifted up 6 points to allow for the underline effect.*

Figure 19. *The **Inhibit hyphens** checkbox allows you to turn on or off the automatic hyphenation for individual words. The **Keep on same line** checkbox keeps one word from being separated from another word by a line break.*

5. If you have more than two characters selected, you can enter a value in the Range kerning field. Positive values increase the space between the letters. Negative values decrease the space between the letters (**Figure 17**).

6. Enter an amount in the Baseline shift field. Positive values raise the text. Negative values lower the text (**Figure 18**).

7. To prevent a word (such as a company name or special term) from being hyphenated, select the text and click the checkbox for Inhibit hyphens (**Figure 19**). *(To turn on automatic hyphenation, see page 178.)*

8. To keep one word with another (such as a title with a last name), select the text and click the checkbox for Keep on same line (**Figure 19**).

Tips

- Drag the top or bottom middle handles of a text block to increase or decrease the leading of an entire text block.
- Hold the Option key and drag a corner handle to change the Horizontal scale of all the text in a text block.
- Drag the left or right middle handles to increase or decrease the Range kerning of an entire text block.
- Hold the Option key as you drag the left or right middle handles of a text block to increase the Range kerning between words.

Change Character Inspector Attributes

173

Chapter 14

Once you've got your text in a text block, you will want to format its paragraph attributes. FreeHand lets you do this by using the Paragraph Inspector.

To use the Paragraph Inspector:

1. With the paragraphs that you want to change selected, choose the Text Inspector and then click on the Paragraph icon (**Figure 20**).
2. To add space above or below the paragraph, enter the amount you want under Paragraph spacing in the Above or Below fields (**Figure 21**).
3. To change the margin indents, enter the amount in the Left, Right, or First fields. (**Figure 22**).

Tips

- Use the Paragraph spacing fields, rather than extra paragraph returns, to add space between paragraphs.
- No space will be added above a paragraph that starts at the top of a column or text block.

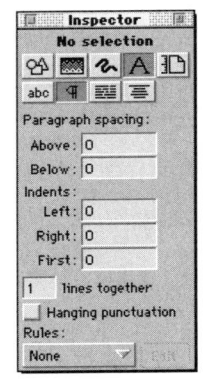

Figure 20. *Clicking on the* **Paragraph** *icon of the* **Text Inspector** *allows you to set various paragraph attributes.*

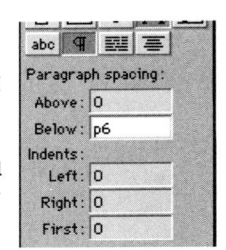

Figure 21. Paragraph spacing *of 6 points (p6) added between the paragraphs by entering an amount in the* **Below** *field.*

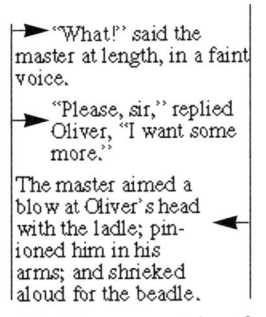

Figure 22. *Three examples of paragraphs with different margin indents. The top paragraph has a* **First line indent**. *The middle paragraph has a* **Left margin indent**. *The bottom paragraph has a* **Right margin indent**. *(The arrows indicate the direction of the indent.)*

Text

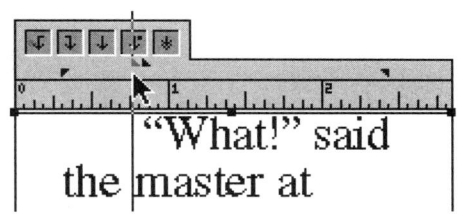

Figure 23. *Dragging the **indent triangles** of the Text Ruler allows you to change margin indents.*

Figure 24. *An example of **keeping lines together**. Notice that although there is room for one more line of text at the bottom of the left column, the lines together setting of 2 has forced the last two liine of the paragraph over to the right column.*

Figure 25. *An example of **hanging punctuation**. Notice how the quotation and punctuation marks hang outside the margins of the paragraphs.*

FreeHand also lets you set margin indents using the text rulers.

To change margin indents using the text rulers:

1. Choose the Text Inspector and then click on the Paragraph icon. Select the paragraphs in which you would like to change the indents.

2. If the text rulers are not visible, choose Text Rulers from the View menu.

3. Drag the bottom part of the left indent triangle to the spot on the ruler you would like the left margin to be (**Figure 23**).

4. Drag the right indent triangle to the spot on the ruler where you would like the right margin to be (**Figure 23**).

5. Drag the top part of the left indent triangle to the spot on the ruler where you would like the first line of the paragraph to be (**Figure 23**).

Tips

■ Dragging the top of the left indent triangle moves just the top.

■ Dragging the bottom of the left indent triangle also moves the top.

To keep lines together:

If you want to keep your paragraph from breaking with fewer than a certain number of lines across columns, enter that amount in the lines together field of the Paragraph Inspector. Press Return or Enter (**Figure 24**).

To create hanging punctuation:

If you want your punctuation to "hang" outside the margins, click in the checkbox for Hanging punctuation in the Paragraph Inspector. This keeps paragraphs from looking ragged (**Figure 25**).

175

Chapter 14

To change paragraph alignment:

With the paragraph or paragraphs selected, click on the Text Inspector and then choose the Alignment icon. Choose the alignment you want from the four Alignment icons (**Figure 26**).

Tip

- Use the following keystrokes to set the alignment of a selected paragraph:

    Command-Option-Shift-L for Left alignment.

    Command-Option-Shift-M for Centered alignment.

    Command-Option-Shift-R for Right alignment.

    Command-Option-Shift-J for Justified alignment.

FreeHand also offers the ability to align text using tabs. There are five different types of tabs. Each one aligns the text in a specific way (**Figure 27**).

To align text using tabs:

1. Begin typing the text you want to align.

2. As you are typing, press the Tab key on the keyboard to insert a tab character into the text.

3. The tabbed text will automatically be spaced at a .5" interval from the rest of the text. The default tab settings are at .5" intervals (**Figure 28**).

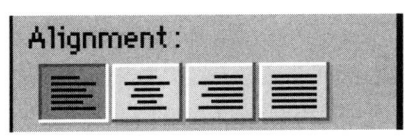

Figure 26. *The four **alignment** icons are (from left to right) **Left**, **Centered**, **Right**, and **Justified**.*

Figure 27. *Examples of the different types of **tabs** (from top to bottom): **Left**, **Right**, **Centered**, **Decimal**, and **Wrapping**. The gray arrows indicate where the tabs were entered.*

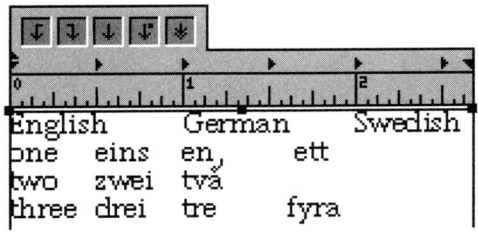

Figure 28. *The **default tab settings** are at .5" intervals and are indicated by the small triangles.*

176

Text

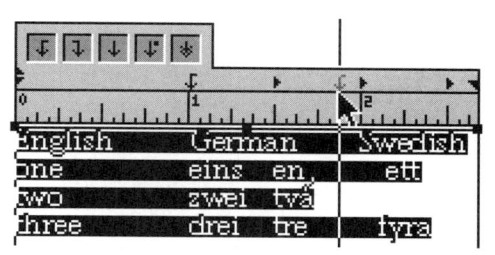

Figure 29a. *To set a tab position, drag a **tab arrow** onto the **text ruler**.*

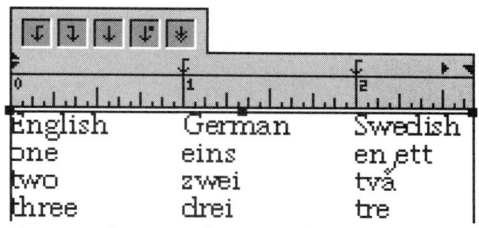

Figure 29b. *Text aligns itself along the tab arrow.*

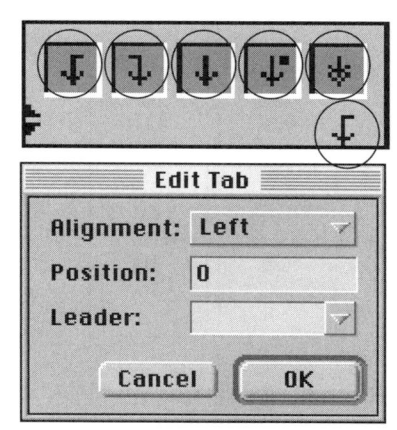

Figure 30. *Double-click on any of the tab icons or the tab arrows on the text ruler (circled) to open the **Edit Tab** dialog box. This allows you to set your tabs numerically and add tab leaders.*

To set the tabs by dragging:

1. Select the paragraphs in which you want to change the tabs.
2. If the text block does not have a text ruler visible, choose Text Rulers from the View menu.
3. Drag the left-aligned tab arrow from the top of the text ruler down to the area just above the numbers (**Figure 29a**).
4. Let go when the tab arrow is in the position you want. The text will be realigned at the spot where you positioned the tab arrow (**Figure 29b**).

To set the tabs numerically:

1. Double-click on any of the tab icons at the top of the ruler. You should see the Edit Tab dialog box (**Figure 30**).
2. Choose the type of tab you want from the Alignment pop-up menu.
3. Enter a number for where you want the tab to be in the Position field. This number is in relation to the left side of the text block.

Tips

- Use the Leader field or pop-up menu to choose a repeating character that will automatically fill the space between the words that are aligned.
- To change the repeating characters of a tab leader, double-click on the repeating characters as they appear in the text and change their size, font, color, etc.

To change existing tabs:

1. To delete a tab from the text ruler, drag the tab arrow down off the ruler and then release.
2. To move a tab to a new position, drag the tab arrow along the ruler to the position you want.

177

Chapter 14

Another set of paragraph attributes are the options for automatic hyphenation. This allows you to hyphenate text at the end of lines.

To turn on hyphenation:

1. With the text block or paragraphs selected, choose the Spacing-and-Hyphenation icon of the Text Inspector.
2. To turn hyphenation on or off, click in the Automatic checkbox.
3. To prevent capitalized words from being hyphenated, click in the Skip capitalized checkbox.
4. To limit the number of hyphens in a row, enter the number in the Consecutive field. Press Return or Enter (**Figure 31**).

Tip

- Clicking the Spacing-and-Hyphenation icon also lets you set the Miniumum, Optimum, and Maximum amounts for wordspacing and letterspacing.

Figure 31. *Checking the* **Automatic** *box turns hyphenation on or off. The* **Skip capitalized** *box prevents capitalized words from being hyphenated. The* **Consecutive** *field lets you enter how many hyphens in a row are allowed.*

FreeHand gives you the ability to divide text blocks into columns and rows. (**Figure 32**).

To create columns and rows:

1. With the text block selected, choose the Object Inspector and then the Column-and-Row icon (**Figure 33**).
2. Enter the number of columns you want in the Count field under Column. Press Return or Enter.
3. If you want to change the Height of the columns, or the Spacing between each column, enter those amounts in their fields. Then press Return or Enter.

Figure 32. *Special effects created with columns and rows.*

Text

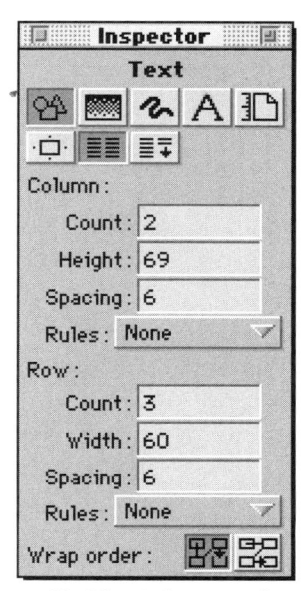

Figure 33. *The **Column** and **Row** settings of the **Object Inspector**.*

Figure 34. *Two examples of the **rules** between columns or rows. The rules on the left were set to **Inset**. The rules on the right were set to **Full height** and **Full width**.*

4. Enter the number of rows you want in the Count field under Row. Press Return or Enter.
5. If you want to change the Width of the rows, or the Spacing between each row, enter those amounts in their fields. Then press Return or Enter.
6. Click on the Wrap order icon to direct the text flow first down or first across the columns and rows.

FreeHand also lets you create rules that fit in the spaces between columns or rows (**Figure 34**).

To add rules to columns and rows:

1. Select the text block you want to add rules to. Click on the Object Inspector and then click on the Column-and-Row icon.
2. Select a rule style from the Rules pop-up menu under Column or Row. The choices are Inset, which will break in the space between the columns or rows, and Full width or Full height, which will cross over the space between the columns or rows.
3. With the text block still selected, choose the Stroke Inspector to apply the stroke. Choose the styles, color, width, etc.

179

Chapter 14

While it is very easy to create columns within a text block, you may want to have text flow from one text block to another. Or you may want text to flow onto an open path or into a closed path. You can link text in these ways by using the Link box of the text block.

To link text between objects:

1. Select a text block you would like to link to another object.

2. Using the Selection tool, drag from the Link box of the block. You will see a wavy line extend out.

3. Drag the wavy line onto the object you want to link your text to (**Figure 35a**). Let go of the mouse.

4. If you had an overflow of text, you will see arrows in the Link box and the text will flow into the new object (**Figure 35b**).

5. If you did not have an overflow, you will see arrows in the Link box. If you add text or decrease the size of the first text box, the text will appear in the new object.

Tip

■ You can link text within a page or across pages.

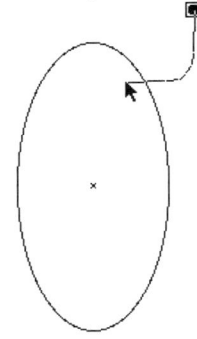

Figure 35a. *To link text, drag from the **Link box** to the text block or object you want the text to link to.*

Figure 35b. *After linking, the text will flow from one box to another.*

Link Text

180

SPECIAL TEXT EFFECTS 15

With FreeHand, you can create looks for text that would be difficult, if not impossible, to create using an ordinary page layout program. In this chapter, you will learn how to align type to a path and how to adjust that alignment. You will also learn how to apply FreeHand's special text effects, including inline graphics. You will learn how to wrap text around a graphic element. And finally, you will learn how to convert text into artwork to create other effects.

One of the most popular effects is to align text to a path. The path can be open or closed, with curve or corner points. The text can even be linked to other paths or text blocks.

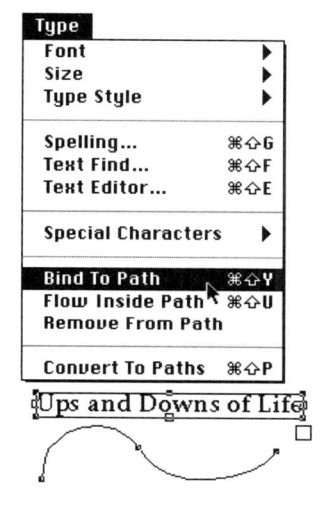

Figure 1a. *With both a path and a text block selected, choose **Bind To Path** from the Type menu to align text to a path.*

Figure 1b. *The results of binding text to a path.*

Figure 2. *As the text was typed a return was inserted after the word "Pixel." The Bind to Path command was applied, and the text was automatically aligned on either side of the oval.*

To bind text to a path:

1. With the Selection tool, select both the text block you want to align to the path and the path you want the text aligned to.

2. From the Type menu, choose Bind To Path (**Figures 1a–b**). The text will automatically align onto the selected path.

Tips

- If you are aligning text to a closed path, such as an oval, and you insert a paragraph return in the text, the text will align on both sides of the path (**Figure 2**).

- If the path is not long enough to display all the text, the overflow box will be filled.

181

There are different ways to change how the text is aligned to the path.

To change the direction that the text flows:

1. Hold the Option key and click with the Selection tool on the path. This selects just the path.
2. Choose Reverse Direction from the Path Operations submenu of the Arrange menu. The text will then flow in the opposite direction on the path (**Figure 3**).

Figure 3. *The* **Reverse Direction** *command will cause the text (top) to change its direction (bottom).*

To move the text along the path:

1. Click with the Selection tool on the path. A small white triangle will appear at the left, center, or right of the text depending on the text alignment.
2. Drag that triangle to move the text along the path (**Figure 4**).

Figure 4. *Drag the small white triangle next to text on a path to move the text along the path.*

Special Text Effects

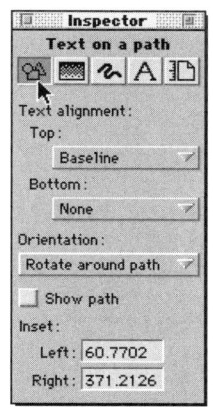

Figure 5. *The **Object Inspector** shows the **Text on a path** options.*

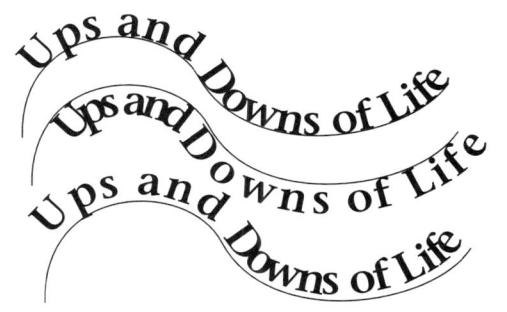

Figure 6. *The various ways text can be aligned to a path: **Baseline** (top), **Ascent** (middle), and **Descent** (bottom).*

Figure 7. *The various ways text can be oriented to a path (from top to bottom): **Rotate around path**, **Vertical**, **Skew horizontal**, and **Skew vertical**.*

To work with text on a path:

1. Use the Selection tool to select the text on a path.

2. Click the Object icon of the Inspector palette to show the Text on a path options (**Figure 5**).

3. To change how the text is aligned to the path, choose Baseline, Ascent, or Descent from the Text alignment pop-up menu (**Figure 6**). The Top pop-up menu controls any text before the paragraph return. The Bottom pop-up menu controls the text after the paragraph return.

4. To change how the the text is oriented to the path, choose Rotate around path, Vertical, Skew horizontal, or Skew vertical from the Orientation pop-up menu (**Figure 7**).

5. To move the text, you can drag the text using the white triangle or you can enter exact values in the Left and Right Inset fields. Once you enter the values, press the Return key to apply them to your path.

6. To see the fill and stroke attributes of the path that the text is aligned to, check the Show path box.

Tips

- An alignment setting of "None" will cause the text to disappear.

- To remove the text from the path, select the path and choose Remove From Path from the Type menu.

- Text can be highlighted while on the path by using the Text tool. Once it's highlighted, the text can be modified using any of the functions of the Type menu or the Type palette.

Text on a Path Options

183

Several of FreeHand's most popular features are the automatic special effects that can be applied to text. These effects can be applied to entire blocks of text or to individual characters or words within a text block. Highlight creates a color or tint that is applied as a block around the text (**Figure 8**). Inline creates outlines of strokes and colors that surround the text (**Figure 9**). Shadow creates an automatic drop shadow behind the text (**Figure 10**). Strikethrough creates a line that runs across the text (**Figure 11**). Underline creates a line that runs underneath the text (**Figure 12**). Zoom creates a three-dimensional effect where the text starts as one color and turns into another (**Figure 13**).

"Where do you come from?" said the Red Queen. "And where are you going? Look up, speak nicely, and don't twiddle your fingers all the time."

Figure 8. *The **Highlight** effect on text.*

QUEEN ALICE

Figure 9. *The **Inline** effect on text.*

JABBER WOCKY

Figure 10. *The single look for the **Shadow** effect on text.*

Twas bright brillig, and the lithe slithy badgers toves Did jump gyre and play gimble in the elearning wabe: All

Figure 11. *The **Strikethrough** effect on text.*

"When I use a word," Humpty Dumpty said, in a rather scornful tone, "it

Figure 12. *The **Underline** effect on text.*

TWEEDLEDEE

TWEEDLEDUM

Figure 13. *The **Zoom** effect on text.*

Special Text Effects

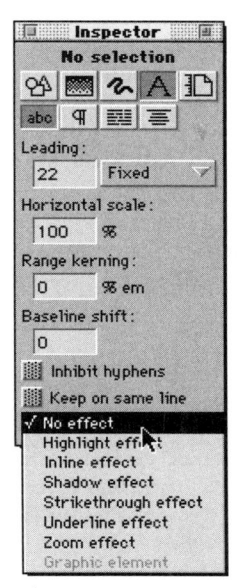

Figure 14. *Use the **Effects** pop-up menu of the **Text Inspector** to apply the special text effects.*

To apply any of the special text effects:

1. After using one of the methods described in the previous chapter to create text *(see page 165)*, select the text you want to apply the special effect to. You can select the text by highlighting it or by selecting the text block with the Selection tool.

2. Choose the Text icon of the Inspector palette and then click on the Character icon. Unless you have previously applied an effect to your text, "No effect" will be checked in the pop-up menu at the bottom of the palette.

3. Choose one of the special effects from the pop-up menu: Highlight, Inline, Shadow, Strikethrough, Underline, or Zoom (**Figure 14**).

Tips

- You can turn the visual display of the text effects on or off, by changing your Preferences settings *(see page 271)*.

- Text effects may slow your screen redraw. Apply them after you have finished most of your work, or work in the Keyline mode.

Chapter 15

Once you have applied a special effect to text, you may find that you want to modify the effect. This is done using the Edit button.

To edit the Inline effect:

1. Select the text that has the Inline effect applied to it and click the Edit button next to the pop-up menu of the Text inspector palette. The Inline Effect dialog box will appear (**Figure 15**).

2. In the Count field, enter the number of sets of outlines you want to surround the text. The Inline effect adds two outlines, a Stroke Width and a Background Width, for each number in the Count field.

3. In the Stroke Width field, enter the width (in points) of the stroke that will be on the outside of the effect.

4. To change the color of the stroke, drag a color or tint from the Color List onto the Stroke drop box.

5. In the Background Width field, enter the width (in points) of the background color that will be between the stroke and the text.

6. To change the background color, drag a color or tint from the Color List onto the Background drop box.

7. When you are satisfied with your choices, click the OK button.

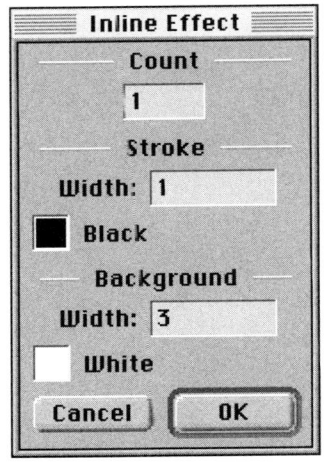

Figure 15. *The **Inline Effect** dialog box allows you to alter the look of the Inline effect.*

Special Text Effects

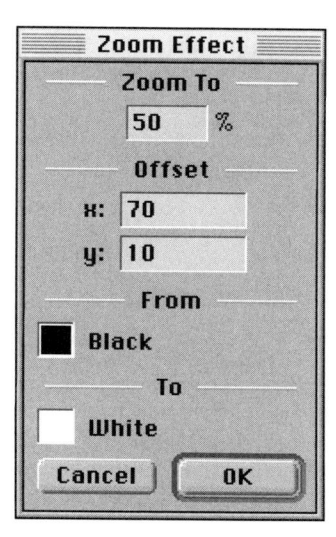

Figure 16. *The **Zoom Effect** dialog box allows you to alter the look of the Zoom effect.*

To edit the Zoom effect:

1. Select the text that has the Zoom effect applied to it and click the Edit button next to the pop-up menu of the Text Inspector palette. The Zoom Effect dialog box will appear (**Figure 16**).

2. In the Zoom To field, enter the percentage of the size of the final object when compared to the original object. For example, if you enter 50%, the final object in the Zoom effect will be half the size of the original text. If you enter 200%, the final object will be twice the size of the original text.

3. In the x and y Offset fields, enter the distance that you want the final object moved from the original text. The x value moves the final object to the right (positive values) or left (negative values). The y value moves the final object up (positive values) or down (negative values).

4. To change the color of the final object, drag a color or tint from the Color List onto the From drop box. This color will also be applied as a thin stroke around the outside of the original text.

5. To change the color of the original text, drag a color or tint from the Color List onto the To drop box.

6. When you are satisfied with your choices, click the OK button.

Chapter 15

Once you open the dialog boxes to edit the Highlight, Underline, and Strikethrough effects, you will notice that all three are really just variations on the same effect.

To edit the Highlight, Underline, and Strikethrough effects:

1. Select the text that has the effect applied to it and click the Edit button of the Text Inspector palette. The dialog box will appear (**Figure 17**).

2. In the Position field, enter the distance from the baseline that you want the effect to appear.

3. In the Stroke Width field, enter the value (in points) of the thickness of the effect.

4. To change the color of the effect, drag a color or tint from the Color List onto the drop box in the dialog box for each effect.

5. To apply a dash pattern to the effect, choose a pattern from the Dash pop-up menu in the dialog box for each effect.

6. To allow the effect to overprint the original text, click the Overprint checkbox. Overprinting will be seen only when separations are made.

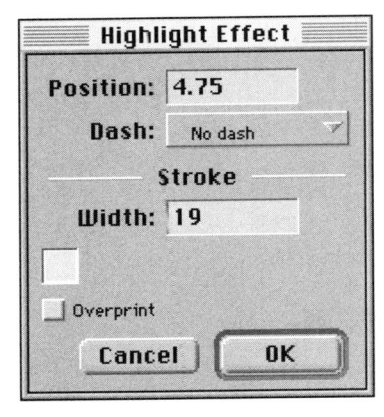

Figure 17. *The three dialog boxes to edit the* **Highlight**, **Underline**, *and* **Strikethrough** *effects are all the same. The differences in the effect are created in the settings.*

To use the Shadow effect:

Choose Shadow effect from the Effects pop-up menu of the Text Inspector. There is no dialog box for editing the Shadow effect. The values of the Shadow effect are fixed. The shadow is always a 50% gray. Its position is always down and to the right of the original text.

Special Text Effects

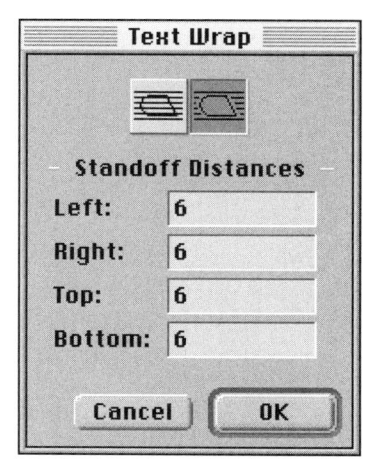

Figure 18. *The **Text Wrap** dialog box. Choosing the top right icon lets you enter the Standoff Distances for the four sides of the object.*

Figure 19. *An example of text wrapping around a graphic. In this case, only Ben's outline was selected as the object to be wrapped.*

FreeHand lets you position graphics so that the text automatically flows around the graphic. This is called text wrap.

To wrap text around a graphic element:

1. Select the graphic element you want the text to wrap around. Do not group it.

2. Move the graphic so that it is in the position you want in relation to the text.

3. If the graphic is not in front of the text block, choose Bring To Front from the Arrange menu.

4. With the graphic still selected, choose Text Wrap (Command-Shift-W) from the Arrange menu. This will display the Text Wrap dialog box (**Figure 18**).

5. Click the top right icon of the dialog box to display the Standoff Distances fields.

6. The Standoff Distances are the amount of space that will be kept between the text and the edges of the graphic. Enter the amount for each side of the graphic.

7. If the object already has a text wrap applied to it, you can edit the Standoff Distances by changing the amounts in the fields. Or you can turn off the Text Wrap by clicking the top left icon of the dialog box.

8. Click OK when you are finished and the text will automatically flow around the graphic (**Figure 19**).

Tip

■ If you want more control over the text wrap, draw a simple outline around the object. Style this outline with no fill or stroke. Choose this invisible outline as the object to have the text wrap around. You can then add or delete points and manipulate the outline to create a more precise text wrap.

189

Chapter 15

In Version 5.5, FreeHand has added the ability to create inline graphics. With inline graphics, you can create graphic elements, such as ornate capital letters or logos, that are incorporated into the text flow. This means that if the text reflows due to editing or format changes, the inline graphic flows along with the text.

To create an inline graphic:

1. Create the graphic you would like to place inline. Your graphic may be FreeHand objects, text on a path, text blocks, or placed TIFF or EPS images. (If the graphic contains any text, make sure you group the object so it is interpreted as a graphic, not as text.)
2. Use the Selection tool to select the graphic, and choose Copy or Cut from the Edit menu (**Figure 20a**).
3. Use the Text tool to place an insertion point where you would like the inline graphic to appear (**Figure 20b**).
4. Choose Paste from the Edit menu. The inline graphic will appear (**Figure 20c**).

Figure 20a. *To create an inline graphic, select the graphic and choose Copy or Cut.*

Figure 20b. *The next step in creating an inline graphic is to use the Text tool to put the insertion point at the spot in the text where the graphic should appear.*

Figure 20c. *The inline graphic as it appears within the text.*

Special Text Effects

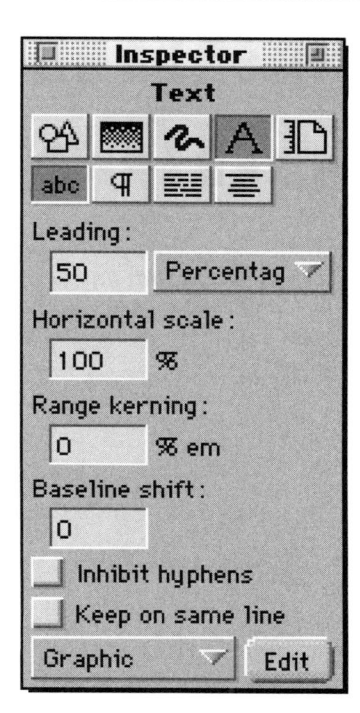

Figure 21. *When an inline graphic is selected in a text block, the Effects pop-up menu in the Character Inspector shows the **Graphic** choice. Click on the **Edit** button next to the pop-up menu to change the Standoff Distances around the inline graphic.*

Tips

- To remove an inline graphic from text, use the Text tool to drag across the graphic as you would a text character. Choose Cut or Clear from the Edit menu.
- To move the inline graphic up or down on the baseline, use the Text tool to drag across the graphic as you would a text character. Change the Baseline shift amounts in the Text Inspector palette or press Option-up arrow or Option-down arrow.
- If you select an inline graphic, the Effects pop-up menu will display the word "Graphic." Click the Edit button to use the Text Wrap dialog box to add more space around the inline graphic (**Figure 21**).
- If you select all the text in a text block, including the inline graphic, and then change the point size of the text, the inline graphic will scale up or down along with the text.

Chapter 15

So far, all the effects we have created with text have kept the text as text. This means that you can still edit the text. However, there may be times when you want to convert the text into paths that can be edited as artwork.

To convert text into paths:

1. Use the Selection tool to select the text block or text on a path you want to convert.

2. Choose Convert To Paths from the Type menu. If you convert text aligned to a path, the path will be deleted, leaving only the text.

3. To manipulate the individual paths of the characters, choose Ungroup from the Arrange menu or hold the Option key as you click on each individual path (**Figure 22**).

Tips

- You cannot change the font, spelling, or words of text that has been converted to paths.

- The fill of text converted to paths will automatically be set to overprint, indicated onscreen by little "O's."

- Any text characters that have holes in them, such as the letters "A," "O," or "B," will automatically be joined as a composite path *(see pages 211–212)*.

- Text must be converted to paths to use the text as a mask *(see page 213)*.

- You will need to convert text to paths to apply most of the FreeHand and third-party filters that create special effects *(see pages 230–232)*.

Figure 22. *The difference between* **text** *(top) and* **text that has been converted to paths** *(bottom). The converted text can be manipulated as artwork.*

EDIT TEXT 16

Anyone who has worked with a word processing program will recognize the usefulness of the features in this chapter—especially for lengthy text. In this chapter, you will learn: how to use the Text Editor; how to use the Spelling checker; how to insert special typographic characters and formatting commands; and how to use the Find Text feature to automate text editing.

Whenever you select text—either in a text block or on a path—you have the ability either to work with that text directly in the block or path, or to work within the Text Editor. The Text Editor allows you to view the text all in one place, or without formatting that might make the text difficult to see onscreen. The Text Editor is especially useful for reading type on a path.

Figure 1. *To see the Text Editor, choose* **Text Editor** *from the* **Type** *menu or press* **Command-Shift-E**.

Figure 2. *The Text Editor allows you to see text that might be difficult to read as part of your document. The scroll bar at the side of the box lets you scroll through lengthy text.*

To use the Text Editor:

1. Use the Selection tool to select the text block or path, or click with the Text tool to place an insertion point inside the text.

2. Choose Text Editor from the Type menu or press Command-Shift-E to open the Text Editor dialog box (**Figure 1**). The Text Editor will open (**Figure 2**).

3. To change the viewing size of the text in the Text Editor dialog box, click on the 12 Point Black checkbox. This will change the type to 12 points. It will also change any colored type to black.

(Continued on the following page)

193

Chapter 16

4. To change any attributes of the text, highlight the text in the Text Editor and make whatever changes you want via the Type menu or the Text Inspector.

5. To see how the text changes you are making will affect the actual text block or path, click the Apply button. When you are satisfied with your changes, click the OK button.

Tips

- If you hold the Option key as you click in a text block, you will open the Text Editor for that block and be positioned at the point in the text where you clicked.

- If you hold the Option key as you click or drag to create a text block, you will open the Text Editor. You can then type your text directly into the Text Editor.

Figure 3a. *The Spelling checker will check for unknown words, capitalization mistakes, and duplicate words.*

You may want to make sure the text in your document is spelled correctly. To do so, you can use the Spelling checker. This feature checks for spelling mistakes, and also looks for capitalization mistakes and duplicate words.

To use the Spelling checker:

1. Use the Selection tool to select the text block or path.

   or

   Place your insertion point at the point in the text where you would like the Spelling checker to start.

   or

   Deselected the text blocks to check the spelling of the entire document.

2. Choose Spelling from the Type menu or press Command-Shift-G. The Spelling checker will appear (**Figure 3a**).

194

Edit Text

Figure 3b. *The **Change** button will change the word that is found to one of the suggested alternates. The **Change All** button will change all instances of the word to the suggested alternate. The **Ignore** button will skip the word. The **Ignore all** button will skip all instances of the word. The **Add** button will add the word found to the dictionary FreeHand uses when performing a spelling check.*

3. To start checking your text, click the Start button (**Figure 3b**). The Spelling checker will look through the text and stop when it finds an error. (The Start button will be changed to Ignore for the rest of the process.)

4. If the Spelling checker finds a word that it does not know, it will show the word in the top field. If it can, it will show a list of suggested alternates for the word it stopped at.

5. If one of the alternates is correct, click on it and then click the Change button (**Figure 3b**). The incorrect word will be deleted and the correct word inserted.

6. If the original word is correct, click the Ignore button (**Figure 3b**), FreeHand will skip over that instance of the word but will stop at it again elsewhere in the text chain.

or

If the original word is correct, click the Ignore All button (**Figure 3b**). The Spelling checker will ignore all instances of that word until you quit FreeHand.

or

If the original word is correct, click the Add button (**Figure 3b**). This will permanently add the word to the Spelling checker dictionary.

(Continued on the following page)

Chapter 16

7. If the original word is incorrect, choose one of the alternates suggested in the list or type in the correct word and then click the Change button (**Figure 3b**). This will change that instance of the word, but will leave any other instances of the word unchanged.

or

If the original word is incorrect, choose one of the alternates suggested in the list or type in the correct word and then click the Change all button (**Figure 3b**). This will change all instances of the word in the text chain.

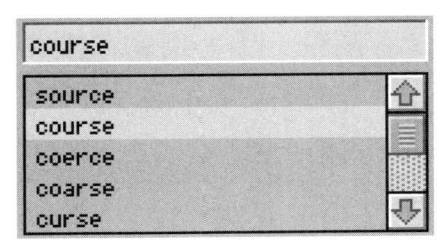

Figure 3c. *Click on the **Suggest** button to see the list of suggested alternates.*

Tips

- To check the spelling of just a portion of a lengthy text block, use the Text tool to select just that portion and then run the Spelling checker.

- To check the spelling of an individual word without checking the entire text chain, type in the word at the top of the Spelling checker and then click the Suggest button. FreeHand will give you a list of suggested spellings for that word (**Figure 3c**).

- To change how the Spelling checker finds words and how words are added to the dictionary, change the Spelling preferences *(see page 274)*.

- To see the section of text currently being checked by the Spelling checker, click the Show selection checkbox

- The Spelling checker is not a grammar checker. It will not find typos such as "He was reel good," since the word "reel" is a known word.

Edit Text

FreeHand allows you to insert special typographic characters into your text that will improve the look of text, as well as characters that help control the flow of text.

To use the Special Characters:

1. Place your insertion point where you would like the special character inserted.

2. In the Type menu, choose one of the characters in the Special Characters submenu (**Figure 4**) or type the keyboard commands shown.

    End Of Column (Shift-Enter) inserts an invisible character that will force the following text to the next column or text block (**Figure 5**). If there is no column or block to flow to, an overflow will occur.

    End Of Line (Shift-Return) inserts an invisible character that will force the following text to the next line (**Figure 6**).

(Continued on the following page)

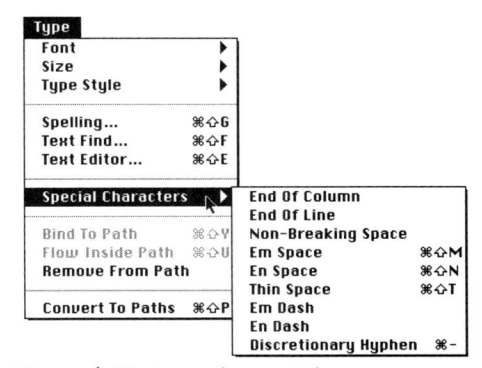

Figure 4. *To insert the special typographic characters, choose* **Special Characters** *from the* **Type** *menu.*

Figure 5. *Text before (left) and after (right) inserting the* **End Of Column** *character.*

Figure 6. *Text before (top) and after (bottom) inserting the* **End Of Line** *character.*

197

Chapter 16

Non-Breaking Space (Option-Space) inserts a space that will not break across lines. This can be used to keep titles such as "Dr." or "Mr." with the names they modify (**Figure 7**).

Em space (Command-Shift-M) inserts a space that is fixed as one em in width (**Figure 8**).

En space (Command-Shift-N) inserts a space that is fixed as one-half of an em in width (**Figure 8**).

Thin space (Command-Shift-T) inserts a space that is fixed as 10% of an em in width (**Figure 8**).

Em dash (Option-Shift-Hyphen) inserts an em dash, which is the length of one em (**Figure 9**).

En dash (Option-Hyphen) inserts an en dash, which is the length of one-half em (**Figure 9**).

We congratulate Dr. DuPrât on her recent promotion. We expect that this will be an important advancement for all the members of

We congratulate Dr. DuPrât on her recent promotion. We expect that this will be an important advancement for all the

Figure 7. *Text before (top) and after (bottom) inserting a **Non-Breaking Space** character.*

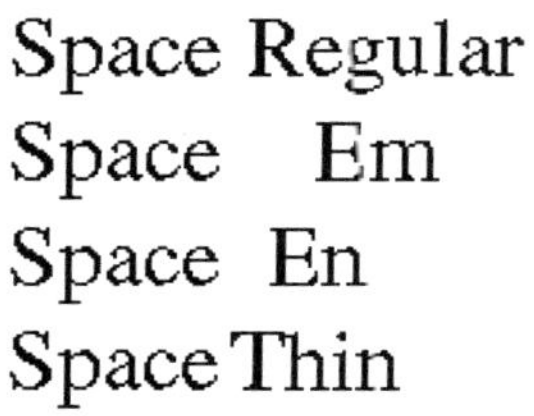

Space Regular
Space   Em
Space En
Space Thin

Figure 8. *The differences between (from top to bottom): a **regular space**, **Em space**, **En space**, and **Thin space**.*

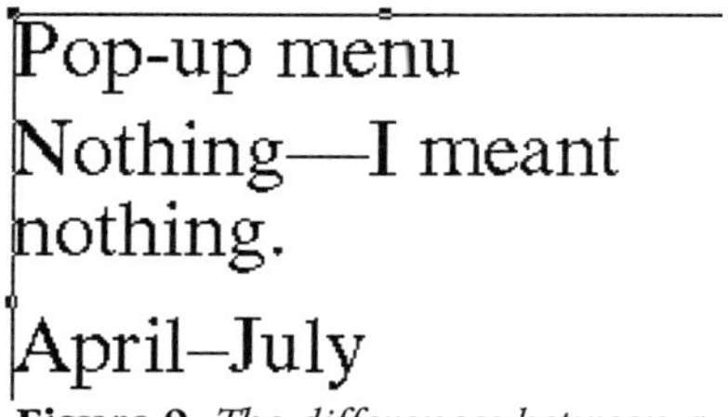

Pop-up menu
Nothing—I meant nothing.
April–July

Figure 9. *The differences between a **regular hyphen** (top), an **Em dash** (middle), and an **En dash** (bottom).*

Edit Text

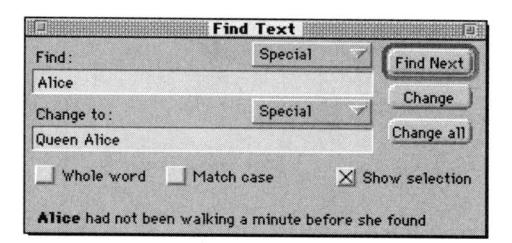

Figure 10. *The **Find Text** dialog box allows you to search and replace text strings or invisible characters.*

If you are working with short amounts of text, it is relatively easy to look through the text to make changes. But if you are dealing with lengthy text chains, you will need to use FreeHand's Find Text dialog box.

To use the Find Text dialog box:

1. Place your insertion point in the text block or use the Selection tool to select the entire text block or path.

2. Choose Text Find from the Type menu or press Command-Shift-F. The Find Text dialog box will appear (**Figure 10**).

3. In the Find field, type the text string or characters you want to search for. In the Change to field, type the text string or characters you want as a replacement.

4. If you want to search for only the whole word listed, click the Whole word checkbox. If you want to search for the text exactly as typed in uppercase and lowercase, click the Match case checkbox.

5. If you want to find or change any Special Characters, use the Special pop-up menus to insert them into either of the fields or type their codes directly into the fields.

6. Click the Find First button to find the first instance of the text string. (The Find First button will change to Find Next for the rest of the process.)

7. If you want to change just that one occurrence of the text, click the Change button. You can then click the Find Next button to find the next instance of the text string.

(Continued on the following page)

Chapter 16

8. If you want to change all occurrences of the text strings, click the Change all button. All instances of the text will be changed and the number of times the change was made will be listed at the bottom of the dialog box.

Tips

- Use the Find Text box to delete double paragraph returns in text.
- Insert the Any single character (^@) to search for any single character (**Figure 11**). For instance, the search string ^@" will find ." ?" and !".
- Insert the Any single letter (^*) to search for any single letter (**Figure 11**). For instance, the search string M^*. will find all instances of both Mr. and Ms.
- Insert the Any single number (^#) to search for any single number (**Figure 11**). For instance, the search string ^#th will find all instances of 4th, 5th, 6th, etc.
- Insert the White space (^w) to search for any type of space between letters, including regular spaces, em spaces, thin spaces, etc (**Figure 11**).
- If you want to see the text currently being searched by the Find Text dialog box, click the Show selection checkbox.

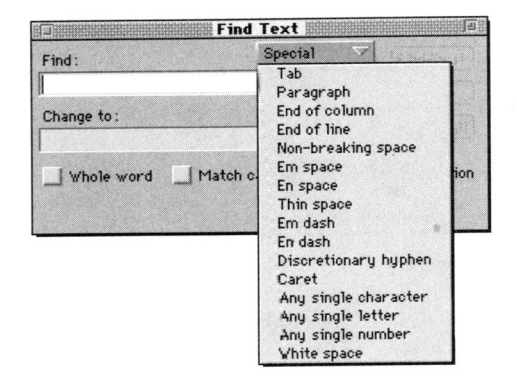

Figure 11. *The **Special** pop-up menus allow you to insert special characters into the Find and Change to fields.*

200

STYLES 17

If you are working on a complicated document, you will find that the Styles palette will help you work more consistently and more quickly. In this chapter, you will learn how to open the Styles palette and work with the two default Styles: Normal and Normal Text. You will learn how to define and name object styles to apply predefined fills and strokes and how to define and name text styles to apply predefined text formatting. You will learn how to redefine or edit styles to make global changes to all objects or text in a document. You will learn how to organize your styles by basing one style on another or making a duplicate of a style. Finally, you will learn how to copy styles from one document to another and how to remove a style from the Styles palette.

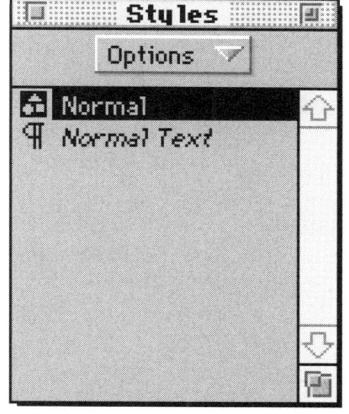

Figure 1. *The **Styles** palette with the two default styles. The Object icon next to Normal indicates it is an object style. The paragraph symbol next to Normal Text indicates it is a text style.*

Styles are controlled by the Styles palette. In order to see the styles in your document, you will need to open the Styles palette.

To view the default styles:

1. Choose Styles (Command-3) from the Window menu. If there is a checkmark next to the word "Styles," then the palette is already open.

2. If you have not added any styles to your document, you will see the two default styles (**Figure 1**).

3. The Normal style has an Object icon next to it. It is the default style for objects.

4. The Normal Text style has a paragraph symbol next to it. It is the default style for text.

201

Chapter 17

There are two ways to define a style: by example or by attributes.

To define a style by example:

1. Draw an object. In this case, draw a circle. (The shape is not important. It is the attributes you assign that create the style.)
or
Type some text.

2. Choose the fill and stroke attributes you want for your object. In this case, choose a dark fill and a thick stroke with a dash pattern (**Figure 2a**).
or
Choose the font, point size, and other attributes you want for your text.

3. With the object still selected, press on the Options pop-up menu of the Styles palette and choose New (**Figure 2b**). A new object style named "Style-1" will appear (**Figure 2c**).
or
With the text still selected, press on the Options pop-up menu of the Styles palette and choose New (**Figure 2b**). The new style will be listed in italic typeface and will have a paragraph symbol (¶) next to it indicating it is a text style (**Figure 3**).

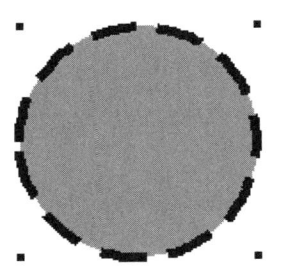

Figure 2a. *To define a style by example, create either the object or text styled the way you want it.*

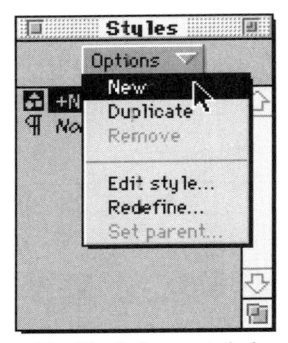

Figure 2b. *To define a style by example, select an object or text that has all the attributes you want for the style and then choose* **New** *from the* **Styles Options** *pop-up menu.*

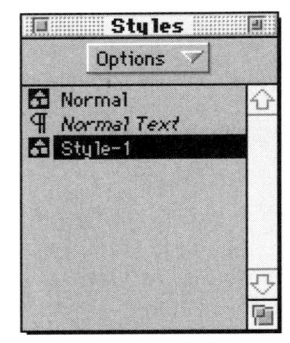

Figure 2c. *A new style is created with the name* "**Style-1**."

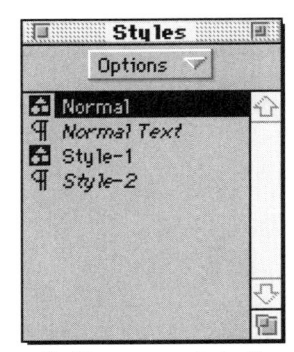

Figure 3. *The* **roman typeface** *and* **object icon** *indicate* **object** *styles. The* **italic typeface** *and* **paragraph symbol** *indicate* **text styles**.

Define a Style by Example

202

Styles

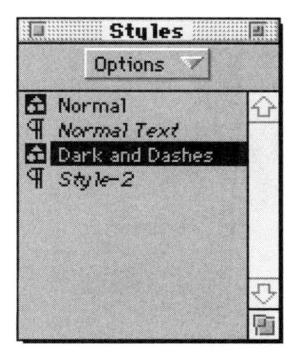

Figure 4. *Double-click on a style name to highlight it and rename it.*

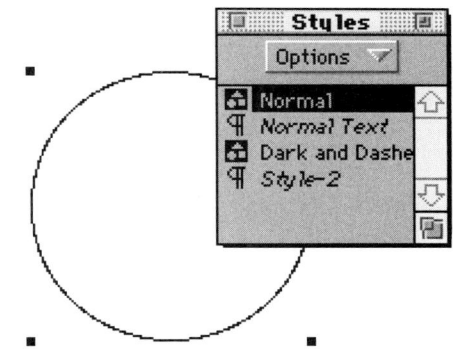

Figure 5a. *To apply a style, select the object or text.*

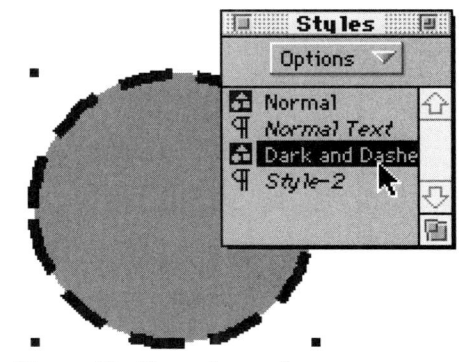

Figure 5b. *To apply a style to an object or text click on the name of the style in the Styles palette.*

To rename a style:

1. Double-click on the name of the style in the Styles palette. The name will be highlighted.

2. Type the new name of the style. For this exercise, we'll call the object style you created in the previous steps "Dark and Dashes" (**Figure 4**).

3. Press the Return or Enter key to apply the new name.

Once you have a Style defined, you can then use it to change the attributes of any objects or text.

To apply a style:

1. Select an object that does not have the same attributes as the style you want to apply (**Figure 5a**).

or

Select text that does not have the same attributes as the style you want to apply.

2. With the new object selected, click on the Dark and Dashes style created previously. The object will automatically take on all the attributes of the Dark and Dashes style (**Figure 5b**). It will not change shape.

or

If you are working with text, the text will automatically take on the attributes of the style you select.

3. If you have any other objects on your page, you can select them singly or together to apply the Dark and Dashes style.

(Continued on the following page)

203

Chapter 17

Tips

- Styles are applied to text on a paragraph basis. You can therefore apply a style to a paragraph simply by placing your insertion point in the paragraph. Any style you select will be applied to the entire paragraph.
- You can also apply styles by dragging the Object icon or paragraph symbol onto an object or paragraph (**Figure 6**).

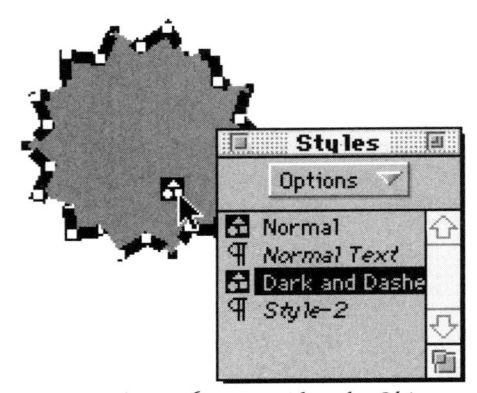

Figure 6. *Drag either the Object icon or the paragraph symbol onto the object or text you want to style.*

You can also create styles without any text or object existing. This is called defining a Style by attributes.

To define a style by attributes:

1. Press the Tab key to deselect all objects and text blocks.
2. If you are defining an object style, make sure that one of the object styles is selected in the Styles palette.

   or

   If you are defining a text style, make sure that one of the text styles is selected in the Styles palette.
3. Use the Inspector palette to choose whichever fill and stroke attributes you would like for the new object style.

   or

   Use the Inspector palette, Type menu, or Color List to choose whichever character and paragraph attributes you would like for the new text style.
4. When you are satisfied with the attributes selected, choose New from the Options pop-up menu of the Styles palette. The new Style will appear with the name "Style-1." This style can be renamed and applied to different objects or paragraphs.

Styles

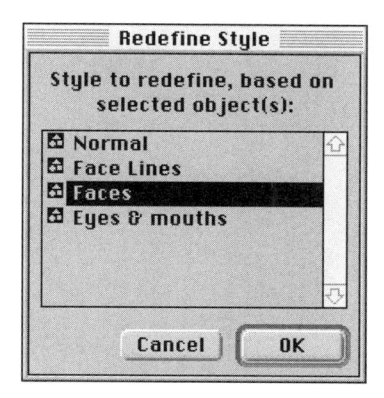

Figure 7. *The **Redefine Style** dialog box allows you to change a style definition to whatever the attributes are of the currently selected object or text.*

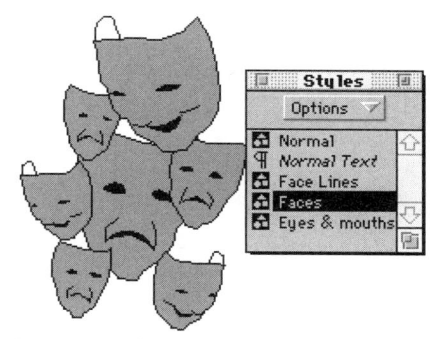

Figure 8a. *The style governing the faces was originally defined with a 2-point stroke and a 50% black fill.*

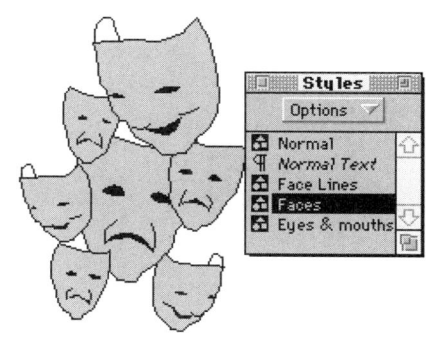

Figure 8b. *Redefining the style for the faces to a thinner stroke and lighter fill changed all the artwork without selecting any object.*

So far, using the Styles palette has meant you could easily apply intricate attributes to objects. In addition, when you redefine a style, you redefine the attributes of all objects in the illustration that have the style applied to them.

To redefine a style:

1. Make sure no objects or text blocks are selected, and select the style you want to change.

2. Use the Inspector palette or Type menu to change the style's attributes. You will notice that a plus sign (+) appears in front of the name of the style. This indicates that the current attributes differ from the original style definition.

3. When you are satisfied with the new attributes, choose Redefine from the Options pop-up menu of the Styles palette. The Redefine Style dialog box will appear, asking you which style you want to redefine. Click on the name of the style you want to redefine and then click OK. (**Figure 7**).

4. You will see a dialog box listing the object or text styles in your document. Choose the style you want to change and then click the OK button. The style definition will change and all objects or text with that style will be updated (**Figures 8a–b**).

205

Chapter 17

In addition to redefining styles, you can also use the Edit Style dialog box to make changes to as many styles as you want at one time.

To use the Edit Style dialog box:

1. Choose Edit style from the Options pop-up menu of the Styles palette. The Edit Style dialog box will appear. If you had an object style selected, the dialog box will reflect object attributes (**Figure 9**).

   or

   If you had a text style selected, the Edit Style dialog box will reflect text attributes (**Figure 10**).

2. Press on the Style pop-up menu to choose the name of the style you want to change.

3. Use any of the settings to change any of the style attributes.

4. If you want to make changes to another style, choose the name of that Style from the pop-up menu. A dialog box will ask you if it is OK to update the style you were just working on Click Update. The second style will be listed, and you can make whatever changes you want to that Style.

5. When you have finished changing the styles, click OK and all your updated styles will be applied.

Tip

■ You can also use the Edit Style dialog box to define all the attributes of a new style. Simply choose New from the Options pop-up menu. With the new style selected, then choose Edit Style from the Options pop-up menu, and make whatever changes you want to the style definition.

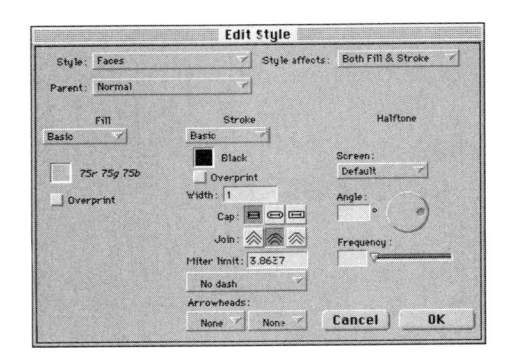

Figure 9. *The **Edit Style** dialog box for **objects** allows you to change all the object attributes at once.*

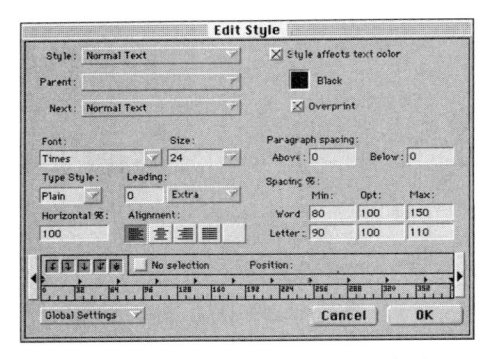

Figure 10. *The **Edit Style** dialog box for **text** allows you to change all the text attributes at once.*

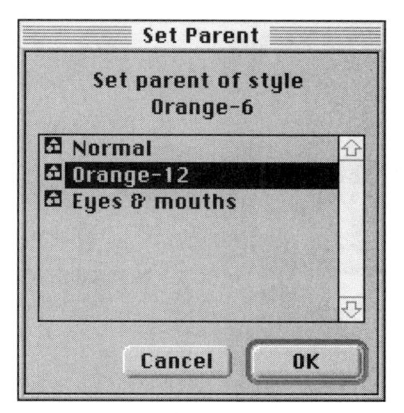

Figure 11. *The **Set Parent** dialog box allows you to base one style on another.*

FreeHand also offers the ability to base one style on another. FreeHand calls this the "Parent" and "Child" relationship of Styles.

To base one style on another:

1. Start by defining a style. For this exercise, create an object style we'll call "Orange-12." Make the style an orange fill with a black stroke of 12 points.
or
Create a text style we'll call "Copy-24." Define the style as the typeface Helvetica, at 24 points, with 28-point leading.

2. Create a second object style called "Orange-6." Make this style the same orange fill as Step 1, but with a black stroke of 6 points.
or
Create a second text style called "Copy-10." Make this style Helvetica, at 10 points, with 12-point leading.

3. Select the Orange-6 style in the Styles palette and choose Set parent from the Options pop-up menu. The Set Parent dialog box will appear; choose the Orange-12 style in it. Click the OK button (**Figure 11**).
or
Select the Copy-10 style in the Styles palette and choose Set parent from the Options pop-up menu. The Set Parent dialog box will appear; choose the Copy-24 style in it. Click the OK button.

4. Once you have set the Parent and Child styles, you will not see any changes in your objects. It is only after you change the Parent style that you will see the changes to the Child style.

Once you have a style based on another, you can see how changing the Parent style affects the Child style.

To work with Parent and Child styles:

1. Use the previous exercise to make sure at least one object has the Orange-12 style and at least one object has the Orange-6 style.

   or

   Make sure at least one paragraph has the Copy-24 style and at least one paragraph has the Copy-10 style.

2. Select the Orange-12 style in the Styles palette and choose Edit style from the Options pop-up menu. The object Edit Style dialog box will appear. The Parent style, Orange-12, should be listed in the Style pop-up menu.

   or

   Select the Copy-24 style in the Styles palette and choose Edit style from the Options pop-up menu. The text Edit Style dialog box will appear. The Parent style, Copy-24, should be listed in the Style pop-up menu.

3. Make whatever changes you want to the style attributes. In this case, change the fill and stroke colors, and the stroke width to 20 points or greater. Click OK.

   or

   Change the typeface to the Times font and change the point size to 18 points. Click OK.

4. Notice how the changes have been applied to the objects or paragraphs For the objects, the colors of the fills and strokes have changed but only the Parent stroke widths have changed. For the text, the typeface has changed, but only the Parent point size has changed (**Figure 12**).

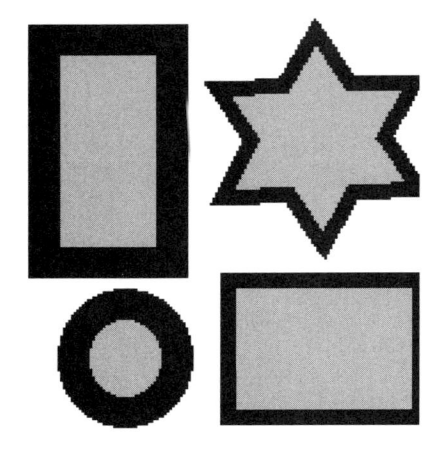

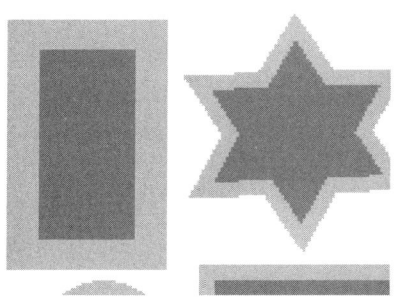

Figure 12. *An example of what happens when a style is based on another in a* **Parent** *and* **Child** *relationship. In this case, the top four objects had the original styles applied to them. The Parent style, had a thicker stroke but shared the same fill and stroke colors as the Child style. The bottom four objects show what happened after the fill, stroke, and stroke weight of the Parent style were changed; the fill and stroke for the objects with the Child style were changed, but the stroke thickness of the objects with the Child style was unaffected.*

Styles

Figure 13. *Choose **Duplicate** from the **Options** pop-up menu of the **Styles** palette to make a copy of a style.*

In addition to basing one style on another, you can also make a duplicate of a style. This allows you to make minor changes to a copy of an intricate style.

To duplicate styles:

1. Choose the object or text style you want to make a copy of.

2. Choose Duplicate from the Options pop-up menu of the Styles palette. A new style with the preface "Copy of" will appear (**Figure 13**).

3. Make any changes you want to this copy of the style.

Once you've defined styles for one document, you may want to bring those styles into other documents. FreeHand lets you do so by using the Copy and Paste commands.

To copy styles between documents:

1. With both documents open, select the objects or text blocks that contain the styles you want to copy.

2. Choose Copy from the Edit menu.

3. Switch to the document that you would like to bring the styles into.

4. Choose Paste from the Edit menu.

5. The object or text styles will appear in the Styles palette of the second document. Once the styles are in the Styles palette, the objects or text blocks that were pasted can be deleted without deleting the styles.

Duplicate Styles; Copy Styles Between Documents

209

Chapter 17

You may find that you no longer need a style listed in the Styles palette. It is relatively easy to delete styles.

To remove a style:

1. Click on the name of the style that you wish to delete.

2. Choose Remove from the Options pop-up menu of the Styles palette. The style will be deleted from the palette (**Figure 14**).

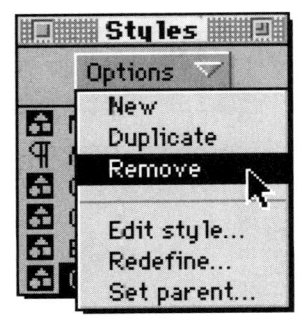

Figure 14. *The **Remove** command deletes a Style from the Styles palette.*

Tip

■ If you delete a style that has been applied to objects or paragraphs, those objects or paragraphs will maintain their attributes. But the name of the style applied to them will change to "Normal" with the plus sign (+) next to it, indicating that other attributes have been applied.

To change the default styles:

You will notice that all documents have a Normal object style and a Normal Text style. These two styles cannot be removed from your documents. You can change the defaults for both of these Normal styles by changing how those styles are defined in the FreeHand Defaults file *(see page 278)*.

PATH OPERATIONS 18

O nce you have created paths, there are many ways you can modify them. In this chapter, you will learn how to create and work with composite paths. You will learn how to turn objects into masks. You will learn how to open or close paths. You will learn how to use the Knife tool to modify paths. You will also learn about the Path Operations commands: Correct Direction; Reverse Direction; Remove Overlap; Simplify; Intersect; Punch; Union; Transparency; Expand Stroke; Inset Path; and Crop. And finally, you will learn how to use the Command-Shift-Plus command to apply Path Operations commands more quickly.

Imagine you have created an illustration of a plate with an intricate pattern. Now image you have created an illustration of a donut with a hole in the center. You want to put the donut on the plate to see through the hole. A composite path gives you the hole in the donut. (Composite paths are sometimes called compound paths in other graphics programs.)

To create a composite path:

1. Use the Rectangle tool to create a rectangle and fill it with one of the pattern fills. This object will be used to show that the composite path has a hole punched in it.

2. Draw another closed object, such as an oval and fill it with a solid color. This object will be used as the outside of the composite path.

(Continued on the following page)

Chapter 18

3. Draw yet another closed object, such as an oval. Make this object smaller and position it completely inside the object created in Step 2.
4. Select the objects created in Step 2 and Step 3 (**Figure 1a**).
5. Choose Join Objects from the Arrange menu (Command-J) (**Figure 1b**). You will now be able to see the pattern through the hole created (**Figure 1c**).

Tips

- If the second object is not completely contained inside the first, the hole will appear only where the objects overlap.
- Composite paths can be created using more than two objects. Where an even number of objects overlap, there will be a transparency or hole. Where an odd number of objects overlap, there will be no transparency.

To work with a composite path:

1. Use the Selection tool to select and move the composite path you created in the previous exercise. Notice that although you clicked on only one portion of the composite, both portions are selected and move together.
2. To select and move individual parts of a composite path, hold the Option key and click on one of the paths. You can now move that path individually from the rest of the composite.
3. If you change the fill or stroke attributes of one of the paths, that change will be applied to all the paths of the composite.

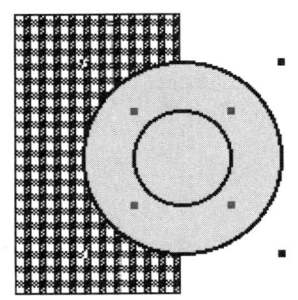

Figure 1a. *Two objects selected before they are joined to make a composite path.*

Figure 1b. *To make a composite path, choose **Join Objects** from the **Arrange** menu.*

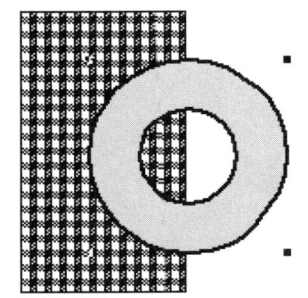

Figure 1c. *Two objects after they have been joined to make a* ***composite path***.

Path Operations

Figure 2a. *A mask will be used to make the rectangles appear only inside the star.*

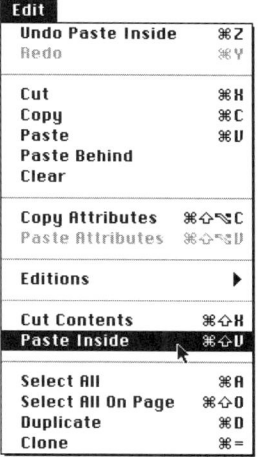

Figure 2b. *To make a mask, choose **Paste Inside** from the **Edit** menu or press **Command-Shift-V**.*

Figure 2c. *When items are pasted into an object, the object acts as a **mask**, and the items can be seen only inside the object.*

To release composite paths:

1. Select the entire composite object.

2. Choose Split Object from the Arrange menu. The paths comprising the composite will be released and will be separate paths again.

While composites punch holes in objects, masks allow you to fill objects so that anything outside the objects will not be seen. The object that is filled is called a mask or clipping path. Masks make it easy to fill objects with different colors; for example, you can easily make a star with stripes of different colors.

To create a mask:

1. Use the Rectangle tool to draw several rectangles filled with different colors. Position these rectangles next to each other. These rectangles will become the stripes of your star.

2. Use the Polygon tool to draw a star that covers the stripes. Choose a contrasting color for the star (**Figure 2a**).

3. Use the Selection tool to select just the rectangles, and choose Cut from the Edit menu.

4. Select the star and choose Paste Inside from the Edit menu (**Figure 2b**). The stripes will now be visible only on the inside of the star (**Figure 2c**).

Release Composite Paths; Create a Mask

213

Chapter 18

Once you have created a mask, you may want to modify one of the elements pasted inside. To do so, you will have to release the mask.

To release a mask:
1. Select the mask and choose Cut Contents from the Edit menu. All the objects that were masked will be released and can be modified or moved.

2. The objects must be cut and then Pasted Inside again to re-create the mask.

Tip
- If you want to transform just the mask, without affecting any of the objects inside the mask, make sure the Contents checkbox is not checked in the Transform palette.

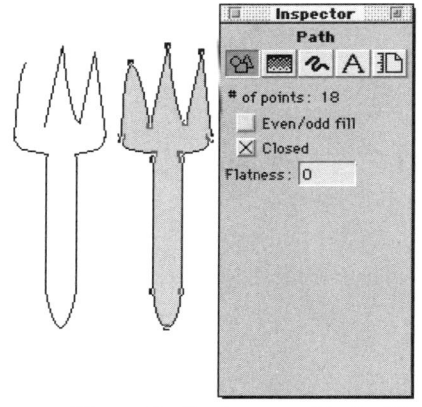

Figure 3. *To close an object with a line between its end points, check the **Closed** checkbox in the **Object Inspector** palette.*

Since only closed paths can act as masks, you may want to take open paths and close them.

To close an open path:
1. Select the open path that you want to close.

2. Click on the Object icon of the Inspector palette.

3. Click on the Closed checkbox. The object will be closed with a straight line from one end point to the other (**Figure 3**).
   or
   Drag one of the end points of the path onto the other end point. This will automatically close the path (**Figures 4a–b**).

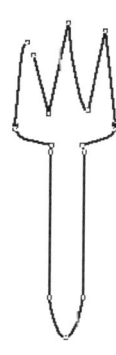

Figure 4a. *You can drag one end point onto another to close an object.*

Figure 4b. *The results of closing an object manually.*

Path Operations

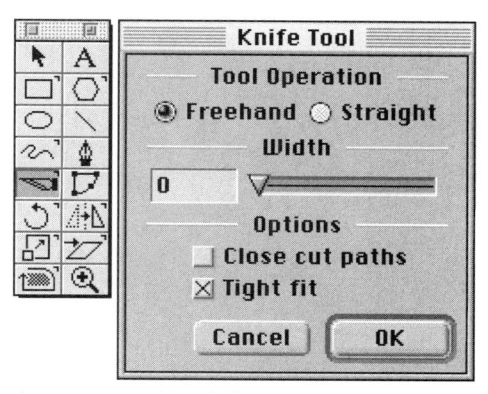

Figure 5. *Double-clicking on the **Knife** tool displays its dialog box.*

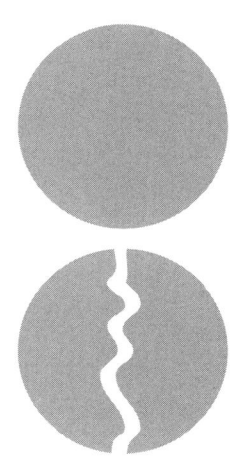

Figure 6. *The **Freehand** setting of the **Knife** tool lets you take a circle (top) and split it into two jagged sections (bottom).*

To open a closed path:
1. Select the closed path that you want to open.
2. Click on the Object icon of the Inspector palette.
3. Click on the Open checkbox. The object will be opened by deleting the segment between the first and last points created on the path.

Some of the most sophisticated path operations can be done by using the Knife tool. With the Knife tool you can open paths, slice objects into parts, punch holes in objects, and even erase parts of objects.

To split paths jaggedly with the Knife tool:
1. Use the Oval tool to create a circle.
2. Double-click on the Knife tool in the toolbox. The Knife Tool dialog box will appear (**Figure 5**).
3. Click on the Freehand radio button so that you can make a jagged cut.
4. Set the Width for 3 or 4 points. This will create a space between the two halves of the circle.
5. Click the checkbox for Close cut paths so that the two halves of the circle are closed paths.
6. Click on the checkbox for Tight fit so that the Knife tool follows the movements of your mouse precisely. Click the OK button.
7. Drag a zig-zag line from one side of the circle to the other.
8. The circle will be cut into two sections, each with a jagged edge, and will look like a broken coin (**Figure 6**).

Open a Closed Path; Split Paths Jaggedly

To split paths evenly with the Knife tool:

1. Use the Oval tool to create a circle.
2. Double-click on the Knife tool in the toolbox. The Knife Tool dialog box will appear.
3. Click on the Straight radio button so that you can make a even cut in the circle.
4. Set the Width for 3 or 4 points. This will create a space between the slices of the circle.
5. Click the checkbox for Close cut paths so that the slices of the circle are closed paths. Click the OK button.
6. Drag a line from one side of the circle to the other. Because you clicked the Straight button, the Knife tool will cut in a straight line. Release the mouse when you reach the other side. The circle will be cut in half. Drag a line from top to bottom to divide the circle into quarters.
7. Use the Knife tool to cut each of the quarters into eighths (**Figure 7**). The circle will be cut into eight pieces like a pizza.

Figure 7. *The **Straight** setting of the **Knife** tool allows you to cut straight segments.*

Tips

- The Knife tool will only cut selected objects. If the Knife tool does not cut an object, it is most likely because that object is not selected.
- Hold the Option key to temporarily set the Knife tool to the Straight setting.
- As you draw with the Knife tool at the Straight setting, hold the Shift key to constrain your cuts to 45° angles.

Path Operations

Figure 8. *The **Knife** tool can also be used as an eraser or hole puncher.*

While the Knife tool can act like a cutting tool, it can also act like an eraser or a hole puncher.

To use the Knife tool to punch holes and erase parts of paths:

1. Use the Rectangle tool to create a rectangle.

2. Double-click on the Knife tool in the toolbox. The Knife Tool dialog box will appear.

3. Click on the Freehand radio button so that you can make irregular holes in the rectangle.

4. Set the Width for 35 points. This will allow you to take large chunks out of the rectangle.

5. Click the checkbox for Close cut paths.

6. Choose Tight fit so that the Knife follows all the movements of the mouse. Click the OK button.

7. Drag with the Knife tool to create a small hole in the rectangle. Repeat at different areas on the rectangle. Wherever the Knife tool is applied, a hole will be created.

8. Use the Knife tool to erase portions of the sides of the rectangle (**Figure 8**). The rectangle will now be modified so that it looks like Swiss cheese. You should be able to create a pretty cheesy rectangle without too much work.

Punch Holes; Erase Parts of Paths

217

Chapter 18

FreeHand also offers several path commands under the Path Operations submenu of both the Arrange menu and the Xtras menu. These commands can also be found in the Operations palette, which can be opened by choosing Operations from the Other submenu of the Window menu or by pressing Command-Shift-I.

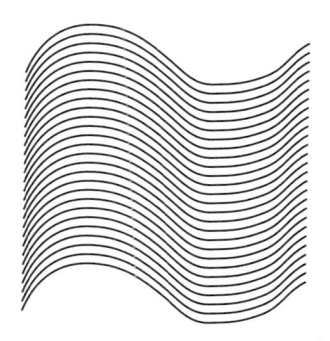

Figure 9a. *When two objects with the same direction are blended, the blend follows a smooth look.*

Ordinarily you will not be concerned with the direction of a path. But you may want to reverse the direction of a path if text is aligned to it *(see page 181)*. You may also want to reverse the direction of a path when it is used in a blend.

To use the Reverse Direction command with blends:

1. Use the Freehand tool to draw two open paths from left to right. Give your paths a stroke so that they are visible.
2. Use the Selection tool to select both paths, and choose Blend from the Path Operations submenu of the Arrange menu.
3. With the blend selected, click on the Object icon of the Inspector palette and change the number of steps to a low number such as 10 or 15 (**Figure 9a**).
4. Hold the Option key and use the Selection tool to select one of the original paths on the end of the blend.
5. Choose Reverse Direction from the Operations palette. (**Figure 9b**)
6. You will notice that the blend seems to "cross over" itself. That is because the two paths have different directions (**Figure 9c**).

Figure 9b. *The **Reverse Direction** command in the **Operations** palette.*

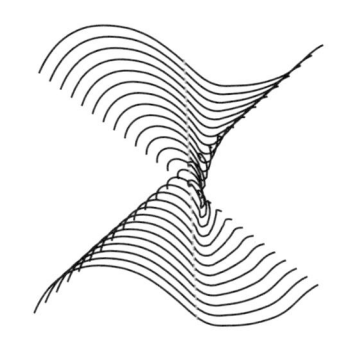

Figure 9c. *When the direction of an object in a blend is changed, the shape of the blend changes.*

218

Path Operations

Figure 10. *The **Remove Overlap** command in the **Operations** palette.*

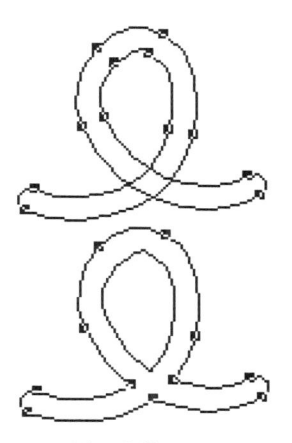

Figure 11. *The difference between an object before (top) and after the **Remove Overlap** command is applied (bottom).*

To use the Remove Overlap command:

1. To see what the Remove Overlap command does, double-click on the Freehand tool in the toolbox and choose the Variable stroke option. Make sure that Auto remove overlap is not checked. Click OK.

2. Set your fill as white and your stroke as black.

3. Drag a looping line with the tool. You will notice that the path created overlaps itself.

4. Choose Remove Overlap from the Operations palette (**Figure 10**). Notice that the overlapping areas are eliminated (**Figure 11**).

Chapter 18

If you have created an object using the Freehand or Autotrace tools, you may find that you have more points on your path than you want. Too many points on a path can cause problems when you print your artwork. You can remove the excess points by using the Simplify command.

To use the Simplify command:

1. Use the Freehand tool to create an intricate path with a number of points.
2. With the path still selected, choose Simplify from the Operations palette (**Figure 12**). The Simplify dialog box will appear (**Figure 13**)
3. Use the triangle slider to change the amount in the Allowable Change field. The greater the number, the more points will be eliminated and the more the shape of the original object may change (**Figure 14**).

Tip

- Hold the Command key as you click on the Simplify icon in the Operations palette. This will apply the previous settings in the Simplify dialog box. This tip also applies to any of the commands in the Operations palette with a dialog box setting.

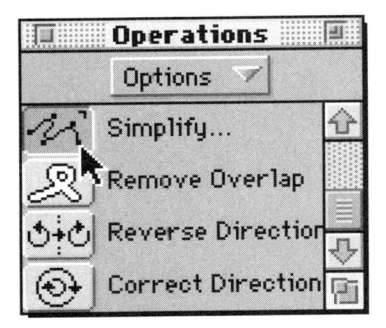

Figure 12. *The **Simplify** command in the **Operations** palette.*

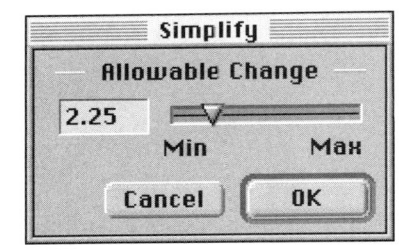

Figure 13. *The **Simplify** dialog box.*

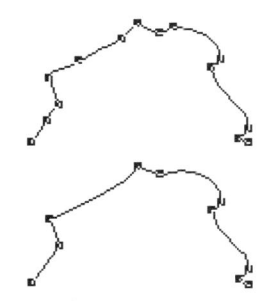

Figure 14. *The difference between an object before (top) and after (bottom) the **Simplify** command has been applied it it.*

Path Operations

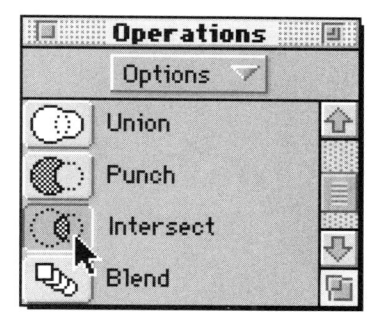

Figure 15. *The Intersect command in the Operations palette.*

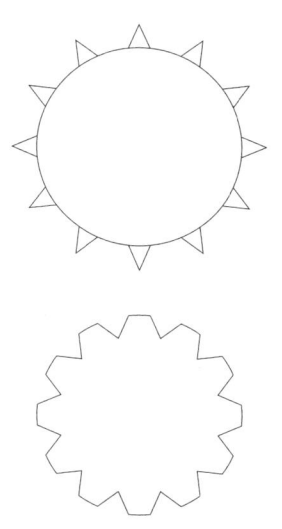

Figure 16. *The difference between an object before (top) and after (bottom) the Intersect command has been applied.*

The next set of commands for path operations can be found under both the Path Operations submenu of the Arrange menu and the Path Operations submenu of the Xtras menu, as well as in the Operations palette. These commands change the shape of paths.

To use the Intersect command:

1. Use the Polygon tool to draw a star.

2. Use the Oval tool to draw a circle that is slightly smaller than the star.

3. Position the circle on top of the star so that the points of the star extend beyond the circle.

4. Choose Intersect from the Operations palette (**Figure 15**).

5. The star will be converted to a star with rounded points (**Figure 16**).

Chapter 18

To use the Punch command:

1. Use the Oval tool to draw a circle.
2. Use the Polygon tool to draw a star.
3. Position the star on top of the circle so that half of the star extends beyond the circle.
4. Choose Punch from the Operations palette (**Figure 17**).
5. The circle will be converted to a partial circle with a star cut out of it (**Figure 18**).

Tips

- If the selected objects do not all overlap, the Intersect command will delete all the objects.
- The Intersect and Punch commands will delete the original objects, leaving only the final result. To create a new object on top of the original objects, you will need to change the Preferences setting *(see page 267)*.
  or
  Hold the Shift key as you apply the Intersect or Punch commands. This will leave the original object and create a new object based on the command.

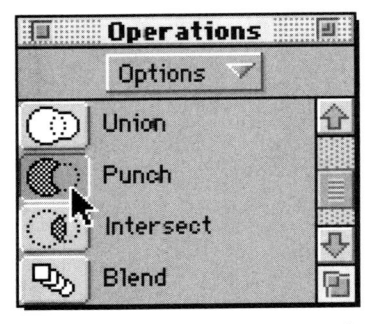

Figure 17. *The **Punch** command in the **Operations** palette.*

Figure 18. *The difference between two objects before (top) and after (bottom) the **Punch** command has been applied.*

Path Operations

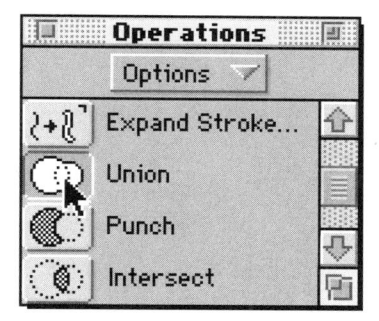

Figure 19. *The **Union** command in the **Operations** palette.*

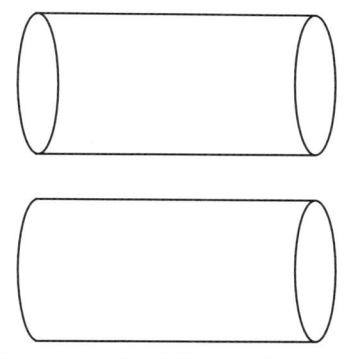

Figure 20. *The difference between an object before (top) and after (bottom) the **Union** command has been applied to the left oval and rectangle. (After the Union command was applied, the resulting object was sent to the back.)*

To use the Union command:

1. Use the Rectangle tool to draw a rectangle. This will become the start of a tube. Set the fill to white and the stroke to black.

2. Because you will want to match the measurements of the rectangle, click on the Object Inspector and note the width and height of the rectangle or enter the measurements you want. For instance, the width can be 150 points and the height 72 points.

3. Use the Oval tool to draw two ovals. These will be the ends of the tube. Make the height of the ovals the same as the height of the rectangle. In this case, we used the height of 72 points and a width of 20 points.

4. Position both ovals so that one is precisely over the left side of the rectangle and the other is over the right side.

5. Select the rectangle and one of the ovals. Since you cannot see both ends of a tube at once, you will need to modify these two shapes.

6. Choose Union from the Operations palette (**Figure 19**).

7. Apply the Send To Back command to the object created by the Union command. You will now have a tube (**Figure 20**).

Tip

- If the selected objects for the Union, Intersect, or Punch commands have different fill or stroke attributes, the final object will take the attributes of the backmost object.

223

Chapter 18

To use the Transparency command:

1. Use the Oval tool to create an oval filled with 50% cyan.

2. Use the Freehand tool, set to the Variable stroke option, to create a "ribbon" that passes across the oval. Fill this object with 100% yellow.

3. Select both the oval and the ribbon and choose Transparency from the Operations palette (**Figure 21**). The Transparency dialog box will appear (**Figure 22**).

4. Set the amount of the transparency to 50%. This will create the look of equal amounts of the front and back colors mixed together. If the transparency amount is less than 50%, the color of the front object will be more obvious. If it is set to more than 50%, the color of the back object will be more obvious. Click OK. You will see the transparency effect (**Figure 23**).

Tip

- The Transparency command does not really let you see through an object. It creates a new object, colored so that it simulates a see-through effect.

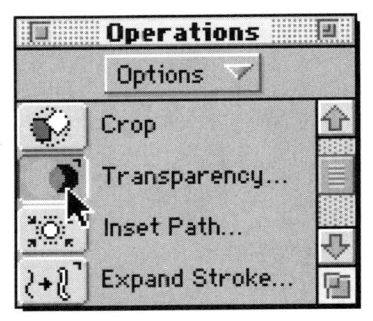

Figure 21. *The **Transparency** command in the Operations palette.*

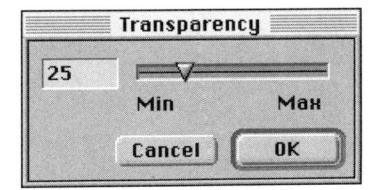

Figure 22. *The **Transparency** dialog box. Moving the triangle slider changes how much the foreground and background colors will be mixed.*

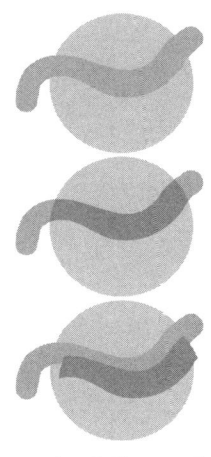

Figure 23. *The difference between an object before (top) and after (middle) the **Transparency** command has been applied. The objects in the bottom illustration were moved to show how the effect was actually created.*

224

Path Operations

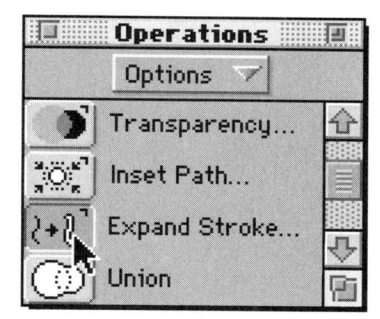

Figure 24. *The **Expand Stroke** command in the **Operations** palette.*

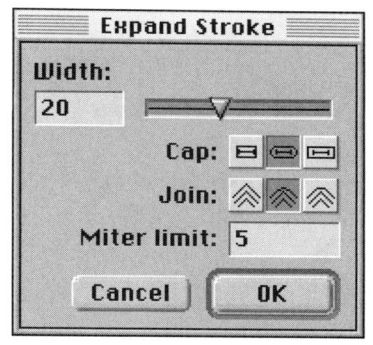

Figure 25. *The **Expand Stroke** dialog box.*

Freehand offers you a way to convert strokes or open paths to closed paths using the Expand Stroke command.

To use the Expand Stroke command:

1. Select the path you wish to convert. Choose Expand Stroke from the Operations palette (**Figure 24**). The Expand Stroke dialog box will appear (**Figure 25**).

2. Enter the Width you want for the final object.

3. Set the Cap, Join, and Miter limit settings. Note that while these settings are the same as the settings for a stroke, the final object will actually be a filled path.

4. Click the OK button. There will be a new filled path that has the stroke settings you chose (**Figure 26**). This new path can be used for other effects, such as the Transparency command or a Tiled fill.

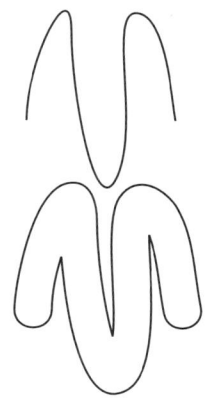

Figure 26. *The difference between an object before (top) and after (bottom) the **Expand Stroke** command has been applied.*

225

Chapter 18

To use the Inset Path command to create a single object:

1. Create a closed path. In this case, use the Polygon tool to create an eight-sided star.
2. Give the polygon a stroke. (The stroke is not necessary for the command to work, but it will make it easier to see the results.)
3. With the path still selected, choose Inset Path from the Operations palette (**Figure 27**). The Inset Path dialog box will appear (**Figure 28**).
4. Use the triangle slider or type in the amount in the Inset field to make an exact copy of the original that is smaller or larger by the amount set. For example, if you enter an amount such as 6 points, the new object will be created so that there is a 6-point reduction from the original object's size. If you enter a negative amount such as -6 points, the new object will be created so that there is a 6-point enlargement from the original object's size. Use the Inset Path command to create objects for a text wrap *(see page 189)* or to outline text that has been converted to paths *(see page 192)*.

Figure 27. *The **Inset Path** command in the **Operations** palette.*

Figure 28. *The **Inset Path** dialog box.*

Tip

- The Inset Path command will delete the original object when it creates the new one unless the Preferences settings are changed for Object Editing *(see page 267)*.
- Hold the Shift key as you apply the Inset Path command. This will leave the original object and create a new object based on the command.

226

Path Operations

To use the Inset Path command to create multiple objects:

1. Create a closed path and choose Inset Path as in the previous exercise.

2. In the Steps field, enter the number of copies you want to create.

3. If you have entered a number greater than 1 in the steps field, you should then choose Uniform, Farther, or Nearer from the pop-up menu.

4. Choose Uniform to make each of the copies the distance away from each other that you specified in the Inset field.

5. Choose Farther to make the first copy the distance away you specified in the Inset field, then the next copy a smaller distance away, and the next copy an even smaller distance away, and so on.

6. Choose Nearer to reverse the Farther effect so that the distance between each copy gets larger until the last distance is the amount you specified in the Inset field.

7. When you are satisfied with your choices, click the OK button. You will have multiple copies of the original object inset from the original (**Figure 29**).

Tip

■ Multiple copies of objects created with the Inset Path command will be created as grouped objects.

Figure 29. *The differences between an object before (top) and after the* **Inset Path** *command has been applied. The bottom three objects had three steps applied at a 4-point inset. The first of the bottom three stars had the* **Uniform** *setting. The second had the* **Farther** *setting. The third had the* **Nearer** *setting.*

Chapter 18

FreeHand 5.5 has added a new command called "Crop." This allows you to use the top object as a "cookie cutter" on the lower objects.

To use the Crop command:
1. Use the Oval tool to create several ovals with different colored fills. Place an irregularly shaped object on top of the ovals. In this case, create a ten-sided star.
2. With all the paths selected, choose Crop from the Operations palette (**Figure 30**).
3. All the ovals will be changed so that only those portions that were under the star will remain (**Figure 31**).

Tips
- The Crop command will delete the original object when it creates the new one unless the Preferences settings are changed for Object Editing *(see page 267)*.
- Hold the Shift key as you apply the Crop command. This will leave the original object and create new objects based on the command.

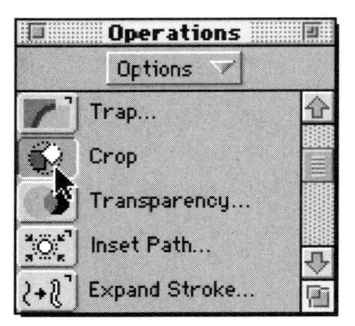

Figure 30. *The* **Crop** *command in the* **Operations** *palette.*

Figure 31. *The difference between an object before (top) and after (bottom) the* **Crop** *command has been applied.*

To use the Command-Shift-Plus command:
If you choose any of the commands from the Xtras menu or the Operations palette, you will notice that the next time you go to that Xtras menu, the last command you chose will be listed at the top of the menu (**Figure 32**).

This means that you can reapply the command using the keystroke Command-Shift-Plus. This allows you to apply the command quickly to a series of objects.

Figure 32. *The very last Xtra you have applied from the Xtras menu or the Operations palette appears at the top of the Xtras menu with the keyboard shortcut Command-Shift-Plus.*

XTRAS 19

Xtras are features that are added to the basic FreeHand program. Because Xtras can perform many different functions—change paths, create objects, convert vectors, etc.—some of the Xtras have been covered in other chapters. In this chapter, you will learn about the majority of FreeHand Xtras, including the Xtra Tools: 3D Rotation, Fisheye Lens, Smudge, and Eyedropper. You will learn about the Colors Xtras that allow you to manipulate the colors in objects and in the Color List. You will learn about the Fractalize Xtra. You will also learn about the Trap, Create Blend, Empty Text Blocks, and Unused Named Colors Xtras. Finally, you will learn about how you can add even more Xtras to FreeHand by obtaining filters from Adobe Illustrator and from other software programs and companies.

Figure 1. *To view the Xtra Tools palette, choose **Xtra Tools** from the **Other** submenu of the **Window** menu.*

The first set of Xtras are found in the Xtra Tools palette. To view this palette, choose Xtra Tools (Command-Shift-K) from the Other submenu of the Window menu (**Figure 1**). The complete Xtra Tools palette (**Figure 2**) contains the 3D Rotation, Arc, Eyedropper, Fisheye Lens, Smudge, and Spiral tools. (*For more information on the Arc and Spiral Xtras, see Chapter 6, "Creation Tools."*)

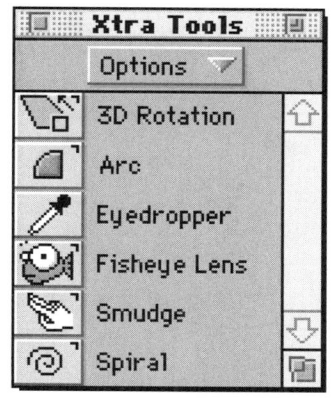

Figure 2. *The **Xtra Tools** palette.*

229

Chapter 19

With the 3D Rotation tool, you can simulate the effect of what would happen to an object if it were rotated in space.

To use the 3D Rotation tool:

1. Select the object or objects you wish to modify with the 3D Rotation tool.
2. Double-click on the 3D Rotation tool in the Xtra Tools palette. The 3D Rotation palette will appear (**Figure 3**).
3. With the Easy setting selected, press on the Rotate from pop-up menu to select what point the rotation should occur from. The choices are: Mouse click, the point you press with your mouse Center of Selection, the physical center of the object; Center of Gravity, the center of the object when weighted for uneven distribution of shapes; and Origin, the bottom-left corner of the bounding box surrounding the selection. Choose Mouse click.
4. The Distance setting controls how much distortion will happen during the rotation. The greater the distance, the less the distortion. For the greatest distortion effect, choose 100.
5. Position your cursor over the spot on the object from which you would like the object to rotate.
6. Press down, do not release the mouse, and move your cursor away from the spot where you pressed. A line will extend from the spot you pressed. The farther along the line you drag, the greater the 3-D rotation will be (**Figure 4**).
7. As you press with the mouse, a triangle sign indicates the point of rotation.
8. When you are satisfied with your rotation, release the mouse and the object will be modified (**Figure 5**).

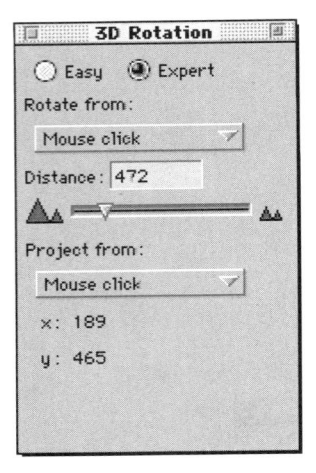

Figure 3. *The **3D Rotation** palette controls how the **3D Rotation** Xtra distorts objects.*

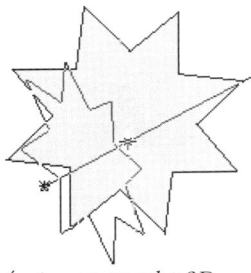

Figure 4. *As you use the 3D Rotation tool, a line extends from the point where you clicked. The farther you drag along this line, the greater the rotation will be.*

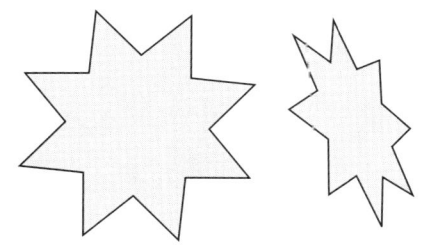

Figure 5. *An object before (left) and after (right) applying a 3-D rotation.*

Xtras

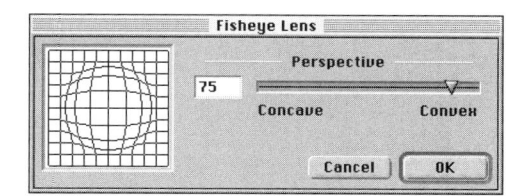

Figure 6. *The **Fisheye Lens** dialog box.*

Figure 7. *When dragging with the Fisheye Lens tool, the oval indicates the area that will be distorted. After the mouse is released the distortion will occur.*

Figure 8. *The results of taking an object (top) and distorting it with the **Fisheye Lens** tool (bottom).*

Tips

- If you want to change the look of the rotation, use the 3D Rotation tool again on a different point in the object.

- In the Easy setting, the point of projection will be the point where the mouse is clicked.

- The Expert setting allows you to choose from which point the projection of the rotation will occur: Mouse click, Center of Selection, Center of Gravity, Origin, and x, y coordinates (which can be entered in the x and y fields).

- In the Expert mode, a plus sign (+) indicates the point from which the rotation is being projected.

To use the Fisheye Lens tool:

1. Select the object you want to modify. For this example, we used text converted to paths.

2. Double-click on the Fisheye Lens tool in the Xtra Tools palette. The Fisheye Lens dialog box will appear (**Figure 6**).

3. Drag the triangle slider or enter the amount you want in the Perspective field. Convex or positive numbers cause the object to bulge. Concave or negative numbers cause the object to be pinched. For this example, we used a Convex setting of 75. Click OK.

4. Drag your cursor to create an oval over the area you want to distort. (**Figure 7**).

5. Let go of the mouse and your selection will be distorted (**Figure 8**).

Tips

- Hold the Option key to create a fisheye lens that goes from the center outward.

- Hold the Shift key to constrain the fisheye lens into a circular shape.

231

Chapter 19

The Smudge tool provides you with a quick and simple way to create a fuzzy or soft edge on an object.

To use the Smudge tool:

1. Select the object or objects you want to modify. For this example, we used the object that was transformed using the 3D Rotation tool previously described.
2. Choose the Smudge tool from the Xtra Tools palette. Your cursor will turn into the Smudge "fingers."
3. Drag with the fingers along the direction you would like the smudge to take. You will see a line extend from your object. This is the length of the smudge (**Figure 9**).
4. When you release the mouse, the smudge will be created (**Figure 10**).

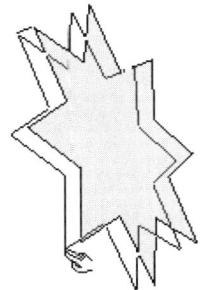

Figure 9. *Dragging with the **Smudge** fingers controls the length of the effect.*

Tips

- Hold the option key to create a smudge that goes from the center outward.
- Double-click on the Smudge tool in the Xtra Tools palette to display the Smudge dialog box (**Figure 11**). You can drop colors from the Color Mixer or Color List in both the Fill and Stroke boxes. This allows you to have the smudge fade to a specific color rather than the default white.
- The number of steps in a smudge is governed by the printer resolution as set in the Document Inspector. If your smudges look jagged, increase the printer resolution.

Figure 10. *An object before (left) and after (right) the **Smudge** tool has been applied.*

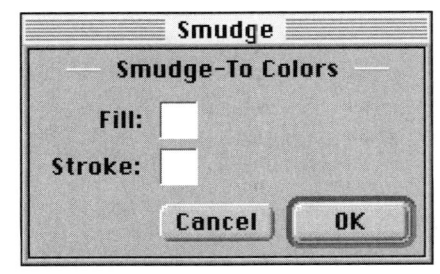

Figure 11. *The **Smudge** dialog box lets you set which colors your fill and stroke will fade to.*

Xtras

Figure 12. *To pick up the color from one object and apply it to another, press the **Eyedropper** on the first object and then drag the color swatch onto the second.*

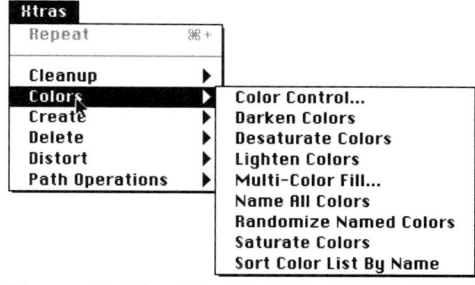

Figure 13. *The Colors Xtras are found in the **Colors** submenu of the **Xtras** menu.*

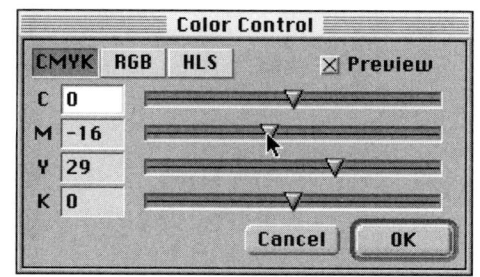

Figure 14. *The **Color Control** dialog box.*

The Eyedropper tool lets you copy colors between objects.

To use the Eyedropper tool:

1. Choose the Eyedropper tool from the Xtra Tools palette. The cursor will change to a little eyedropper.

2. Position the eyedropper over the color that you want to copy.

3. Press down with the eyedropper. Do not let go of the mouse. Your cursor will turn into a little square of the color.

4. Drag that square onto the fill or stroke of another object. The color will be applied (**Figure 12**).

FreeHand also offers the Colors Xtras, located under the Xtras menu (**Figure 13**).

To use the Color Control dialog box:

1. Select the objects you want to adjust.

2. Choose Color Control from the Colors submenu of the Xtras menu. The Color Control dialog box will appear (**Figure 14**).

3. Choose from CMYK, RGB, or HLS color.

4. Use the triangle sliders or the fields to add or subtract color from the objects you have chosen. Positive numbers add color. Negative numbers subtract color.

5. Checking the Preview box lets you see how your adjustments are affecting the selected objects.

6. When you are satisfied with the color changes, click the OK button. Your changes will be applied to the objects.

Tip

■ The Color Control dialog box only works on process colors.

233

Chapter 19

FreeHand also offers automatic commands for changing colors: Darken Colors, Lighten Colors, Saturate Colors, and Desaturate Colors (**Figure 15**).

To use the Darken or Lighten Colors commands:

1. Select the object or objects you want to change.
2. Choose Darken Colors or Lighten Colors from the Colors submenu of the Xtras menu.
3. Darken Colors decreases the Lightness value of the color in 5% increments.
4. Lighten Colors increases the Lightness value of the color in 5% increments.
5. To continue to darken or lighten the colors, press Command-Shift-+, which will repeat the command.

To use the Saturate or Desaturate Colors commands:

1. Select the object or objects you want to change.
2. Choose Saturate Colors or Desaturate Colors from the Colors submenu of the Xtras menu.
3. Saturate Colors increases the Saturation value of the color in 5% increments. This has the effect of making muted colors more vibrant.
4. Desaturate Colors decreases the Saturation value of the color in 5% increments. This has the effect of making colors less vibrant.
5. To continue to saturate or desaturate the colors, press Command-Shift-+, which will repeat the command.

Figure 15. *The flower pot at top was altered using the* **Darken Colors** *(upper left),* **Lighten Colors** *(upper right),* **Saturate Colors** *(lower left), and* **Desaturate Colors** *(lower right) commands. Each command was applied eight times to the artwork*

Xtras

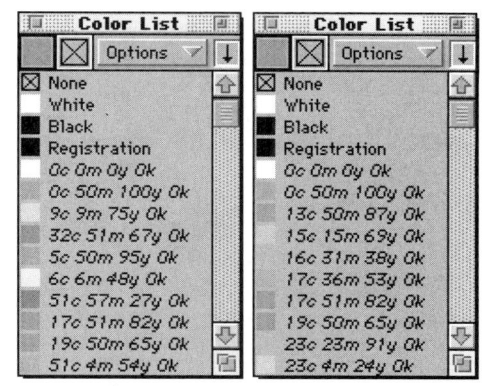

Figure 16. *An unsorted Color List (left) and the same list after applying the **Sort Color List by Name** command (right).*

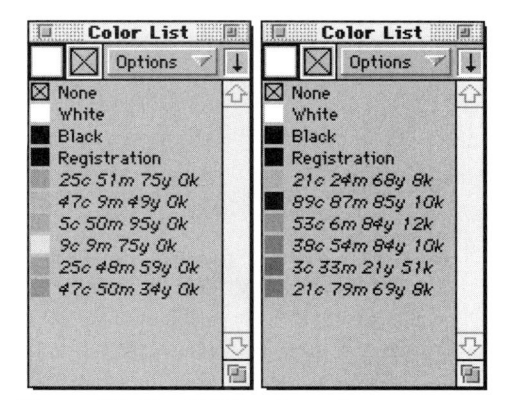

Figure 17. *The CMYK values of a named Color List before (left) and after (right) the **Randomize Named Colors** command has been applied.*

You may use the Color Mixer to create a color and then apply it to an object. This means the color name will not appear in the Color List. FreeHand offers you a quick way to find and name all unnamed colors.

To use the Name All Colors command:

Choose Name All Colors from the Colors submenu of the Xtras menu. All colors used by objects in your document that are not named will be put on the Color List, and their CMYK percentages will be their names.

To use the Sort Color List By Name command:

Choose Sort Color List By Name from the Colors submenu of the Xtras menu. This rearranges the Color List. The default colors appear first, followed by the colors named by their percentages, and then named colors (**Figure 16**).

To use the Unused Named Colors command:

Choose Unused Named Colors from the Delete submenu of the Xtras menu. All colors that are not applied to an object or a style will be deleted from the Color List. The default colors will not be deleted even if they are not being used.

To use the Randomize Named Colors command:

This command changes the values of the named colors in the Color List. All objects that have named colors applied to them will then be changed (**Figure 17**).

Tip

- Use the Randomize Named Colors command to create alternate versions of maps, charts, and other illustrations.

235

Chapter 19

The Fractalize command allows you to distort an object for dramatic effects.

To use the Fractalize command:

1. Select the object that you wish to distort. For this example, we created a six-sided star set to an acute angle.
2. Make sure the Even/odd fill box is checked in the Inspector palette. This will make the final object more dramatic.
3. Choose Fractalize from the Distort submenu of the Xtras menu.
4. Each time you choose the command, FreeHand creates geometric shapes between the points of the path.
5. Repeat the command several times until you are satisfied with the effect (**Figure 18**).

Figure 18. *The original object before (left) and after (right) the* ***Fractalize*** *command was applied three times.*

Tips

- Use the command on multiple objects rather than just one object.
- Mix different objects together, such as a square surrounding a star.
- If you have used the Fractalize command on two or more objects, use the Join Objects command from the Arrange menu to create holes in the final object.

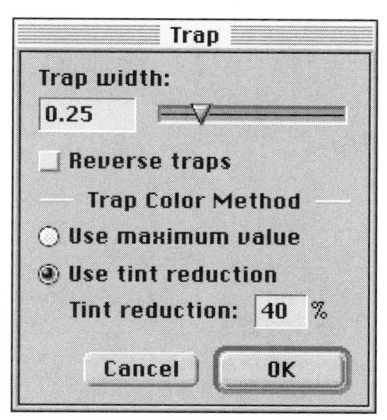

Figure 19. *The **Trap** dialog box.*

Trapping is a technique printers use to compensate for misregistration of colors when multiple color plates are used in the printing process. FreeHand offers you the ability to create the traps. While the trapping command is very easy to apply, setting the proper values takes years of experience. If you do not have experience with trapping, and you want to set traps, consult the print shop that will print your work. Also consult the *Commercial Printing Guide* that came with FreeHand.

To use the Trap command:

1. Select two or more objects in your illustration that you want to trap.

2. Choose Trap from the Create submenu of the Xtras menu. The Trap dialog box will appear (**Figure 19**).

3. Use the sliders or type in the Trap width suggested by your print shop.

4. If your print shop agrees, choose the Use maximum value setting to make the trap color the strongest available.
or
Choose the Use tint reduction setting and enter the reduction amount suggested by your print shop.

5. If you check the Reverse traps box, any traps that would have been spreads will be chokes and any chokes will be spreads. Consult your print shop as to when you should do this.

6. Click OK. The traps will be created.

Tip

■ When you create traps, you are creating new objects that overprint between the two original objects. If you move or delete objects later, be careful that you do not leave the traps behind.

To use the Create Blend command:

This command is identical to the Blend command in the Path Operations submenu of the Arrange menu *(see page 160)*.

To use the Empty Text Blocks command:

If you drag with the Text tool, you will create a text block. If you then decide not to type anything, and deselect the block, it will stay on your page. Choose Unused Text Blocks from the Delete submenu of the Xtras menu to delete all empty text blocks.

To add Xtras from other companies:

In addition to the Xtras that come with the FreeHand, there are other Xtras that are available. These include the plug-ins that come with Adobe Illustrator.

You can also get plug-ins or Xtras from other software companies. Some of these Xtras are KPT Vector Effects from MetaTools, Infinite FX from BeInfinite, DrawTools from Extensis, and Letraset Envelopes from Letraset.

To use Xtras from other companies:

After you install them, Xtras from other companies will be listed either in their own menu or in one of the FreeHand Xtras categories. These third-party Xtras will be listed in an italic typeface (**Figure 20**) They can be used just like any of the original FreeHand Xtras.

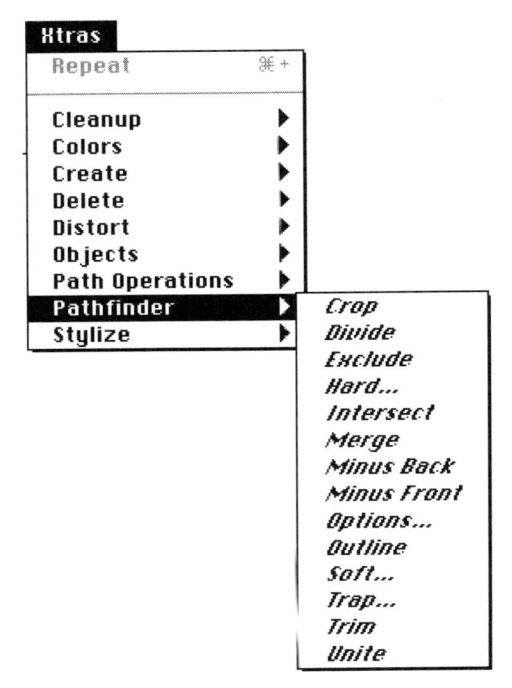

Figure 20. *The* **Adobe Illustrator Pathfinder** *filters as displayed in the* **FreeHand Xtras** *menu.*

OTHER APPLICATIONS 20

No one program can do it all, so on occasion you may need to work with other applications along with FreeHand. In this chapter, you will learn how to place, resize, transform, and modify pixel-based artwork, such as TIFF and PICT files, and vector-based artwork, such as EPS files, in FreeHand. You will also learn how to modify the size, position, and colors of pixel-based artwork and how to apply Photoshop plug-ins. You will learn how to extract an embedded placed image from a file. You will learn how to export your files in the EPS format for use in page layout programs. You will learn how to turn FreeHand files into other formats, such as PICT files, Adobe Illustrator files, text files, or files in earlier versions of FreeHand. You will also learn how to open Adobe Acrobat PDF files in FreeHand. Finally, you will learn how to add Fetch information to your FreeHand file.

You may find that you wish to add files from other programs, such as Adobe Photoshop, to your FreeHand layout. This is called "placing" artwork into FreeHand.

To place artwork into FreeHand:

1. Choose Place from the File menu.

2. Use the dialog box to find the file you want to place. While most print work requires a TIFF or EPS format, you may also place PICT and PICT2 images.

3. When you have chosen the file you want to place, your cursor will change into a corner symbol (**Figure 1**).

(Continued on the following page)

Figure 1. *The **corner symbol** indicates that you have a file ready for placement.*

4. Click the corner symbol to place the file in its original size.

or

To specify a certain size for the placed image, drag the corner symbol to fill the size you want (**Figure 2**).

Tip

- Unless you have changed the Preferences settings for Expert Import/Output *(see page 277)*, your placed image is only linked to the FreeHand file. If you send the FreeHand file to someone else for output, you must include the original placed image along with the FreeHand file or the placed image will not print correctly.

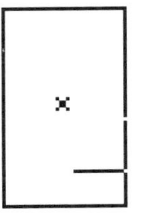

Figure 2. *Dragging the corner symbol sizes the placed image.*

Once you have a placed image, FreeHand gives you many different ways to modify that image.

To resize placed images by dragging:

1. Place the Selection tool on one of the corner handles of the placed image.

2. Drag to change the size of the image (**Figure 3**).

Tip

- Hold the Shift key to constrain the horizontal and vertical proportions of the image.

Figure 3. *Drag the corner handle to change the size of a placed image.*

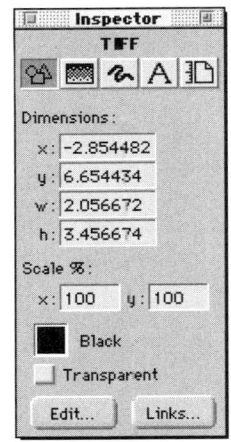

Figure 4. *Click the **Object** icon of the **Inspector** palette to resize placed images.*

Working with Other Applications

Figure 5. *Any of the transformation tools, such as the Rotating tool shown here, may be used on placed images.*

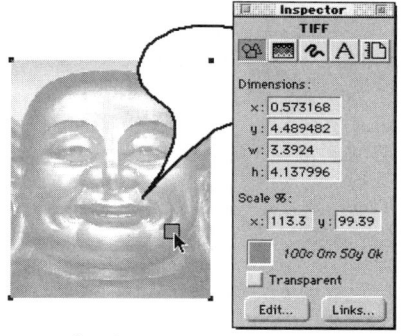

Figure 6. *Black-and-white or grayscale TIFF or PICT images may be colorized by dragging color swatches onto the image or onto the color drop box in the Inspector palette.*

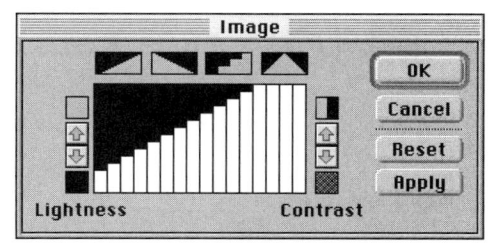

Figure 7. *The **Image** dialog box allows you to adjust the lightness or contrast of the image. Click the Apply button to view your changes before you click OK.*

To resize placed images numerically:

1. With the placed image selected, click on the Object icon of the Inspector palette (**Figure 4**).

2. Use the Scale % x and y fields to change the size of the image.
or
Enter the exact dimensions you want for the image in the w and h fields.

3. Press Return or Enter to apply the changes.

To transform a placed image:

1. Select the placed image.

2. You can modify the image using any of the transformation tools (Rotating, Reflecting, Scaling, or Skewing) either by eye or by using the Transform palette (**Figure 5**).

FreeHand also offers you ways to modify the color and shade of grayscale or black-and-white TIFF and PICT images.

To modify a placed image:

1. With the placed image selected, click on the Object icon of the Inspector palette. If the image is a greyscale or black-and-white PICT or TIFF image, you will see a color drop box in the Inspector palette.

2. To colorize the image, drag a color swatch from the Color List onto the color drop box or onto the image (**Figure 6**).

3. To change the lightness or contrast of grayscale images, click on the Edit button. The Image dialog box will appear (**Figure 7**).

(Continued on the following page)

241

Chapter 20

4. If you want to change the placed file, you can use the Links button to change the image.

5. If you have a grayscale image, you can click on the Transparent checkbox to turn the image from grayscale to a 1-bit image. This will convert all the white areas to clear. This lets objects behind your placed image show through the transparent areas (**Figure 8**).

Tip

- Transforming, colorizing, or modifying the lightness or contrast of a placed image in FreeHand may add to the printing time for the file. If possible, go back to the original image, replicate the changes you've made, and then replace the revised image in the FreeHand file.

FreeHand 5.5 lets you use Photoshop filters to modify placed TIFF images.

To install Photoshop filters in FreeHand 5.5:

1. With FreeHand not running, open the Xtras folder in the Macromedia folder in the System Folder.

2. Place a copy or alias of whichever Photoshop filters you want installed into FreeHand in the Xtras folder. You can also make an alias of the plug-ins folder itself and put that into the FreeHand Xtras folder.

3. Close the System Folder and launch FreeHand.

4. Any Photoshop filters that are able to run in FreeHand will be found under the Xtras menu with the label *"[TIFF]"* preceding the name of the filter (**Figure 9**).

Figure 8. *The placed image before (top) and after (bottom) the **transparent** option was applied.*

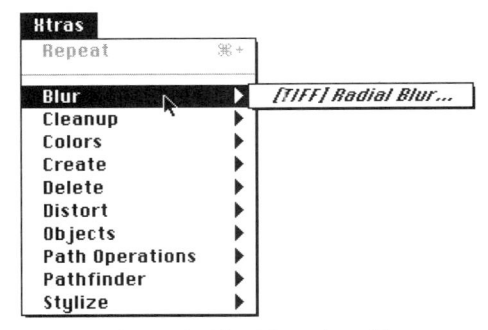

Figure 9. *The Photoshop filter **Radial Blur** as it appears in the **Xtras** menu.*

Working with Other Applications

Figure 10. *The **Radial Blur** filter as applied to a placed image.*

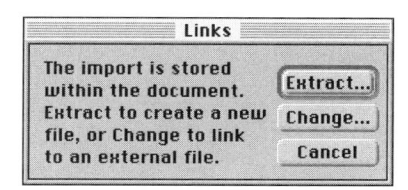

Figure 11. *The **Links** dialog box lets you extract an embedded image into a separate file linked to the FreeHand file. This reduces the size of the FreeHand file.*

To apply a Photoshop filter to a TIFF image:

1. Select the placed TIFF image.
2. From the Xtras menu, choose the Photoshop filter you wish to apply to the image.
3. If a dialog box or settings box appears, follow the steps necessary to adjust the settings for the filter.
4. The filter will automatically be applied to your image (**Figure 10**).

Tip

- When you use any Photoshop filters on TIFF images in FreeHand, the result is an embedded TIFF image. This will cause the size of the FreeHand file to be larger than it was before the TIFF was embedded. If you want to keep the file size lower, use the Extract feature to create a copy of the modified image.

To extract an embedded placed image:

1. Select the image that is embedded in the FreeHand file.
2. Click on the Links button in the Object Inspector. The Links dialog box will appear (**Figure 11**).
3. The Extract button opens the Extract dialog box, which lets you choose a name and destination for the extracted image.
4. The Change button opens the Change dialog box, which lets you change the file to a separate file that will be linked to the FreeHand document.

Apply Photoshop Filters; Extract Embedded Placed Image

243

Chapter 20

FreeHand offers you many different ways of converting or exporting your FreeHand files into formats that can be read by other applications. Because exporting as some formats can change the contents of your file, you must pick your export format according to your needs.

To export files:

1. With the file open, choose Export from the File menu. The Export document dialog box will appear (**Figure 12a**).

2. At the bottom of the box you will see a field where the name of the file will be. The name of the file to be exported will automatically be followed by a period and a suffix that reflects the nature of the exported file.

3. The Format pop-up menu lists all the formats that the FreeHand export feature supports (**Figure 12b**).

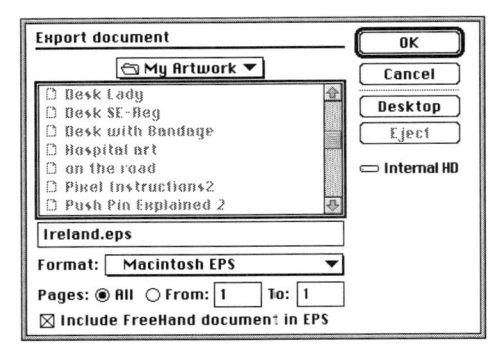

Figure 12a. *The **Export** document dialog box.*

Figure 12b. *The **Format** pop-up menu gives you the options for exporting your file to different formats.*

To export as an EPS file:

1. Choose Export from the File menu.

2. If you are going to place your EPS file in a Macintosh application, choose Macintosh EPS from the Format pop-up menu.

3. If you are going to place your EPS file in a Windows application, choose MS-DOS EPS.

4. If you do not know which platform your file will be placed in, choose Generic EPS. (The Generic EPS format will print, but does not show a preview onscreen.)

5. The name of the exported file automatically gets the suffix ".eps."

244

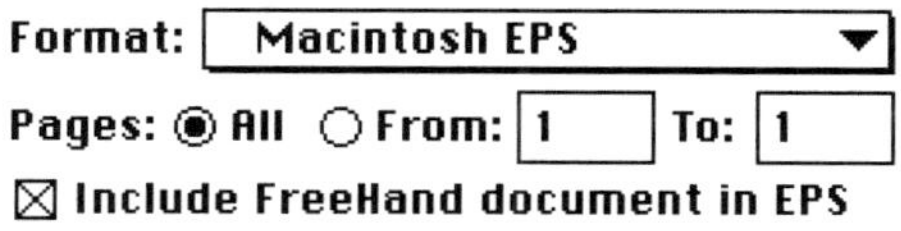

Working with Other Applications

```
Format: [ Macintosh EPS      ▼]
Pages: ● All  ○ From: [1]  To: [1]
☒ Include FreeHand document in EPS
```
Figure 13. *The setting controls for the **Export document** dialog box.*

6. If your FreeHand file has only one page, you do not have to pick anything in the Pages radio button section. Your exported EPS file will consist of that one page of artwork.

7. If your FreeHand file has more than one page, you will need to choose how many pages to convert to EPS artwork. If you want all the pages to be exported, make sure the All radio button is picked.

8. If you want just some of the pages to be exported, choose the From radio button and enter the page numbers in the From and To fields. When you export multiple pages as EPS files, each page will be converted into its own file with the suffix ".eps-1," ".eps-2," etc., indicating each page.

9. If you want to be able to open the EPS file later to make changes, check the Include FreeHand document in EPS checkbox (**Figure 13**). This lets you open the EPS file later.

Tip

■ If you export a file without including the FreeHand document in the file, you will be able to open that exported EPS, and you will be able to place it in page layout programs but you will not be able to edit the artwork. In order to edit the file, you will need to save the original FreeHand file, sometimes called the "native" FreeHand file.

You may find it necessary to export your files in the Adobe Illustrator format.

To export as an Adobe Illustrator file:

1. Choose Export from the File menu.

2. Choose one of the Adobe Illustrator formats from the Format pop-up menu (**Figure 14**).

3. You will notice that the name of the file automatically gets the suffix ".art."

4. If your FreeHand file has only one page, you do not have to pick anything in the Pages radio button section. Your Illustrator file will consist of that one page of artwork.

5. If your FreeHand file has more than one page, you will need to choose how many pages to convert to the Illustrator format. If you want all the pages to be exported, make sure the All radio button is picked.

6. If you want just some of the pages to be exported, choose the From radio button and enter the page numbers in the From and To fields. When you export multiple pages as Illustrator files, each page will be converted into its own file with the suffix ".art-1," ".art-2," etc., indicating each page.

Tips

- If you are uncertain what features, if any, will be lost when you export your file, make sure you keep a copy of the file in the FreeHand format.

- If you choose Photoshop EPS from the Format pop-up menu your file will be saved as an Illustrator file. This format can then be read by Photoshop and converted into a Photoshop file.

Adobe Illustrator 1.1™
Adobe Illustrator 88™
Adobe Illustrator® 3
Adobe Illustrator™ **5.5**

Figure 14. *The four choices for exporting FreeHand files in the* ***Adobe Illustrator*** *format.*

Working with Other Applications

FreeHand 3.1
FreeHand 3.1 text editable

Figure 15. *The two choices for exporting FreeHand files in previous **FreeHand** formats.*

You may need to send your file to someone who does not have the latest version of FreeHand. In that case, you will need to export the file as an earlier version of FreeHand.

To export as a FreeHand file:

1. Choose Export from the File menu.
2. Choose FreeHand 3.1 from the Format pop-up menu (**Figure 15**).
3. You will notice that the name of the file automatically gets the suffix ".fh3."
4. Because the FreeHand 3.1 format does not support multiple pages, all artwork on your pasteboard will be saved into a single file, regardless of which pages that artwork was on.
5. Because FreeHand 3.1 does not support certain text features, exporting in the FreeHand 3.1 format will break up text blocks to make the text look as similar as possible to the FreeHand 5.5 formats.
6. If you choose the FreeHand 3.1 text editable format, the exported file will keep the text blocks together. The resulting layout won't be as close to the original document, but it will let you edit your text as a complete story.

To export as other formats:

1. Choose Export from the File menu.
2. To open your files in MacDraw or Canvas applications, choose either PICT file or PICT2 file from the Format pop-up menu.
3. To send the text of your file in the Microsoft Rich Text Format, choose RTF text from the Format pop-up menu.
4. To send the text without the formatting, choose ASCII text from the Format pop-up menu.

Chapter 20

FreeHand 5.5 offers you a different way to change the format of your artwork. This is the Create PICT Image Xtra. This converts whichever items are selected, both vector and pixel images, into just pixel-based art. That art can be used in applications that require pixel-based artwork.

To create a PICT image:

1. Select the object or objects you wish to convert.
2. Choose Create PICT Image from the Xtras menu or the Operations palette.
3. The Create PICT dialog box will appear (**Figure 16**) *(see the following section on the options for your image).*
4. Choose Copy. This creates a pixel-based copy of the image that will be temporarily stored on the Macintosh Clipboard. The pixel-based copy can then be pasted back into FreeHand, into the Scrapbook, or into other applications.
5. Choose Save to save the image as a separate PICT file. This separate file can be placed back into FreeHand or used by other applications.

Tip

- If you hold the Shift key while you select Create PICT Image, you will skip the dialog box and copy the PICT image to the Clipboard using current settings.

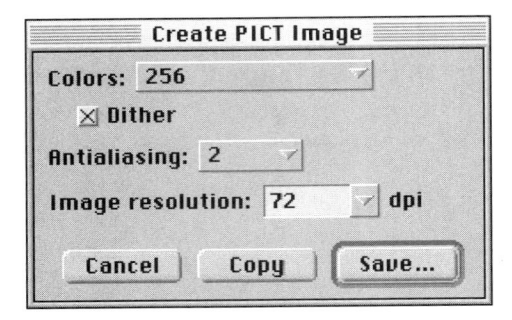

Figure 16. *The **Create PICT image** dialog box lets you set how your artwork will be converted into a PICT image.*

Figure 17a. *A PICT image created using 256 colors, the dithering turned on, an anti-aliasing of none, and a 72-dpi resolution.*

Figure 17b. *A PICT image created using millions of colors, anti-aliasing of 4, and entering a 150-dpi resolution.*

Working with Other Applications

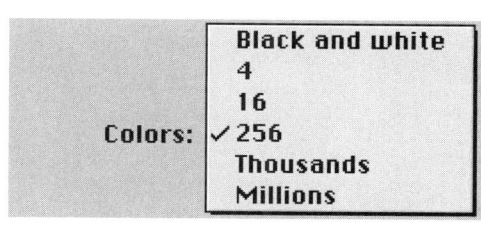

Figure 18. *The Colors choices of the Create PICT image dialog box.*

Figure 19. *The Antialiasing choices of the Create PICT image dialog box.*

Figure 20. *The Image resolution choices of the Create PICT image dialog box.*

How you choose the PICT image options depends on what you are going to do with the image created (**Figures 17a–b**).

To choose the PICT image options:

1. The Colors pop-up menu (**Figure 18**) of the Create PICT Image dialog box lets you control the number of colors used to convert your artwork. Most print work needs the Millions setting. But if you are creating files for multimedia, you may only need 256 colors.

2. The Dither checkbox controls how colors are created when anything less than Thousands or Millions is chosen. When checked, the final colors of the created image will be a little closer to the colors of the original image.

3. The Antialiasing pop-up menu (**Figure 19**) lets you control how much "fuzziness," or anti-aliasing, is added to the edges of your artwork. None means no anti-aliasing will be added. The anti-aliasing amounts increase from 2 to 4. Anti-aliasing eliminates the jagged edges that occur when vector-based artwork is converted to pixel-based artwork.

4. The Image resolution field (**Figure 20**) lets you enter the dpi, or dots per inch, of the PICT file you are creating. For most multimedia work or screen presentations, a resolution of 72 is sufficient. For most print work, higher resolutions are needed.

Tip

■ The higher the number of colors, anti-aliasing, and resolution, the more RAM will be needed. If you do not have enough RAM to create your image, you will need to increase the RAM allotted to FreeHand.

Chapter 20

FreeHand 5.5 also lets you open documents saved in the Adobe Acrobat PDF format.

To open an Acrobat PDF within FreeHand:

1. With FreeHand running, choose Open from the File menu.

2. Find the Acrobat PDF that you wish to open and open it as you would any FreeHand file.

3. Multipage Acrobat files will be converted to multipage FreeHand files.

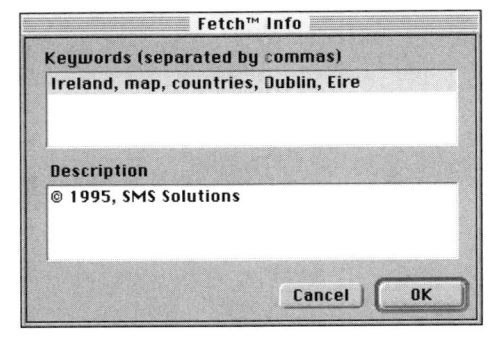

Figure 21. *The **Fetch Info** dialog box allows you to create keywords and descriptions that can help you search through the Fetch database.*

FreeHand also lets you add information you can use to catalog your files with the Adobe Fetch program.

To add Fetch Info:

1. With the file open, choose Fetch Info from the File menu. The Fetch Info dialog box will appear (**Figure 21**).

2. Type in the keywords and description information you want for your Fetch catalog.

3. Click OK. The Fetch information will be saved when you save the file.

4. To add a preview to your FreeHand file so it can be seen in the Fetch program, you need to check the Preferences settings for Importing/Exporting *(see page 269)*.

PRINTING 21

Once you've finished your illustration, you will probably want to print it. This chapter is divided into two parts. The first part covers the print options for printing to a simple desktop printer. In that section, you will learn about the settings in the printer dialog box: setting the number of copies; setting which pages to print; picking the paper source; setting the tiling options; scaling the illustration or making it automatically fit the size of the page; and choosing separations or composite proof.

The second part covers the print options for printing to high-resolution imagesetters: adding crop marks and registration marks; adding the name of the file and adding separation-name labels; setting the imaging options; setting global trapping; selecting and setting the proper PostScript Printer Description file (PPD); setting halftone screens; setting the transfer function; setting which inks will print or overprint; and setting the screen angles. You will also learn about the Output Options: splitting complex paths; printing the objects on invisible layers; choosing the image data; converting RGB TIFF images to CMYK; and setting the maximum number of color steps; setting the flatness. You will learn how to create a report about your document. Finally, you will learn which files you need to include when you send your work to be printed at a service bureau.

Chapter 21

BASIC PRINTING

Before you print your document, you should determine what kind of printer you will be using. If your printer is not a PostScript Level 1 or Level 2 device, for example, the Custom, Textured, or PostScript fills and strokes will not print. If you are in doubt as to the type of printer you have, check the specifications that came with the printer.

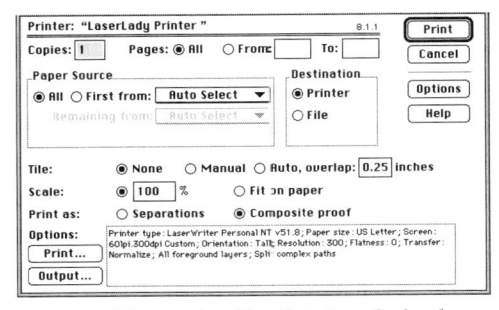

Figure 1a. *The **Printer** dialog box.*

To open the Printer dialog box:

Choose Print from the File menu or press Command-P. The Print dialog box will appear (**Figure 1a**). Some of the options that appear in this dialog box may change depending on the type of printer you have and the LaserWriter software you have installed in your System Folder.

To set up the Printer dialog box:

1. In the Copies field, enter the number of copies you want to print.

2. For the Pages choices (**Figure 1b**), choose All if you want all the pages in your document to print.

or

Choose the From radio button and then fill in the page numbers that you want to print. You can choose a range of pages by entering different numbers in the From and To fields, or you can print just a single page by entering its number in both the From and To fields.

3. Choose the Paper Source that you want your printer to use (**Figure 1c**). This can be a paper cassette, a manual feed option, or other choices specific to your printer.

Figure 1b. *The **Pages** choices in the **Printer** dialog box.*

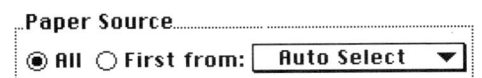

Figure 1c. *The **Paper Source** choices in the **Printer** dialog box.*

Printer Dialog Box

Printing

Tile: ● None ○ Manual ○ Auto, overlap: 0.25

Figure 1d. *The **Tile** choices in the **Printer** dialog box.*

Scale: ● 100 %   ○ Fit on paper

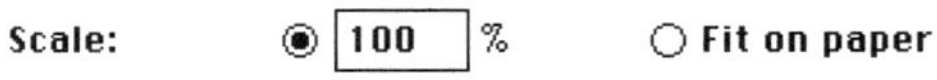

Figure 1e. *The **Scale** choices in the **Printer** dialog box.*

Print as: ○ Separations ● Composite proof

Figure 1f. *The **Separations** or **Composite proof** choices in the **Printer** dialog box.*

4. If you wish to tile your illustration to fit on the paper you are printing on, choose Manual or Auto from the Tile options (**Figure 1d**) *(see next page)*.

5. If you want to change the size of your illustration, enter an amount in the Scale field (**Figure 1e**). This allows you to enlarge or reduce your illustration.
or
If you want the artwork page to fit on the paper you are printing on, choose Fit on paper (**Figure 1e**). This will reduce or enlarge the artwork page accordingly.

6. If your artwork has color in it, you will need to choose Separations or Composite proof under the Print as options (**Figure 1f**). If you are printing to an ordinary desktop printer, you will most likely want to print your job as a composite proof. This means that all the colors of the image will appear on one page. If you are outputting to a high-resolution printer, you will want to make separations. This means that each of the colors of your artwork will be separated into individual prints or plates of film.

Printer Dialog Box

253

Chapter 21

If your artwork is bigger than the paper in your printer, you will not be able to print the entire illustration at actual size on one page. FreeHand lets you "tile" your illustration onto multiple pieces of paper that can then be assembled to form the larger illustration.

To tile an oversized illustration

1. In the Printer dialog box, choose Manual or Auto from the Tile options.
2. If you choose Auto, FreeHand will automatically divide your artwork into different pages.
3. If you choose Auto, you have the choice of how much overlap there will be between each page.
4. If you choose Manual, you will need to move the zero point from the ruler down onto the artwork to set the lower-left corner (**Figure 2**). FreeHand will print whatever is up and to the right of that zero point.

Tips

- When you choose Manual tiling, you need to reset the zero point and then choose Print from the File menu. You will need to repeat this process as many times as necessary to print all the sections of your document.
- Manual tiling can be useful in printing just those elements of your artwork that you do not want to run across a cut line.

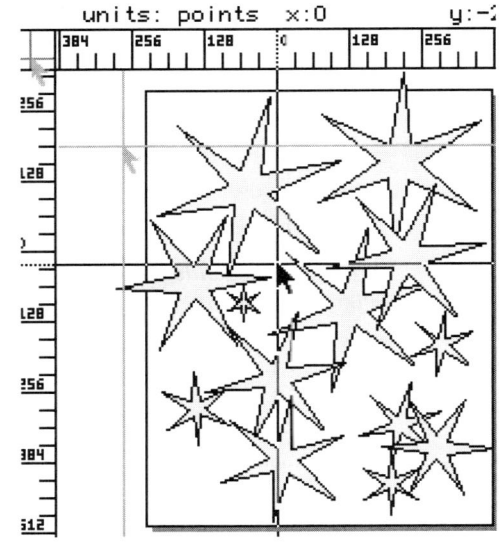

Figure 2. *Drag the zero point from the ruler to set the position of the page for* ***Manual*** *tiling.*

Printing

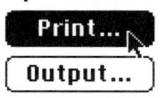

Figure 3a. *The* ***Print*** *button under Options in the* ***Printer*** *dialog box gives you the* ***Print Options***.

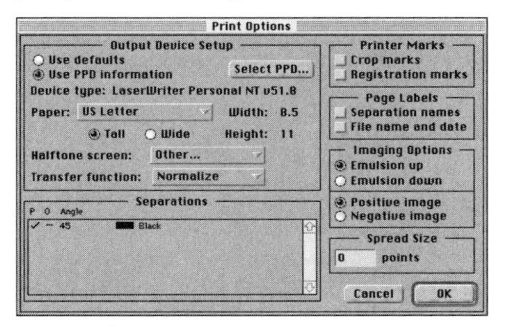

Figure 3b. *The* ***Print Options*** *dialog box.*

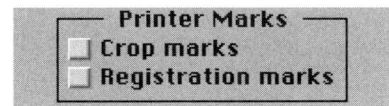

Figure 4. *Click the* ***Crop marks*** *and* ***Registration marks*** *checkboxes to have these printer marks print outside your artwork.*

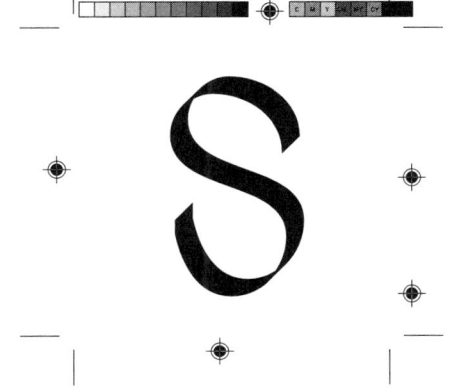

Figure 5. *Artwork printed with* ***Crop marks*** *and* ***Registration marks***. *Color bars are also added when the Registration marks box is checked.*

ADVANCED PRINTING

To change the print options:

With the Printer dialog box open, click on the Print button (**Figure 3a**) under the word Options. This opens the Print Options dialog box (**Figure 3b**).

To add printer marks:

1. Click the Crop marks (**Figure 4**) checkbox to add crop marks at the corners of your pages (**Figure 5**).

2. Click the Registration marks (**Figure 4**) checkbox to add registration marks at the sides of your pages. This option will also add color bars at the top of the page (**Figure 5**).

To add page labels:

1. Click the Separation names (**Figure 6**) checkbox to add to the printed page a label with the name of the color plate that is being printed. If you are not printing separations, then the label will be "Composite."

2. Click the File name and date (**Figure 6**) checkbox to add to the printed page the name of the file, the date and time that the file is being printed, and the page number.

Tip

■ The Separation names and File name and date labels are printed outside the live area of your artwork.

Figure 6. *Click the* ***Separation names*** *and* ***File name and date*** *checkboxes to have these page labels print outside your artwork.*

The imaging options (**Figure 7**) are usually chosen only when artwork is being printed for final output on high-resolution devices.

To choose the imaging options:

1. Choose Emulsion up for printing to paper. When printing to film separations, Emulsion up means the image reads correctly when the emulsion of the film is up or facing the reader.

2. Choose Emulsion down for paper prints only when you want to make a mirror image of your artwork. When printing to film separations, Emulsion down means the image reads correctly when the emulsion of the film is down or facing away from the reader.

3. Choose Positive image for printing to paper. This keeps the image as black on a white background.

4. Choose Negative image for paper prints only when you want to invert the image to white on a black background. Negative image is the usual choice when printing to film separations.

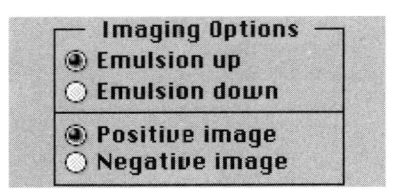

Figure 7. *The four **Imaging Options**.*

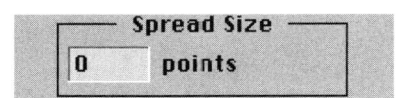

Figure 8. *The **Spread Size** field allows you to have all artwork "spread" a certain amount to compensate for misregistrations in the final printing.*

In addition to the trapping created by the Trap Xtra *(see page 237)*, FreeHand provides a trapping option called "spread."

To choose the spread size:

In the Spread Size field (**Figure 8**), enter the amount that you want basic fills and strokes to expand. This compensates for misregistrations in the final printing. Trapping amounts vary depending on the type of printing press, paper, inks, etc. Do not enter any amount unless you have spoken to the print shop where your artwork will be printed.

Printing

Figure 9. *Press the **Select PPD** button in the **Print Options** dialog box to choose the proper printer description.*

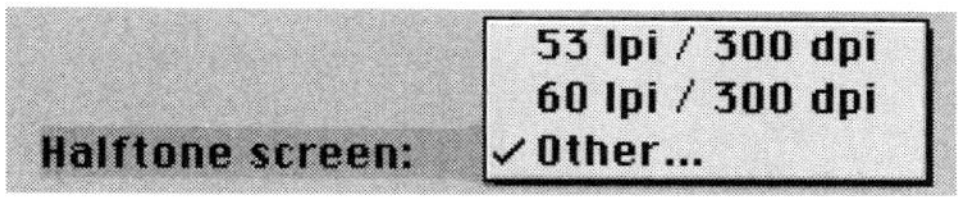

Figure 10. *The **Halftone screen** pop-up menu for a typical laser printer.*

Unlike other programs that use the Page Setup dialog box for certain settings, FreeHand uses the PPD (PostScript Printer Description) information. If you want to set choices such as paper size and orientation, you will need to select the correct PPD for the type of printer you are using.

To select the PPD:

1. Press the Select PPD button (**Figure 9**) in the Print Options dialog box to set the Output Device Setup.

2. Choose the printer you want to print to from the list of PPDs that are installed in the Printer Descriptions folder in the Extensions folder of your System Folder.

3. Click the Open button when you are done. This will put the proper PPD information into the Print Options dialog box.

If your artwork has any screened objects, you may want to set the Halftone screen.

To set the halftone screen:

1. If you have a PPD selected, you will see a pop-up menu for Halftone screen.

2. Choose from the list of common screens (**Figure 10**) for your output device. A 300-dpi laser printer has screens of 53 lines per inch (lpi) or 60 lpi. High-resolution imagesetters commonly have screens of 150 lpi or 133 lpi.

Tip

■ If you are printing to a laser printer and are getting banding in your blends, try lowering the screen frequency to something like 35 lpi or 40 lpi. While your screens may look a little "dotty," it should reduce banding.

257

Chapter 21

In addition to setting the halftone screen for the entire illustration, you can set the halftone screen for individual objects.

To set halftone screens for individual objects:

1. Select the object that you want to set the halftone screen for.

2. Choose Halftone from the Window menu or press Command-H. The Halftone palette will appear (**Figure 11**).

3. Choose from the Screen pop-up menu to change the shape of the screen dot. The Default setting gives you the default shape of the output device you are printing to. The other choices are Round dot, Line, and Ellipse. Consult with your print shop on which shape of screen dot they prefer.

4. Enter the angle of the screen in the Angle field or rotate the wheel to set the screen angle. If no value is in the Angle field, the default setting of 45° is used.

5. Enter the frequency of the screen in the Frequency field or use the slider to set the number. If no value is in the Frequency field, the default setting of your output device is used.

Figure 11. *The **Halftone** palette lets you change the halftone screen for individual objects.*

Figure 12. *The **Transfer function** choices.*

To set the Transfer function:

1. With the Print Options dialog box open, you will see a pop-up menu for Transfer function (**Figure 12**).

2. If you are printing to an output device that has been specially calibrated, press on the pop-up menu and choose Unadjusted.

3. If you are printing to an ordinary laser printer, choose Normalize.

Printing

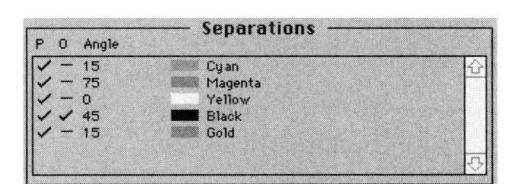

Figure 13. *The **Separations** box lets you select which colors will print (indicated by a check in the P column) and which colors will overprint (indicated by a check in the O column).*

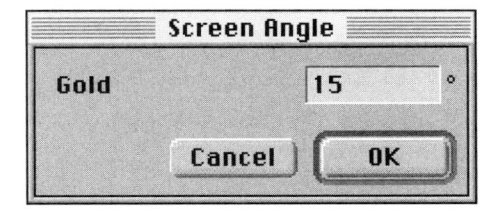

Figure 14. *The **Screen Angle** dialog box lets you set the angle that a color's screens will be printed.*

4. If you wish to speed up the time it takes to print your image, and don't mind sacrificing the quality of your image, choose Posterize. This will reduce the number of levels of screens that are printed in your illustration.

FreeHand also gives you choices as to which color plates will or will not print in your artwork. These are called "separations."

To set the separations:

1. Choose Print from the File menu. The Printer dialog box will appear.

2. Click on the Print button at the bottom of the Printer dialog box. The Print Options dialog box will appear.

3. At the bottom of the Print Options dialog box the colors of your document will be listed (**Figure 13**). You should see the four process colors (Cyan, Magenta, Yellow, and Black), as well as any spot colors used in your document.

4. To prevent a color from printing, click in the P column to delete the checkmark for that color.

5. To set a color to overprint, click in the O column to create a checkmark for that color.

6. To set the screen angle for a color, double-click on the color name. The Screen Angle dialog box will appear (**Figure 14**). Enter the angle you want for that color and click OK. Repeat for each color.

Tip

■ Do not adjust the screen angles, screen frequency, or overprinting options unless you know what you are doing. Consult with the print shop that will be producing your job.

259

Chapter 21

FreeHand also offers you various output options for printing to a PostScript output device. These options are also contained inside the file when it is exported as an EPS file *(see page 244)*.

To open the Output Options dialog box:
Choose Output Options from the File menu. The Output Options dialog box will appear (**Figure 15**).
or
Choose Print from the File menu. Under the Options section, click on the Output button. This will bring up the Output Options dialog box.

To choose the output options:
1. If you want objects that are on hidden layers to print, check the Include invisible layers checkbox.

2. If you check the Split complex paths checkbox, FreeHand will, if necessary, split up long, complex paths that could produce errors in printing.

3. Click ASCII encoding only if you are having trouble printing a file with bitmapped images. Otherwise, click Binary data. Click None (OPI comments only) if your TIFF images will be replaced by a high-resolution version at a color electronic prepress system.

4. Check the Convert RGB TIFF to CMYK checkbox only if you are sending your work to a program that does not convert RGB TIFF images to CMYK.

5. Enter a number from 8 to 255 in the Maximum Color Steps field only if you are having trouble converting a file using an electronic prepress system.

6. Enter a number from 1 to 100 in the Flatness field if the Print Monitor reports a limitcheck error when printing your file.

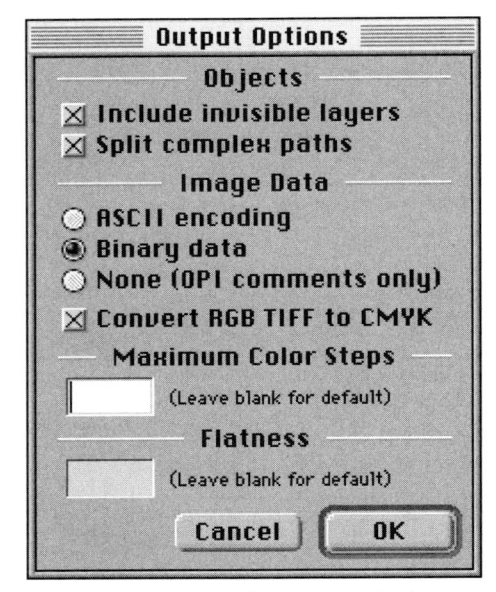

Figure 15. *The Output Options dialog box.*

Printing

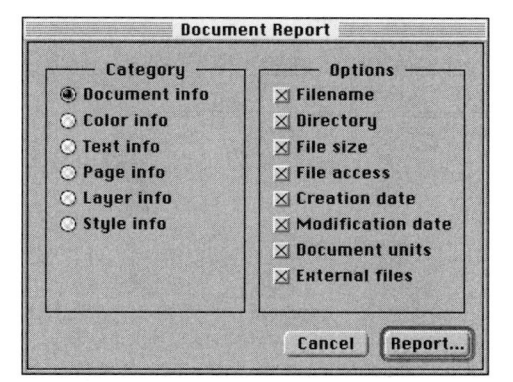

Figure 16. *The **Document Report** dialog box lets you select the information to be included in the document report.*

There may be times when you want a record or report of all the information about your FreeHand file. FreeHand provides you with a very sophisticated report for all your documents.

To create a document report:

1. With the document open, choose Report from the File menu. The Document Report dialog box will appear (**Figure 16**).

2. Click on each one of the six categories listed on the left side of the Document Report dialog box.

3. Use the checkboxes on the right side to indicate which information in each category you want listed.

4. Click the Report button to see the Document Report Viewer. This is where you can read the complete document report or click the Save button to create a permanent text file of your report.

Chapter 21

Unless you have your own high-resolution imagesetter, you will want to transfer your work onto a floppy disk or some type of removable cartridge and then send this disk or cartridge to a service bureau where the file will be output. There are certain files you will want to include, depending on your FreeHand settings.

To send a file out for imagesetting:

1. If the file has no placed images, such as PICT, TIFF, or EPS images from other programs, then all you have to do is copy the FreeHand file onto the disk or cartridge that you are sending out.

2. If your file does have placed images in it, then you need to check if the images have been embedded or linked to your FreeHand file. This can be done by checking the option for External Files found in the Document Info category of the document report.

3. If you have external files listed in the document report, it means that those placed images are linked, not embedded, in your FreeHand file. This means that, in addition to the FreeHand file, you need to send the original files of the linked images to your service bureau (**Figure 17**).

4. If you have no external files listed in the document report, it means that any placed images are embedded in the FreeHand document. You do not have to send the original files of these embedded images along with the FreeHand file. However, FreeHand files with embedded placed images can grow to very large sizes.

5. To turn on and off the option to embed images, change the Preferences settings for Expert Import/Output (*see page 277*).

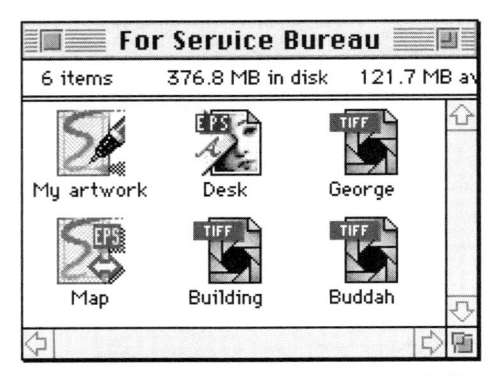

Figure 17. *When a **FreeHand file** is sent to a service bureau, the files of all placed images that are not embedded in the FreeHand document should also be included.*

Send a File for Imagesetting

262

PREFERENCES 22

Just because FreeHand comes with certain settings doesn't mean you have to keep those settings. FreeHand gives you a wealth of choices as to how your application will operate. In this chapter, you will learn how to set the preferences for a wide variety of features. You will also learn how you can change the default settings for new documents.

Preferences control the entire application. This means that any changes you make to the Preferences settings will be applied to all documents, past, present, and future.

To change the preferences:

1. Open FreeHand.
2. Choose Preferences from the File menu.
3. The Preferences settings are divided into fifteen different categories listed on the left side of the Preferences box. Click on the category you want.

Figure 1. *The **Preferences** settings for the **Color** category.*

The Color category controls how colors are displayed both in the Color List and onscreen (**Figure 1**).

To change the Color preferences:

1. Choosing the Use CMYK values option means that colors created in the Color Mixer and then imported into the Color List will be listed with their CMYK amounts (**Figure 2**).
2. Choosing the Use RGB values option means colors will be listed with their RGB values (**Figure 2**).

Figure 2. *The first six colors listed were named using their CMYK values. The last six colors listed were named using their RGB values.*

(Continued on the following page)

263

3. Choosing the Container color option means that when a text block is selected, the Fill color in the Color List shows the fill color of the block, not the text inside the block.

4. Choosing the Text color option means that when a text block is selected, the Fill color in the Color List shows the fill color of the text, not the block.

5. Checking the Auto-rename changed colors option will change the name of any colors when their CMYK or RGB values are changed using the Color Mixer or the Randomize Named Colors command in the Xtras menu.

6. Checking the Color Mixer uses split color well option allows you to compare any changes to a color in the Color Mixer with the original color.

7. Checking the Dither 8-bit colors option changes how colors are displayed onscreen. If you are working on a monitor with only 256 colors, you should turn this option on to see a better representation of your colors.

8. Checking the Adjust display colors option gives you the Calibrate button. Click on that button to see the Display Color Setup dialog box with seven different colors (**Figure 3**). Click on each box to use the Macintosh color wheel to change how the color is displayed onscreen.

9. Checking the Guide color or Grid color boxes allows you to use the Macintosh color wheel to change the colors FreeHand uses for guides and the dots of the visible grid.

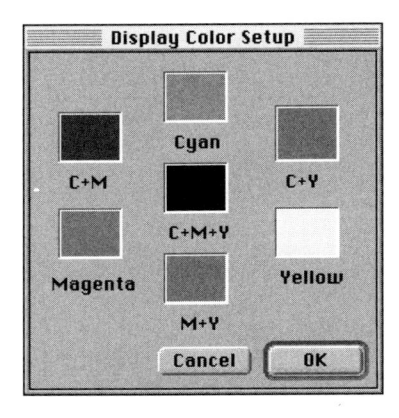

Figure 3. *Choosing the* **Calibrate** *button gives you the* **Display Color Setup** *dialog box. Clicking on each of these colors gives you the Macintosh color wheel, where you can change how the colors are displayed onscreen.*

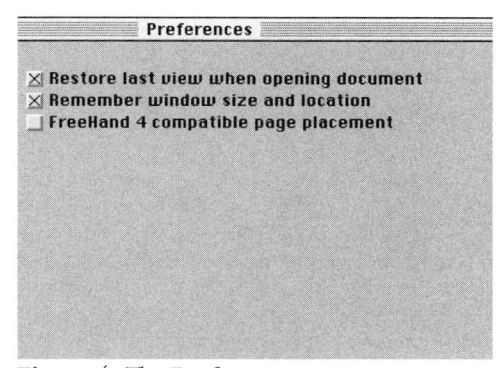

Figure 4. *The **Preferences** settings for the **Document** category.*

The Document category controls how FreeHand opens documents. It also controls the size of the pasteboard of the documents (**Figure 4**).

To change the Document preferences:

1. Checking the Restore last view when opening document option allows you to have FreeHand "remember" the last view of a document before it was closed.

2. Checking the Remember window size and location option allows you to have FreeHand "remember" the size and position of the title bar of the window that holds the file.

3. Checking the FreeHand 4 compatible page placement option allows you to see the area on the pasteboard that will be kept when a FreeHand 5.5 file is converted to FreeHand 4 (**Figure 5**).

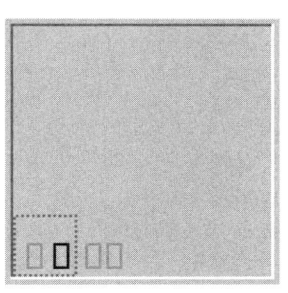

Figure 5. *The dotted line around two of the pages shows the area of the pasteboard that will be kept when the FreeHand 5.5 document is converted to FreeHand 4. In this case, two of the pages lie outside the area.*

Chapter 22

The Editor category is divided into three areas. Editing General controls the overall editing features (**Figure 6**).

To change the Editing General preferences:

1. The Number of undo's field lets you enter the number of times you can undo your actions. You can enter any number between 1 and 100.

2. The Pick distance field lets you change how close you have to come with the Selection tool to manipulate a point or handle. You can enter a number up to 5 pixels.

3. The Cursor key distance field lets you set how far any of the four arrow keys (up, down, left, and right) on your keyboard will move objects. This amount is measured in the current unit of measurement.

4. The Snap distance field lets you control how close you have to come when you are snapping one object to another. The largest number is 5 pixels.

5. Checking the Dynamic scrollbar option lets you see your illustration move as you drag on the scrollbars of the window.

6. Checking the Remember layer info option means that if an object is pasted from one document to another, it will be pasted into the new document onto the same layer it originally had.

7. Checking the Dragging a guide scrolls the window option means that if you drag a guide into the ruler you will scroll to a different section of your artwork. When this option is not selected, dragging a guide into the ruler will remove the guide from the screen and will not scroll the window.

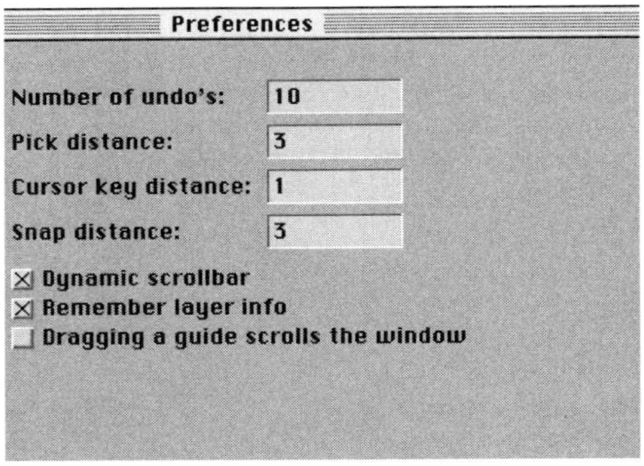

Figure 6. *The **Preferences** settings for the **Editing General** category.*

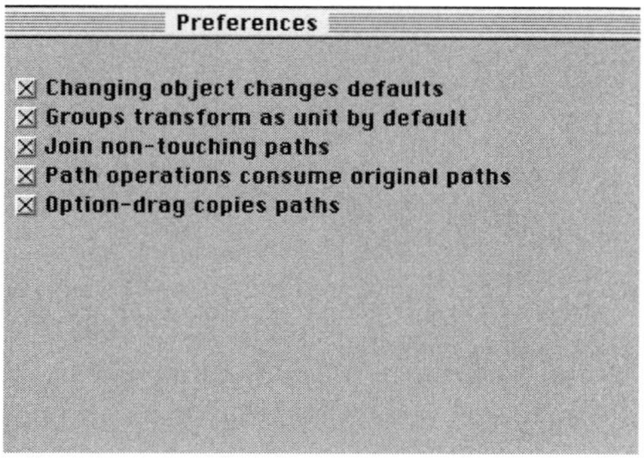

Figure 7. *The **Preferences** settings for the **Object Editing** category.*

The Object Editing category controls how your objects are modified (**Figure 7**).

To change the Object Editing preferences:

1. Checking the Changing object changes defaults option means that if you change an object's fill or stroke, the next object you create will have the same attributes as the previous one.

2. Checking the Groups transform as unit by default option means that all items in a group will automatically transform together and may result in unwanted distortions. When this option is not selected, you have to turn on the Transform as unit option or each object will transform individually.

3. Checking the Join non-touching paths option means that if you choose the Join Objects command for two objects that do not touch, FreeHand will draw a line segment between the two nearest end points.

4. Checking the Path operations consume original paths option means that when you apply Path Operations commands such as Punch and Intersect, the original paths will be deleted, leaving only the object that results from applying the commands.

5. Checking the Option-drag copies paths option controls whether or not holding the Option key and dragging or transforming an object will create a copy.

Tip

- If you want to leave the Path operations consume original paths option on, you can hold the Shift key as you apply any Path Operations commands; this will override the Preferences setting.

Chapter 22

The Text Editing category controls how text and text blocks are modified (**Figure 8**).

To change the Text Editing preferences:

1. Checking the Always use Text Editor dialog option means the Text Editor dialog box will come up when the text tool is clicked.
2. Checking the Track tab movement with vertical line option means a line will extend through the text when tab stops are placed on the ruler (**Figure 9**).
3. Checking the Show text handles when text ruler is off (slower) option lets you see the text block handles and boundary when you are in a text block (**Figure 10**).
4. Checking the New default-sized text containers auto-expand option means that if you click with the Text tool, the text block will continue to expand as you type.
5. Choosing the Build paragraph styles based on First selected paragraph option means the style attributes will come only from the first paragraph in the selection.
6. Choosing the Build paragraph styles based on Shared attributes option means the style attributes will come from all the paragraphs in the selection.
7. Choosing the Drag and drop a paragraph style to change single paragraph option means that if you drag a style icon onto a paragraph, only that paragraph will change.
8. Choosing the Drag and drop a paragraph style to change The entire text container option means that if you drag a style icon onto a text block, all the paragraphs in the block will change.

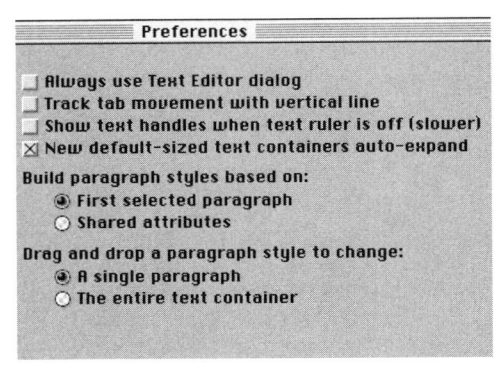

Figure 8. *The **Preferences** settings for the **Text Editing** category.*

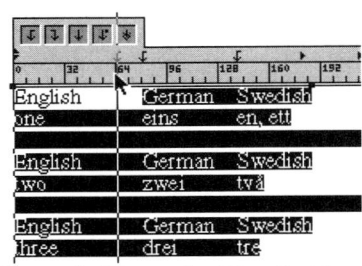

Figure 9. *The vertical line that is visible when the **Track tab movement with vertical line** option is selected.*

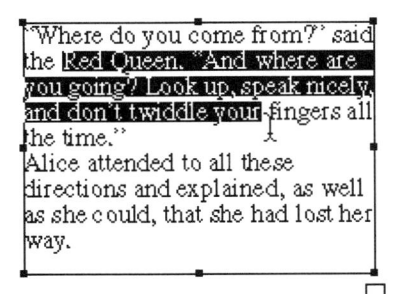

Figure 10. *Working in a text block with the **Show text handles when text ruler is off (slower)** preference on.*

Preferences

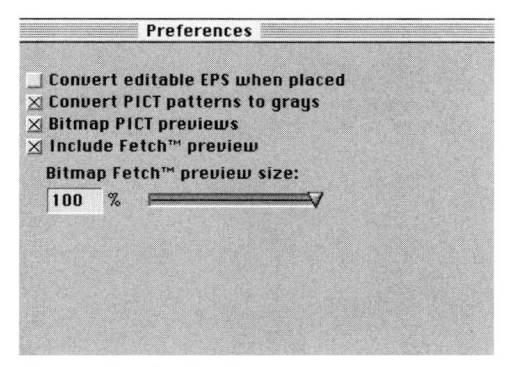

Figure 11. *The **Preferences** settings for the **Importing/Exporting** category.*

The Importing/Exporting category controls how graphics are imported and exported from FreeHand (**Figure 11**).

To change the Importing/Exporting preferences:

1. Checking the Convert editable EPS when placed option means that, if possible, EPS files that are placed in your FreeHand file are converted, so that their objects or points can be selected and modified.

2. Checking the Convert PICT patterns to grays option means that when bitmapped patterns in MacDraw Pro and Canvas PICT files are imported, the patterns will be gray.

3. Checking the Bitmap PICT previews option means that when you export your file as an EPS file to a page layout program such as QuarkXPress or Adobe PageMaker, the preview will be bitmapped (which will mean a faster screen redraw in the layout program).

4. Checking the Include Fetch preview option means that a preview of the image will be created that can be used with the graphics cataloging program Fetch.

5. When the Include Fetch preview option is selected, you can then enter an amount in the Bitmap Fetch preview size field. This lets you control the size of the preview created for the graphics cataloging program Fetch. Use the triangle slider or type the size you want in the field.

Chapter 22

The Palettes category controls how the palettes are displayed (**Figure 12**).

To change the Palettes preferences:

1. Checking the Hiding palettes hides the Toolbox option means that the toolbox will be hidden when the Hide Palettes command is chosen.

2. Checking the Remember location of zipped palettes option means that FreeHand "remembers" the position of the palette in its zipped state and will move the palette back to that position when it is zipped.

3. Checking the Black and white interface option means the gray shading and triangle sliders of boxes and palettes will be replaced by a black and white interface (**Figure 13**).

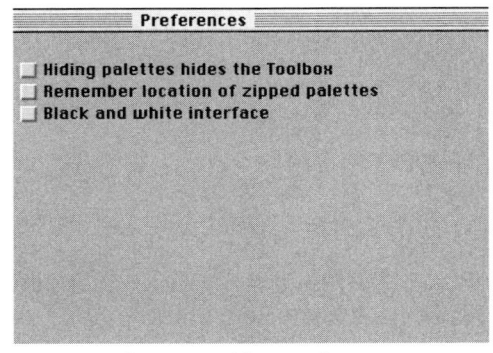

Figure 12. *The **Preferences** settings for the **Palettes** category.*

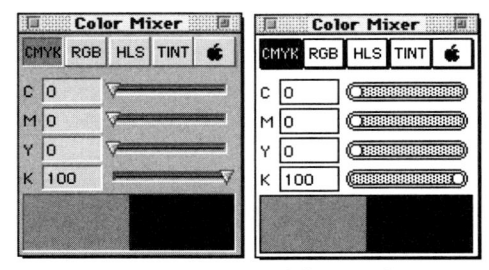

Figure 13. *The difference between the **gray interface** (left) and the **black and white interface** (right).*

Preferences

Figure 14. *The **Preferences** settings for the **Redraw** category.*

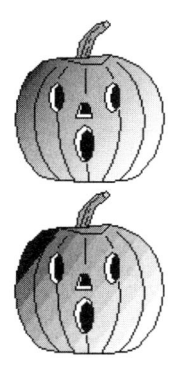

Figure 15. *The difference between the smooth fills (top) and the stepped fills (bottom).*

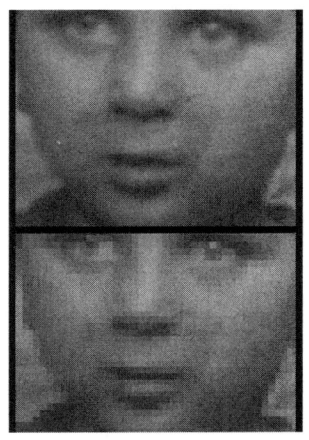

Figure 16. *The difference between a TIFF placed with a high-resolution display (top) and with a lower-resolution display (bottom).*

The Redraw category controls how objects, placed art, and text are displayed (**Figure 14**). None of the Redraw features will affect final output.

To change the Redraw preferences:

1. Checking the Better (but slower) display option means that Graduated and Radial fills are displayed onscreen in distinct steps (**Figure 15**).

2. Checking the Display text effects option means that special text effects such as the Inline effect and the Zoom effect will be visible onscreen.

3. Checking the Buffered drawing (faster but uses more RAM) option means that when you move to a new area or page, FreeHand draws the entire artwork offscreen and then pops it onscreen.

4. Checking the Redraw while scrolling option means that you will see your artwork as you scroll. If Redraw while scrolling is not checked, you won't see your artwork till you stop scrolling.

5. Checking the High-resolution TIFF display option means that TIFF images will be more detailed (**Figure 16**).

6. Checking the Display overprinting objects option means that "O's" are displayed when an object is set to overprint (**Figure 17**).

(Continued on the following page)

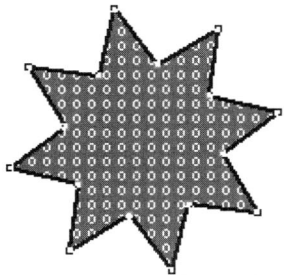

Figure 17. *The "O's" that indicate an object is set to **overprint**.*

271

Chapter 22

7. Entering an amount in the Greek type below pixels field controls which size of text will be "greeked" or turned from letters to a gray band (**Figure 18**).

8. Entering an amount in the Preview drag items field changes how many items are seen as a preview when moved or transformed (**Figures 19a–b**).

Tips

- If you start a drag of several items and then wish to see the preview, press and release the Option key as you drag. You will see then see a preview of all the items regardless of how the preferences are set.

- If you are holding the Option key to make a copy of the items, release the Option key and then press it again while you are still dragging. You will add a preview to the drag and make a copy.

Figure 18. *An example of text that is **greeked** (top) and the same text block with its text visible (bottom).*

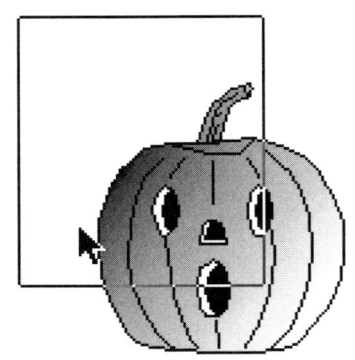

Figure 19a. *Dragging several objects without a preview.*

Figure 19b. *Dragging Several objects with a **preview**.*

Preferences

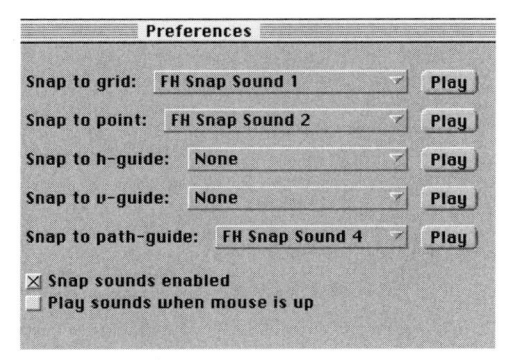

Figure 20. *The Preferences settings for the Sounds category.*

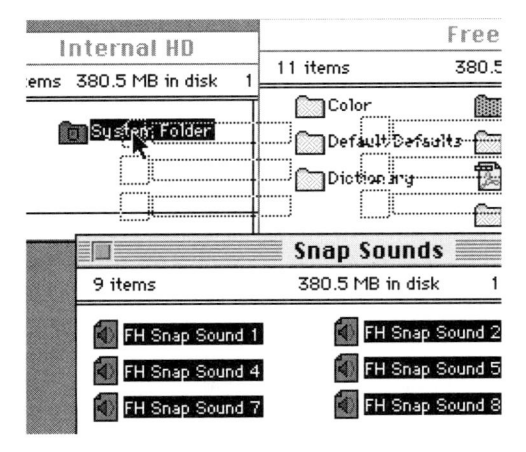

Figure 21. *To install the Snap sounds, drag the FreeHand **Snap Sounds** files onto your **System Folder**.*

The Sounds category controls which sounds are heard when you snap to different objects such as grids, points, guides, etc. (**Figure 20**). In order to use the Snap sounds you will need to install them into your Macintosh system.

To install the Snap sounds:

1. Find the folder called "Snap Sounds"; it should be in the FreeHand application folder.
2. There will be nine sound files inside the Snap Sounds folder. Select them all and drag them onto the System Folder (**Figure 21**).
3. An alert box will appear asking if you wish to store the files in the System file. Click OK. The files will be moved to the System file in the System Folder. The sounds will now be available under the Sounds preferences.

To change the Snap sounds preferences:

1. Press on the pop-up menu next to each of the Snap sounds choices. Choose whichever sound you want. Choose the FreeHand sounds or any other sounds in your System file. Choose None to turn off the sound for any choice.
2. If you would like to hear what each sound is like, click the Play button to the right of each choice.
3. Checking the Snap sounds enabled option will turn on the Snap sounds for all the choices.
4. If you check the Play sounds when mouse is up option, you will hear the snap sound whenever your mouse passes over the snap point, even if the mouse button is not pressed. (Very noisy!)

The Spelling category controls several choices about how the Spelling checker feature works (**Figure 22**).

To change the Spelling preferences:

1. Checking the Find duplicate words option controls if the Spelling checker finds duplicate words such as "the the."

2. Checking the Find captialization errors controls if the Spelling checker finds capitalization errors such as "Really? how did that happen?"

3. Choose the Add words to dictionary Exactly as typed option if you wish to add case-sensitive words. This means that words such as "McKneily," "McKee," or "McCarron" are entered with their capitalization intact.

4. Choose the Add words to dictionary All lowercase option if you do not wish to add the words as case-sensitive.

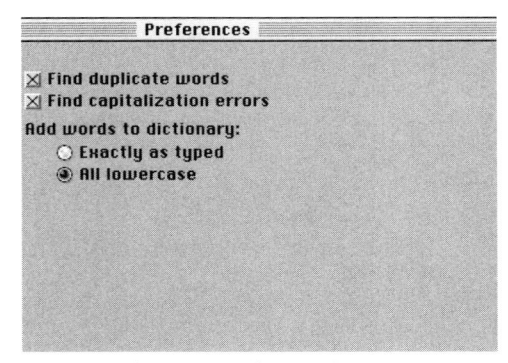

Figure 22. *The **Preferences** settings for the **Spelling** category.*

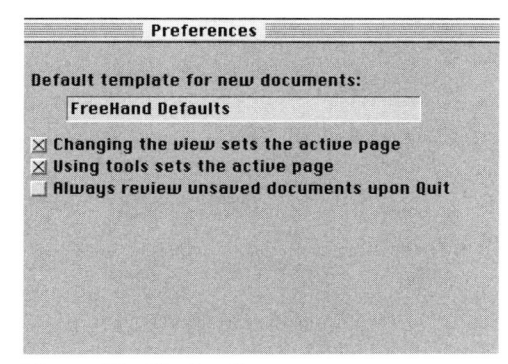

Figure 23. *The **Preferences** settings for the **Expert Document** category.*

There are three Expert categories: Document, Editing, and Import/Output. The Expert Document category controls sophisticated document features (**Figure 23**).

To change the Expert Document preferences:

1. Choosing the Default template for new documents option lets you change the file that FreeHand uses for the defaults file.

2. Checking the Changing the view sets the active page option means that if you scroll from one page to another, the page that comes into view will be the active page.

3. Checking the Using tools sets the active page option means that if you use any of the tools on a page, that page will be the active page.

4. Checking the Always review unsaved documents upon Quit option means that when you quit, you will be presented with a dialog box for each unsaved document. Unchecking the option means that if you quit with unsaved work, you will be presented with a box that tells you there are unsaved documents. You can then review them or not.

Chapter 22

The Expert Editing category controls the changes that you make to objects and text (**Figure 24**).

To change the Expert Editing preferences:

1. Entering numbers in the Default line weights (changes take effect after relaunching) field controls the sizes of the stroke weights listed in the Stroke Widths submenu of the Arrange menu. You can add as many widths as you want as long as there is a space between each number. All the sizes listed here are in points.

2. Checking the Auto-apply style to selected objects option means that if an object is modified and that modified object is used to define a new style, the new style will automatically be applied to any selected objects.

3. Checking the Define style based on selected object option means that a style will take its attributes from the selected object.

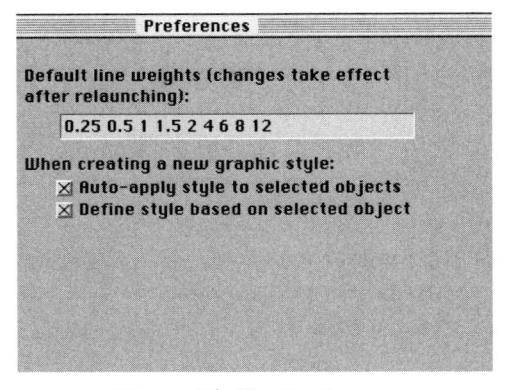

Figure 24. *The **Preferences** settings for the **Expert Editing** category.*

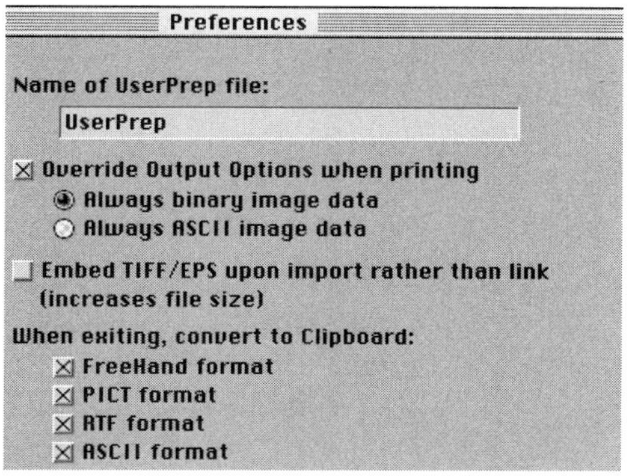

Preferences

Figure 25. *The* **Preferences** *settings for the* **Expert Import/Output** *category.*

The Expert Import/Output category controls how files are printed, how images are placed into FreeHand, and how the contents of the clipboard are handled (**Figure 25**).

To change the Expert Import/Output preferences:

1. The Name of UserPrep file field lets you choose which file FreeHand looks for when printing a document. Unless you have printing problems, you should not have to define a UserPrep file. For more information, see the ReadMe file in the UserPrep folder.

2. Checking the Override Output Options when printing checkbox lets you control the output for printing and exporting here rather than in the Output Options of the File menu or the Print Options. Your file will print faster if you choose the Always binary image data option rather than the Always ASCII image data option.

3. Checking the Embed TIFF/EPS upon import rather than link (increases file size) option means that all the information necessary to print placed images is embedded into the FreeHand document rather than linked.

4. Checking the choices for the When exiting, convert to Clipboard option controls how information is kept on the Clipboard when you switch from FreeHand to another application. The choices are FreeHand format, PICT format, RTF format, and ASCII format.

To save your Preferences settings:

While most changes you make to the Preferences will take effect immediately, those changes are not saved onto your hard disk until you quit FreeHand.

Chapter 22

FreeHand also lets you change the default settings for your documents. Defaults are the settings that you have when you open a new FreeHand document. Default settings include such things as how many and which colors will be listed in the Color List, how many pages a document should have, and how many layers a document should have. To change the defaults, you need to work with the FreeHand Defaults file.

To change the FreeHand Defaults file:

1. With FreeHand open, choose Open from the File menu and find the FreeHand Defaults file in the application folder. Choose Open.
   or
   In the Finder, double-click on the FreeHand Defaults file. This will launch FreeHand and open the FreeHand Defaults file (**Figure 26**).

2. Make whatever changes you would like in this file. For instance, if you would like to have certain colors in the Color List, you can create those colors or use the Options pop-up menu in the Color List to import colors. *(For more information on creating colors, see Chapter 10, "Color.")*

3. Save the file in the same folder where you found it under the same name. When asked to replace the existing file, click Replace.

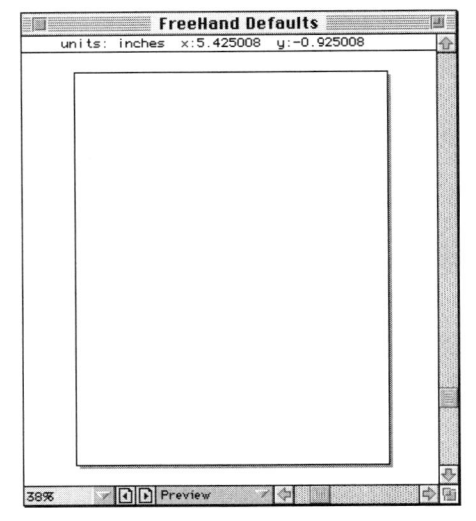

Figure 26. *With the file called **FreeHand Defaults** open, any changes you make to that file will become the default settings for all new files.*

Appendix A: Keyboard Shortcuts

The following are lists of most of the keyboard shortcuts available. Try to use one or two each week until they are familiar to you.

Cmd.	=	Command key
Opt.	=	Option key
L arr.	=	Left arrow key
R arr.	=	Right arrow key
D arr.	=	Down arrow key
U arr.	=	Up arrow key

Menu commands

Blend . . . . Cmd.-Shift-B
Bring Forward . . . . Cmd.-[
Bring To Front . . . . Cmd.-F
Clone . . . . Cmd.-=
Copy . . . . Cmd.-C or F3
Copy Attribute . . . . Cmd.-Opt.-Shift-C
Cut . . . . Cmd.-X or F2
Cut Contents . . . . Cmd.-Shift-X
Deselect All . . . . Tab
Duplicate . . . . Cmd.-D
Export . . . . Cmd.-E
Group . . . . Cmd.-G
Info Bar . . . . Cmd.-Shift-R
Join Elements . . . . Cmd.-J
Lock . . . . Cmd.-L
New . . . . Cmd.-N
Open . . . . Cmd.-O
Paste . . . . Cmd.-V or F4
Paste Attributes . . . . Cmd.-Opt.-Shift-V
Paste Inside . . . . Cmd.-Shift-V
Place . . . . Cmd.-Shift-D

Preview . . . . Cmd.-K
Print . . . . Cmd.-P
Quit . . . . Cmd.-Q
Redo . . . . Cmd.-Y
Repeat Last Xtra . . . . Cmd.-Shift-+
Rulers . . . . Cmd.-R
Save . . . . Cmd.-S
Save As . . . . Cmd.-Shift-S
Select All . . . . Cmd.-A
Send Backward . . . . Cmd.-]
Send To Back . . . . Cmd.-B
Snap To Grid . . . . Cmd.-;
Snap To Guides . . . . Cmd.-\
Snap To Point . . . . Cmd.-'
Split Elements . . . . Cmd.-Shift-J
Text Ruler . . . . Cmd.-/
Transform Again . . . . Cmd.-,
Undo . . . . Cmd.-Z or F1
Ungroup . . . . Cmd.-U
Unlock . . . . Cmd.-Shift-L

Appendix A

General commands

50% magnification	Cmd.-5
100% magnification	Cmd.-1
200% magnification	Cmd.-2
400% magnification	Cmd.-4
800% magnification	Cmd.-8
Close knife path cut	Cmd.-Knife Tool
Close multiviews	Opt.-Click Close Box
Close document	Cmd.-Opt.-W
Deselect all	Cmd.-Tab
Fit all	Cmd.-0 (zero)
Fit in window	Cmd.-W
Grabber hand	Space Bar
Help cursor	Cmd.-Shift-? or Help key
Hide all palettes	Cmd.-Shift-H or F2
New window	Cmd.-Opt.-N
Next page	Cmd.-Page Down
Previous page	Cmd.-Page Up
Stop screen redraw	Cmd.-period
Thicker stroke	Cmd.-Opt.-Shift->
Thinner stroke	Cmd.-Opt.-Shift-<
Calligraphic pen size down	1 or [or L arr.
Calligraphic pen size up	2 or] or R arr.
Zoom in	Cmd.-Space Bar-Click or Drag
Zoom out	Cmd.-Opt.-Space Bar-Click

Text commands

Baseline Shift down (1 pt.)	Opt.-D arr.
Baseline Shift up (1 pt.)	Opt.-U arr.
Bind To Path	Cmd.-Shift-Y
Bold type	Cmd.-Opt.-Shift-B or F6
Bold italic type	Cmd.-Opt.-Shift-O or F8
Centered alignment	Cmd.-Opt.-Shift-M
Convert To Paths	Cmd.-Shift-P
Decrease point size (1 pt.)	Cmd.-Shift-<
Discretionary hyphen	Cmd.--
Em space	Cmd.-Shift-M
En space	Cmd.-Shift-N
Find Text palette	Cmd.-Shift-F
Flow Inside Path	Cmd.-Shift-U
Highlight effect	Cmd.-Opt.-Shift-H
Increase point size (1 pt.)	Cmd.-Shift->
Italic type	Cmd.-Opt.-Shift-I or F7
Justified alignment	Cmd.-Opt.-Shift-J
Kern/Track by -1% em	Opt.-L arr.
Kern/Track by -10% em	Opt.-Shift-L arr.
Kern/Track by +1% em	Opt.-R arr.
Kern/Track by +10% em	Opt.-Shift-R arr.
Left alignment	Cmd.-Opt.-Shift-L
No effect	Cmd.-Opt.-Shift-N
Non-Breaking Space	Opt.-Space Bar
Plain type	Cmd.-Opt.-Shift-P or F5
Right alignment	Cmd.-Opt.-Shift-R
Spelling	Cmd.-Shift-G
Text Editor	Cmd.-Shift-E
Text Wrap	Cmd.-Shift-W
Thin space	Cmd.-Shift-T
Underlined type	Cmd.-Opt.-Shift-U

Appendix B: **Fills and Strokes**

Custom fills

The ten Custom fills appear onscreen as a series of "C's" in the artwork. The examples below show how each of the fills print. The gray circles show which of the Custom fills allow background objects to show through their transparent areas.

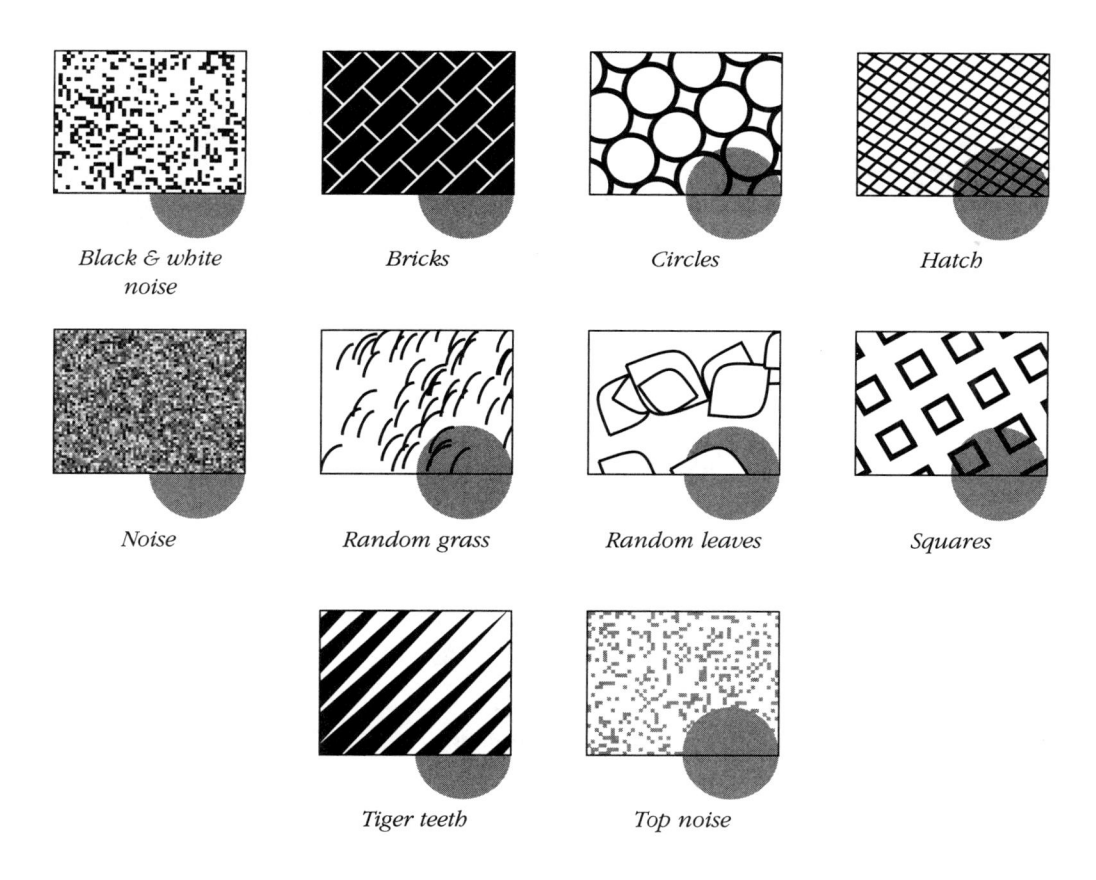

Black & white noise	Bricks	Circles	Hatch
Noise	Random grass	Random leaves	Squares
	Tiger teeth	Top noise	

Figure 1. *The ten **Custom fills** at their default settings.*

281

Appendix B

Textured fills

The nine Textured fills appear onscreen as a series of "C's" in the artwork. The examples below show how each of the fills will print at their default settings. The final example shows how only the black area responds to a change in color.

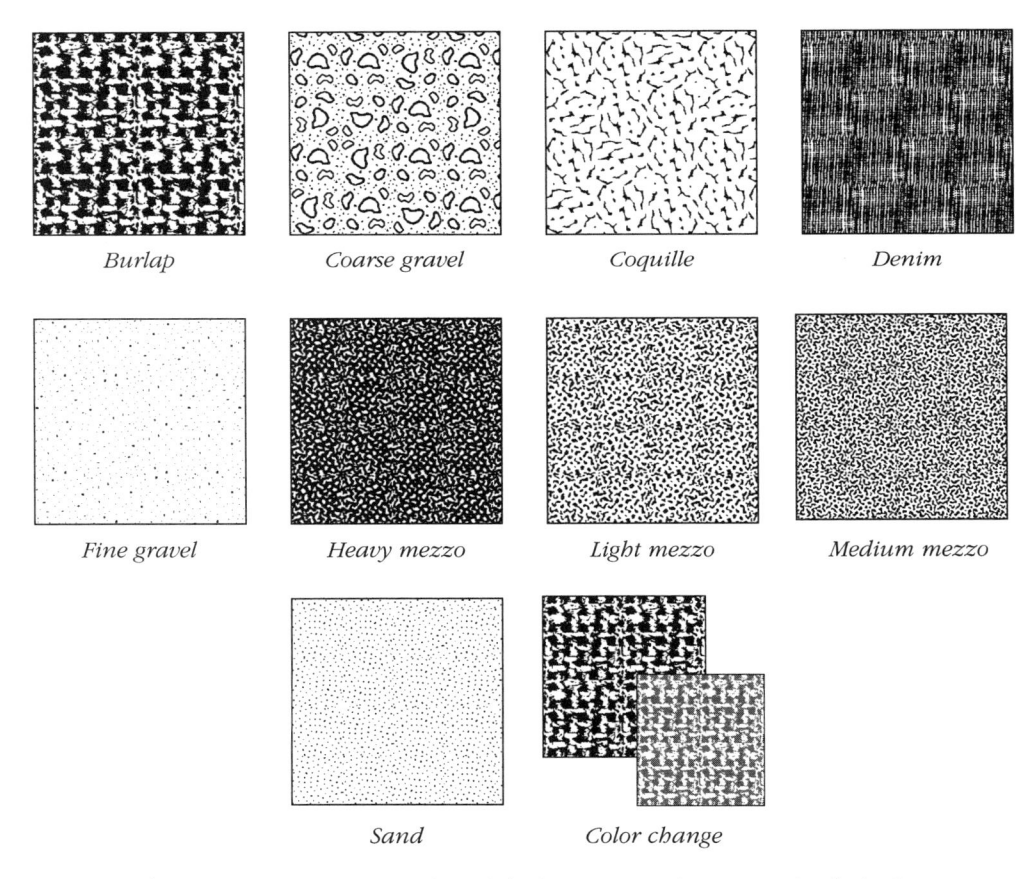

Burlap   *Coarse gravel*   *Coquille*   *Denim*

Fine gravel   *Heavy mezzo*   *Light mezzo*   *Medium mezzo*

Sand   *Color change*

Figure 2. *The nine* **Textured fills** *at their default settings and an example of which areas respond to a color change.*

Pattern fills and strokes

The Pattern fills and strokes are bitmapped patterns that appear onscreen and print as shown below. In addition to these default settings, each of the patterns either may be inverted or may have its pixels edited one by one.

Figure 3. *The sixty-four* **Pattern fills** *and* **strokes** *at their default settings.*

283

Appendix B

Custom strokes

The twenty-three Custom strokes appear onscreen as solid strokes (*see example in lower-right corner of this page*). The examples below show how each of the fills will print at their default settings. The gray circles indicate which of the Custom strokes have opaque white areas and which have transparent white areas.

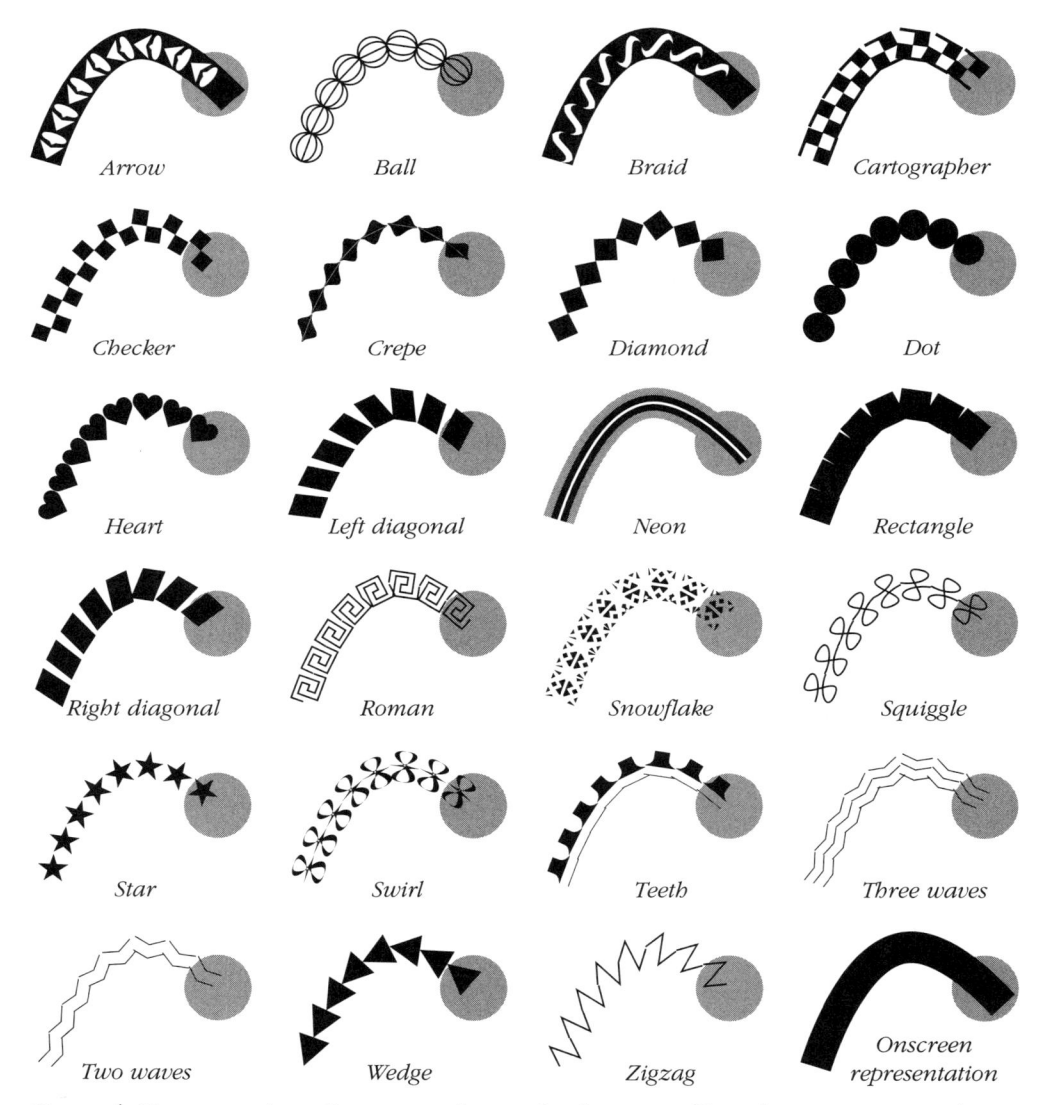

Arrow *Ball* *Braid* *Cartographer*

Checker *Crepe* *Diamond* *Dot*

Heart *Left diagonal* *Neon* *Rectangle*

Right diagonal *Roman* *Snowflake* *Squiggle*

Star *Swirl* *Teeth* *Three waves*

Two waves *Wedge* *Zigzag* *Onscreen representation*

Figure 4. *The twenty-three* **Custom strokes** *and a depiction of how they are represented onscreen.*

Index

~ (Tilde key), 81
3-D buttons, creating
    with Graduated fills, 133
    spherical, with Radial fills, 135
3D Rotation palette, 230–231
    Easy setting, 231
    Expert setting, 231
    illustrated, 230
    See also palettes
3D Rotation tool, 17, 230–231
    line extension, 230
    triangle sign, 230

A

Acrobat PDF format, 250
Add Guides dialog box, 37
Add Pages dialog box, 24
Adobe Gallery Effects, 18
Adobe Illustrator, 13
    plug-ins, 238
Adobe Illustrator files, exporting, 246
Adobe PageMaker, 14, 269
Adobe Photoshop, 13
alignment
    paragraph, 176
    text, 176
Alignment pop-up menu, 177
Align palette, 10
    See also palettes
anchor points, 17, 75
    group, 78, 80
    See also points
angle (Info Bar), 104
Arc dialog box, 72
arcs
    closed, 72
    concave, 72
    flipping, 72
    open, 72
Arc tool, 70
    Command key and, 72
    Control key and, 72
    example illustration, 70
    Option key and, 72
    settings, choosing, 72–73
Arrange menu
    Bring Forward command, 47
    Bring To Front command, 46, 189
    function of, 6
    Group command, 78
    illustrated, 7
    Join Objects command, 212, 236
    Lock command, 56
    Path operations submenu
        Blend command, 160, 218
        Crop command, 228
        Expand Stroke command, 225
        Insert Path command, 226–227
        Intersect command, 221
        Punch command, 222
        Remove Overlap command, 219
        Reverse Direction command, 79, 182, 218
        Simplify command, 220
        Transparency command, 146, 224
        Union command, 223
    Send Backward command, 47
    Send To Back command, 46
    Split Object command, 213
    Text Wrap command, 189
    Ungroup command, 81, 192
    Unlock command, 56
Arrowhead Editor dialog box, 155
arrowheads, 154–156
    applying, 154–155
    creating, 155–156
    editing, 155
    size of, 154
    transferring, 155
    See also paths
Arrowheads pop-up menu, 154
arrow key movement, 266
artwork
    colorizing, 241
    drawing offscreen, 271
    embedded, 262
    extracting, 243
    modifying, 241–242
    placing in FreeHand, 239–240
    resizing, 241
    resizing by dragging, 240
    transforming, 241
    viewing while scrolling, 271
    See also placed images
ASCII encoding, 260
ASCII text, 170
attributes, defining styles by, 204–205
Auto tiling, 254

B

"banding," 164
baseline shift, 173, 191
Basic fills, 130–132
    applying, 130
    changing color of, 130–132
    See also fills
Basic strokes, 147–148
BeInfinite, 238
Bevel joins, 150
Bézier handles, 16
Bézigon tool, 16, 69
    advantages of using, 95
    bumpy curved path creation with, 97
    connector point creation with, 101–102
    function of, 93
    illustrated, 4
    Option-click with, 97
    path continuation with, 102
    Pen tool vs., 93–94

Index

plus sign (+) cursor, 94
point handles, 95
smooth curved path creation with, 95
straight-to-bumpy path creation with, 99
See also Pen tool
Bitmapped artwork. See pixel images
bleed area, 27
bleeds, 25
    defined, 27
    setting size of, 27–28
blends, 159–164
    with banding, 164
    choosing points and, 161
    creating, 160–161
    defined, 159
    illustrated, 159, 161
    limitations, 163
    live, 162
    number of steps in, 161
    printing, 164
    progression of, 159
    reversing path direction with, 218
    rules for, 163
    smoother display of, 163
    viewing, 163
    ways of using, 160
borders, text block, 168–169
bounding box, 77
bumpy curved paths
    with Bézigon tool, 97
    illustrated, 97, 98
    with Pen tool, 98–99
    See also paths
Butt caps, 149

C

Calligraphic pen, 69
Canvas files, 247, 269
caps
    Butt, 149
    Round, 149
    Square, 149
    See also strokes
Character Inspector, 172–174
characters. See text; text blocks
Child styles, 207–208
    See also Parent styles; styles
circles
    converting to partial, 222
    creating, 61–62
Clipboard, information storage, 277
clipping paths. See masks
close box, 3
closed objects, 90
closed paths, 89
    aligning text to, 181
    determining, 90
    opening, 215
    See also open paths; paths

CMYK mode, 17
    color definition, 119
    defined, 117
color bars, 255
Color Control dialog box, 233
Color List, 117
    adding colors to, 120–121
    Fill drop box, 130, 131, 145
    function of, 10
    illustrated, 10
    opening, 120
    Options pop-up menu, 120
    rearranging, 235
    Stroke drop box, 148
color-matching system libraries, 126–127
Color Mixer, 117
    CMYK mode, 117
    Color Well, 120
    function of, 10
    hiding/showing, 119
    HLS mode, 118
    opening, 119
    RGB mode, 117
    Tint mode, 118
    See also Color List
Color Preference dialog box, 121
Color Preferences, 263–264
colors, 17, 117–128
    adding
        to color list, 120–121
        from color-matching system libraries, 126–127
        from copied objects, 126
        from custom color libraries, 126
        from EPS files, 126
        to Multi-Color fills, 144
    changing values of, 235
    Crayon, 127
    darkening, 234
    defining, 119–120
    deleting, 124–125
        groups, 124
        in Multi-Color fills, 144
    desaturate, 128
    desaturating, 234
    dragging
        for Graduated fills, 133–134
        for Radial fills, 135–137
    duplicating, 124
    fill, 130–132
    Greys, 127
    Highlight effect, 188
    importing, 278
    lighten/darken, 128
    lightening, 234
    names of, 121, 122
        finding, 235
        moving, 124
        unnamed, 128
    number of, 127
    on-screen display, 264

Index

overprinting, 259
printing, preventing, 259
process, 123
renaming, 122–123
saturating, 128, 234
screen angle for, 259
selecting, 122
spot, 123–124
Strikethrough effect, 188
stroke, 148
Underline effect, 188
Zoom effect, 187
See also Color List; Color Mixer
Colors submenu. See Xtras menu, Colors submenu
color systems
    choosing, 118
    CMYK, 17, 117
    HLS, 17, 118
    Macintosh color wheel, 118
    RGB, 17, 117
    tint, 118
columns, 178–180
    adding rules to, 179–180
    creating, 178–179
    height, 178
    spacing, 178
    See also text
Command key
    Arc tool and, 72
    See also keyboard shortcuts
commands, 5
    See also specific menus and commands
Commercial Printing Guide, 237
composite paths, 211–213
    creating, 211–212
    defined, 211
    moving, 212
    releasing, 213
    selecting parts of, 212
    working with, 212
    See also paths
compound paths. See composite paths
connector points, 83
    creating, 101–102
    point handles, 85
    types of, 83
    See also points
constrain angle, 94
Control key
    Arc tool and, 72
    dragging color swatches and, 133
    text blocks and, 167
copying
    objects, 105
        during transformation, 110
    Option key and, 272
    styles between documents, 209
corner points, 82
    converting curve points to, 100
    with one handle, 100

point handles, 85
retracting handles, 86
types of, 82
See also points
Corner radius, rectangle, 60
corner symbol, 239
    dragging, 240
Crayon colors, 127
Create color library dialog box, 128
Create PICT image dialog box, 248–249
    Antialiasing option, 249
    Colors option, 249
    Dither checkbox, 249
    illustrated, 248
    Image resolution option, 249
Create submenu. See Xtras menu, Create submenu
crop marks, 255
curve points, 83
    converting to corner points, 100
    point handles, 84
    types of, 83
    See also points
custom color libraries, 126, 128
    adding colors from, 126
    creating, 128
    deleting, 128
    exporting, 128
Custom fills, 140–141
    applying, 140
    default settings, 281
    defined, 140
    illustrated, 281
    printing, 140
    scaling, 140
    transparent backgrounds, 140
    See also fills
Custom strokes, 156
    illustrated, 284
    See also strokes
cx (Info Bar), 104
cy (Info Bar), 104

D

Dash Editor dialog box, 151–152
dash patterns, 151–154
    applying, 151
    editing, 152
    list of, 151
    multi-colored, 153
    Option key and, 152
    "string of pearls," 153
    See also strokes
Dash pop-up menu, 151
Delete submenu. See Xtras menu, Delete submenu
deleting
    colors, 124–125
        in Multi-Color fills, 144
    custom color libraries, 128
    guides, 35, 36
    inline graphics, 191

287

Index

layers, 51
objects, 88
points, 88–89
styles, 210
tabs, 177
text blocks, 168, 238
text on paths, 183
Deneba Canvas, 13
dialog boxes
    illustrated, 12
    setting devices, 12
    See also specific dialog boxes
Display Color Setup dialog box, 264
Display mode pop-up menu, 3
dist (Info Bar), 104
Distort submenu. See Xtras menu, Distort submenu
document grid, 3
    changing intervals, 39
    defined, 39
    illustrated, 39
    snapping to, 40–41
    viewing, 39
Document Inspector palette, 9
    Basic fill application with, 130
    Closed checkbox, 90
    closing path with, 90–91
    Corner Point icon, 85
    Curve handles icons, 86
    Curve Point icon, 84
    Dimensions-and-Inset icon, 166, 167
    Document icon, 39
    Document Setup icon, 21, 39
    extending handles with, 86–87
    Fill icon, 129, 130, 141, 142
    Fill icon pop-up menu
        Basic command, 130
        Custom command, 140
        Graduated command, 132
        Pattern command, 142
        PostScript command, 143
        Radial command, 134
        Textured command, 141
        Tiled command, 137
    Grid size field, 39
    Group palette, 91–92
    Magnification icon, 25, 26
    Object icon, 84, 90
    opening, 21
    opening path with, 90–91
    Options pop-up menu, 24
    Pages icon, 22, 24, 27
    retracting handles with, 86
    Stroke icon, 147, 148
    Strokes icon pop-up menu
        Basic command, 147
        Custom command, 156
        Pattern command, 157
        PostScript command, 158
    Tall icon, 23, 24
    Taper pop-up menu, 132

    Wide icon, 23, 24
    xy coordinates, 91
Document Preferences, 265
Document Report dialog box, 261
Document Report Viewer, 261
documents
    closing, 29
    copying styles between, 209
    creating, 20–21
    launching, 19
    number of steps in, 162
    report of, 261
    saving, 28
document window, 3
    components, 3
    illustrated, 2
    Preview pop-up menu, 32
    rulers, 33
DrawTools, 238
drawing, with Freehand tool, 66
dx (Info Bar), 104
dy (Info Bar), 104

E

Edit Guides dialog box, 37
Editing General Preferences, 266
Edit menu
    Clear command, 88, 191
    Clone command, 110, 153
    Copy command, 105, 190, 209
    Cut command, 48, 105, 190, 191
    Duplicate command, 105, 110, 111
    function of, 6
    illustrated, 6
    Paste Behind command, 48
    Paste command, 105, 190, 209
    Paste Inside command, 213
Edit Style dialog box, 206, 208
Edit Tab dialog box, 177
Effects pop-up menu, 185, 191
ellipses
    creating, 61–62
    grouping, 79
Ellipse tool, 61–62
end points, 89
    See also points
EPS files
    adding colors from, 126
    editing, 245
    exporting, 244–245
    opening, 245
    placed, 124
    preferences, 269
Expand Stroke dialog box, 225
Expert Document Preferences, 275
Expert Editing Preferences, 276
Expert Import/Output Preferences, 277
Export Colors dialog box, 128
Export document dialog box, 244–247

Index

exporting
    as Adobe Illustrator file, 246
    as Canvas file, 247
    as EPS files, 244–245
    files, 18, 244
    as FreeHand file, 247
    as MacDraw file, 247
    output control for, 277
    preferences, 269
    See also importing; Importing/Exporting Preferences
Extensis, 238
Extract dialog box, 243
Eyedropper tool, 233

F

Fetch Info dialog box, 250
Fetch preview, 269
File menu
    Close command, 29
    Export command, 244, 246, 247
    Fetch Info command, 250
    function of, 7
    illustrated, 6
    New command, 20
    Open command, 20, 250, 278
    Place command, 73, 170, 239
    Preferences command, 273
    Print command, 252, 254, 260
    Quit command, 30
    Report command, 261
    Revert command, 30
    Save command, 28
files
    Acrobat, 250
    EPS, 126, 244–245
    exporting, 18, 244
    external, 262
    FreeHand Defaults, 278
    "native" FreeHand, 245
    placing, 73
    sending for imagesetting, 262
    UserPrep, 277
Fill icon pop-up menu
    Basic command, 130
    Custom command, 140
    Graduated command, 132
    Pattern command, 142
    PostScript command, 143
    Radial command, 134
    Textured command, 141
    Tiled command, 137
fills, 16, 113, 114, 115, 116, 129–146
    applying, 129
    Basic, 130–132
    choosing, 129
    Custom, 140–141, 281
    Graduated, 132–134
    Multi-Color, 144–145
    None, 145
    Overprint feature and, 146
    Pattern, 142–143, 283
    PostScript, 143–144
    Radial, 134–137
    Textured, 141–142, 282
    Tiled, 137–140
    types of, 129
Find Text dialog box, 199–200
Fisheye Lens dialog box, 231
Fisheye Lens tool, 17, 231
Flatness setting, 260
Format pop-up menu, 244
    FreeHand 3.1 command, 247
    illustrated, 244
    Photoshop EPS command, 246
Fractal Design Painter, 13
FreeHand
    3.1 format, 247
    file, exporting as, 247
    as graphics/drawing program, 13
    icon, 19
    launching, 19
    as layout program, 14–15
    as multipage program, 15
    object orientation and, 13–14
    objects in, 15–16
    Photoshop filters in, 242
    placing artwork in, 239–240
    quitting, 30
    text in, 16–17
    utilities, 17–18
FreeHand Defaults file, 278
Freehand tool, 16, 224
    Calligraphic pen button, 69
    Calligraphic settings, 65
    dragging with, 66
    drawing with, 66
    Freehand settings, 65
    illustrated, 4
    Option key and, 66
    plus sign (+) cursor, 66
    Variable stroke button, 67
    Variable stroke settings, 65
Freehand Tool dialog box, 65–66

G

Graduated fills, 132–134
    3-D button creation with, 133
    applying, 132–134
    color changes and, 136
    defined, 132
    displayed in distinct steps, 271
    Linear, 132
    Logarithmic, 132
    mixing color types and, 136
    Multi-Color, 145
    using black and, 136
    See also fills
graphics
    bleeding, 25

Index

inline, 190–191
programs, 13
Greys, 127
grouped objects, 78–79
    moving numerically, 91
    sizing numerically, 92
    See also objects
groups
    levels of, 80
    nested, 81
    path, 78
    transforming together, 267
guides, 34–39
    adding numerically, 37–38
    creating, 34–36
    deleting, 35, 36
    distance between, 37
    dragging, 34–35
    horizontal, 34
    in Keyline mode, 35
    layers, 38
    locking, 38
    moving, 35
    multiple page documents and, 37
    paths into, 38
    in Preview mode, 35
    snapping to, 38–39
    vertical, 34
    See also rulers
Guides dialog box, 36, 37

H

Halftone palette
    function of, 10
    illustrated, 10, 258
    opening, 258
    Screen pop-up menu, 257, 258
    See also palettes
halftone screen, setting, 257–258
    for individual objects, 258
Hand tool, 18
hanging punctuation, 175
height (Info Bar), 104
Highlight effect, 184
    applying, 185–186
    colors, 188
    dash pattern, 188
    editing, 188
    See also text, effects
high-resolution printers, 253
HLS color system, 17
    color definition, 119
    defined, 118
horizontal ruler, 3
hyphenation
    inhibiting, 173
    turning on, 178

I

icons
    Alignment, 176
    Bevel join, 150
    Butt cap, 149
    Column-and-Row, 178, 179
    Corner Point, 85
    Curve Point, 84
    Dimensions-and-Inset, 166, 167, 168, 169
    Document Setup, 21
    Fill, 129, 130, 141, 142
    FreeHand, 19
    FreeHand Document, 28
    FreeHand Template, 28
    Magnification, 25, 26
    Miter, 150
    Move, 112
    Object, 84, 90, 204
    Pages, 22, 24, 27
    Reflection, 116
    Rotation, 113
    Round cap, 149
    Round join, 150
    Scale, 114
    Skew, 115
    Spacing-and-Hyphenation, 178
    Square cap, 149
    Stroke, 147, 148
    Tall, 23, 24
    Wide, 23, 24
    Wrap order, 179
Infinite FX, 17, 238
Image dialog box, 241
images. *See* artwork
imagesetting, 262
importing
    colors, 278
    text, 170–171
    See also exporting
Importing/Exporting Preferences, 269
Info Bar, 3, 103–104
Inline effect, 184
    applying, 185–186
    background, 186
    editing, 186
    outlines, 186
    See also text, effects
Inline Effect dialog box, 186
inline graphics, 190–191
    deleting, 191
Innovative Data Design, 13
Inset Path dialog box, 226–227
Inspector palettes, 1, 9
    Character, 172–174
    choices, 18
    Document, 9, 21
    icons, 9
    Object, 9

Index

Paragraph, 174–175
Text, 9, 166–172
See also palettes

J

joins
    Bevel, 150
    defined, 150
    Miter, 150, 151
    non-touching paths, 267
    Round, 150

K

Kai's Power Tools, 18
kerning, 172–173
keyboard shortcuts, 279–280
    general commands, 280
    menu commands, 279
    text commands, 280
Keyline mode, 31
    defined, 31
    guides in, 35
    illustrated, 31
    screen redrawing and, 32
    viewing in, 32–33
    See also Preview mode
Knife tool, 215–217
    dragging with, 217
    for erasing path parts, 217
    functions, 215
    illustrated, 4
    for punching holes, 217
    splitting paths evenly with, 216
    splitting paths jaggedly with, 215
Knife Tool dialog box
    Close cut paths option, 215, 216, 217
    constraining cuts with, 216
    Freehand button, 215, 217
    illustrated, 215
    Straight button, 216
    Tight fit option, 215, 217
KPT Vector Effects, 18, 238

L

layers, 45–56
    default, 49
    display of, 55–56
    dragging, 52, 54
    duplicating, 50
    Guides, 50, 52
        objects on, 54
    invisible, 55
    locking, 53, 56
    moving objects
        between, 53–54
        front/back and, 46–47
        within, 47–48
    names
        check mark next to, 55
        dots next to, 55
        padlock next to, 56
        X next to, 55
    nonprinting, 54
    pasting objects and, 266
    placing images on, 73
    printing, 54–55
    removing, 51–52
    renaming, 50
    reordering, 52–53
    unlocking objects on, 56
    viewing objects of, 56
Layers palette
    default layers, 49
    dividing, 54
    function of, 10
    illustrated, 10, 49
    opening, 49
    Options pop-up menu, 50, 51
    printing/nonprinting layers, 54
    using, 49–50
leading, 172
Learning PostScript: A Visual Approach, 143, 158
Letraset, 238
    Letraset Envelopes, 17, 238
libraries. See color-matching system libraries; custom color libraries
Library dialog box, 127
Limitcheck error, 260
Linear fills, 132
lines
    creating, 64–65
    dragging on with Option key and, 87
Line tool, 16
    illustrated, 4
    Shift key and, 64
    using, 64–65
Link box, 168, 180
    black circle in, 171
    white, 171
    working with, 171
Links dialog box, 243
Live Blends, 162
Logarithmic fills, 132

M

MacDraft, 13
MacDraw files, 247, 269
Macintosh color wheel, 118
    color definition, 119
    opening, 264
MacPaint, 13, 142
magnification
    changing, 26–27
    exact amounts, 43–44
    of pages, 25–26
    settings, 26
    See also zooming
Magnification submenu. See View menu, Magnification submenu
Magnifying tool, 4, 42

Index

Manual tiling, 254
margin indents
    in Paragraph Inspector, 174
    from text rulers, 175
masks, 213–214
    creating, 213
    defined, 213
    releasing, 214
    transforming, 214
menu bar, 2–3
menus, 18
    Arrange, 7
    choosing, 5
    Edit, 6
    File, 6
    Type, 8
    View, 7
    Window, 8
    See also specific menus and commands
MetaTools, 238
Miter joins
    changing limit of, 151
    defined, 150
Multi-Color Fill dialog box, 144–145
Multi-Color fills, 144–145
    adding colors to, 144
    applying, 144
    changing colors in, 144
    creating, 145
        Graduated, 145
        Radial, 145
    deleting colors in, 144
    See also fills
multiple pages, 15

N

nested objects, 80
    grouping, 81
    ungrouping, 81
    See also objects
nesting
    levels, 80
    objects, 80–81

O

Object Editing Preferences, 226, 267
Object Inspector palette, 9
    Closed checkbox, 214
    Column-and-Row icon, 178, 179
    Dimensions-and-Inset icon, 158, 169
    Links button, 243
    Open checkbox, 215
    Text on a path options, 183
object-oriented programs, 13–14
objects, 15–16
    Bézier handles, 16
    in bleed area, 27
    closed, 90
    copying, 105
        during transformation, 110

creating with straight sides, 94–95
cutting, 105
deleting, 88
deselecting, 77
dragging, 77
filling, 16
grouped, 78–79
Guide layer, 54
linking text between, 180
locking on layer, 56
modifying shape of, 16
moving, 77–78
    front/back, 46–47
    within layer, 47–48
    between layers, 53–54
    locked, 49, 56
    with Transform palette, 112
    using Paste Behind, 48–49
nesting, 80
outline, 107, 109
overlapping, 45
pasting, 105
points in, 15
previews, 272
reflecting, 108
resizing, 78
rotating, 106–107
scaling, 107
selecting, 77–78
    grouped, 78
    locked, 56
    multiple, 77
    with selection marquee, 76
shape of, 14
side by side, 45
skewing, 109
snapping, 266
Snap To Grid and, 40
snap to sounds, 41
stroking, 16
styles, 202, 204
transforming, 17
transparency, 224
ungrouping, 81
unlocking on layer, 56
one-third rule, 83–84
open paths, 89
    closing, 90, 214
    deselecting, 94
    determining, 90
    See also closed paths; paths
Operations palette, 218
    Create PICT Image command, 248
    Crop command, 228
    Expand Stroke command, 225
    function of, 10
    illustrated, 11
    Insert Path command, 226–227
    Intersect command, 221

Index

Punch command, 222
Remove Overlap command, 219
Reverse Direction command, 218
Simplify command, 220
Transparency command, 146, 224
Union command, 223
See also palettes
Option key
    Arc tool and, 72
    composite paths and, 212
    copying and, 272
    dash patterns and, 152
    dragging color swatches and, 135
    dragging from points and, 87
    dragging on lines and, 87
    during transformation, 110
    Fisheye Lens tool and, 231
    Freehand tool and, 66
    grouped objects and, 79
    Knife tool and, 216
    Live Blends and, 162
    Magnifying tool and, 42
    nested groups and, 81
    object copy, 105
    object move and, 105
    object selection and, 153
    Rectangle tool and, 60
    Text Editor and, 194
    See also keyboard shortcuts
Options pop-up menu
    Color List
        Duplicate command, 124
        Export command, 128
        Make process command, 123
        Make spot command, 123
        New command, 120
        Remove command, 124
    Document Inspector palette, 24
    Layers palette, 50, 51
        Duplicate command, 50
        Remove command, 51
    Styles palette
        Duplicate command, 209
        Edit command, 208
        New command, 202, 204, 206
        Redefine command, 205
        Remove command, 210
        Set Parent command, 207
orientation, changing, 23–24
Other submenu. See Window menu, Other submenu
Output Options dialog box, 260
    See also printing
Oval tool, 15, 215, 221, 223, 224, 228
    illustrated, 4
overlapping, removing, 219
overprinting, 146
    "O"s display, 271

P

padlock (Info Bar), 104

page labels, 255
pages. See work pages
Pages pop-up menu, 22
palettes, 18
    3D Rotation, 230
    Align, 10
    black and white interface, 270
    expanding, 44
    Halftone, 10
    hiding, 44
    Inspector, 1, 9, 18, 21, 166–174
    Layers, 10
    Operations, 10, 11, 218
    Style, 10, 11
    Transform, 10, 11
    Type, 10, 11
    Xtras, 10, 11, 17
    zip box, 44
    zipped location, 270
    zipping, 44
Palettes Preferences, 270
Pantone model, 17, 126
Paragraph Inspector palette, 174–175
    Hanging punctuation box, 175
    opening, 174
    See also palettes
paragraphs
    alignment, changing, 176
    applying styles to, 204
    margin indents, 174
    spaces between, 174
    style attributes, 268
    style icon in, 268
    See also text; text blocks
Parent styles, 207–208
    See also Child styles; styles
Paste Inside, 213–214
    See also Masks
pasteboard
    arranging pages on, 25–26
    defined, 20
    illustrated, 20
    seeing area of, 265
Path Operations submenu. See Arrange menu, Path Operations submenu
paths, 75
    adding points to, 89
        path end, 102
    anchor points, 17, 75
    applying arrowheads to, 154
    bumpy curved
        with Bézigon tool, 97
        with Pen tool, 98–99
    changing shape of, 76, 221–228
    clipping. See masks
    closed, 89
    closing, 89–90
        with Inspector palette, 90–91
        open, 214
    complex, splitting, 260

Index

composite, 211–213
continuing, 102
determining closed/open, 90
fractalizing, 236
grouping, 78
into guides, 38
open, 89
opening
    closed, 215
    with Inspector palette, 90–91
operations, 17, 211–228
reshaping, 88
reversing direction of, 218
simplifying, 220
smooth curved
    with Bézigon tool, 95
    with Pen tool, 96–97
straight-to-bumpy
    with Bézigon tool, 99
    with Pen tool, 100–101
text
    binding to, 181–182
    conversion to, 192
    deleting, 183
    highlighting, 183
    moving, 182, 183
    orientation, 183
    working with, 183–184
See also points
Pattern fills, 142–143
    default settings, 283
    illustrated, 283
    opaque backgrounds, 142
    printing, 143
    See also fills
Pattern strokes, 157–158
    applying, 157
    colors, 158
    default settings, 283
    defined, 157
    illustrated, 283
    opaque backgrounds, 157
    printing, 158
    See also strokes
PDF format. See Acrobat PDF format
Pen tool, 16, 69
    advantages of using, 95
    Bézigon tool vs., 93–94
    bumpy curved path creation with, 98–99
    connector point creation with, 101–102
    function of, 93
    illustrated, 4
    path continuation with, 102
    plus sign (+) cursor, 94
    point handles, 96
    smooth curved path using, 96–97
    straight-to-bumpy path creation with, 100–101
    See also Bézigon tool
Photoshop filters
    applying to TIFF images, 243

finding, 242
installing in FreeHand, 242
Radial Blur, 243
PICT images
    colorizing, 241
    creating, 248
    illustrated, 248
pixel images, 239
    difference from object-oriented, 13–14
    Pixel, 181
Place dialog box, 73
placed images
    colorizing, 241
    embedded, 262
    extracting embedded, 243
    modifying, 241–242
    placing in FreeHand, 239–240
    printing information, 277
    resizing, 241
    resizing by dragging, 240
    transforming, 241
    See also artwork
point handles
    Bézigon tool, 95
    connector point, 85
    corner point, 85
    curve point, 84
    defined, 82
    extending, 86–87
    illustrated, 82
    Pen tool, 96
    retracting, 86–88
    smooth curved path, 95
points, 75, 82–88
    adding to path end, 102
    anchor, 17, 75, 78
    black dot, 77
    blends and, 161
    changing, 85
    connector, 83
    converting, 84–85
    corner, 82
    curve, 83
    deleting, 88–89
    dragging from with Option key, 87
    dragging on, 78
    end, 89
    excess, removing, 220
    grouping, 78, 80
    manipulating, 84–85
    moving, numerically, 91
    one-third rule, 83–84
    selecting
        additional, 76
        by clicking, 75–76
        individual, 79
        with selection marquee, 76
    types of, 75
    See also paths; point handles
polygons, 62

Index

Polygon tool, 16, 221, 226
    illustrated, 4
    plus sign (+) cursor, 62
    using, 62
Polygon Tool dialog box, 62–63
    Polygon option, 62
    Star option, 63
PostScript fills, 143
PostScript Printer Description (PPD)
    file, 251
    information, 257
    selecting, 257
PostScript printers
    Level 1, 143, 158, 164, 252
    Level 2, 143, 158, 164, 252
PostScript strokes, 158
Power Duplicating
    defined, 110
    transformation tools for, 110–112
preferences, 263–278
    changing, 263
    color, 263–264
    functions of, 263
    saving, 277
    See also Preferences settings
Preferences settings
    Color, 263–264
    Document, 265
    Editing General, 266
    Expert Document, 275
    Expert Editing, 276
    Expert Import/Output, 277
    Importing/Exporting, 269
    Object Editing, 226, 267
    Palettes, 270
    Redraw, 271–272
    Snap Sounds, 273
    Spelling, 196, 274
    Text Editing, 268
Preview mode, 31, 32
    defined, 31
    guides in, 35
    illustrated, 31
    viewing in, 32
    See also Keyline mode
previews, 272
Printer dialog box
    Composite proof button, 253
    Copies field, 252
    illustrated, 252
    opening, 252
    Pages choices, 252
    Paper Source choices, 252
    Print button, 255
    Scale choices, 253
    Separations button, 253
    setting up, 252–253
    Tile choices, 253
printers, changing resolution of, 21–22, 162

printing, 18, 251–262
    advanced, 255–262
    basic, 252–254
    bleed area and, 27
    blends, 164
    colors, preventing, 259
    Custom fills, 140
    emulation up/down, 256
    halftones and, 257–258
    layers, 54–55
    output control for, 277
    overprinting, 259
    Pattern fills, 143
    Pattern strokes, 158
    placed images, 277
    positive/negative images, 256
    at service bureaus, 262
    Textured fills, 141
    transfer function, 258–259
    See also Output Options dialog box
Print Options dialog box
    color listing, 259
    Crop marks checkbox, 255
    File name and date checkbox, 255
    Halftone screen option, 257–258
    illustrated, 255
    Imaging Options list, 256
    Registration marks checkbox, 255
    Select PPD button, 257
    Separation names checkbox, 255
    Separations box, 259
    Spread Size option, 256
    Transfer function option, 258–259
process colors, 123
    conversion to spot colors, 123–124
    See also colors

Q

QuarkXPress, 14, 269
quitting FreeHand, 30

R

Radial Blur filter, 243
Radial fills, 134–137
    3-D button creation with, 135
    applying
        by dragging colors, 135–137
        with Document Inspector, 134–135
    center location, 134
    color changes and, 136
    defined, 134
    displayed in distinct steps, 271
    Inside drop box, 134
    mixing color types and, 136
    Multi-Color, 145
    Outside drop box, 134
    using black and, 136
    See also fills
radius (Info Bar), 104

295

Index

rectangles, 57
    constraining into squares, 59
    Corner radius setting, 60
    creating, 58–59
    creating from center point outward, 60–61
    grouping, 79
    rounded-corner, 60
Rectangle tool, 217, 223
    dragging with, 58
    illustrated, 4
    Option key and, 60
    plus sign (+) cursor, 58
    uses, 57
Rectangle Tool dialog box, 60
Redefine Style dialog box, 205
Redraw Preferences, 271–272
reflecting
    angle, 116
    by eye, 108
    with Transform palette, 116
    See also transformations
Reflecting tool, 17
    illustrated, 4
    star cursor, 108
    using, 108
reflection axis, 108
registration marks, 255
resize menu, 3
resolution, printer, 21–22
Revert Changes dialog box, 30
Review dialog box, 30
RGB color system, 117
rotating
    by eye, 106–107
    with Transform palette, 113
    See also transformations
Rotating tool, 17
    illustrated, 4
    star cursor, 106
    using, 106
rotation axis, 106
Round caps, 149
Round joins, 150
rows, 178–180
    adding rules to, 179–180
    creating, 178–179
    spacing, 179
    width, 179
    See also text
RTF text, 170
ruler guides, 3
rulers
    dragging guide into, 266
    illustrated, 33
    opening, 33–34
    text, 165
    viewing, 33
    See also guides
rules, adding to columns/rows, 179–180
Rules pop-up menu, 179

S

Save Changes dialog box, 29
Save dialog box, 28
saving
    documents, 28
    as FreeHand template, 28
    preferences, 277
scaling
    by eye, 107
    outline, 107
    with Transform palette, 114
    See also transformations
Scaling tool, 4, 17, 107
Screen Angle dialog box, 259
Screen pop-up menu, 258
scroll arrow, 3
Selection tool, 75–76
    deleting guides and, 35
    dragging with, 76
    four-headed cross cursor, 77
    illustrated, 4
    moving guides and, 35
    opening, 75
    Shift key and, 76
separations, 253
    setting, 259
service bureaus, 262
Set Parent dialog box, 207
Shadow effect, 184
    applying, 185–186
    using, 188–189
    See also text, effects
Shift key
    Create PICT Image command and, 248
    Crop command and, 228
    Fisheye Lens tool and, 231
    group anchor points and, 78
    Inset Path command and, 226
    Intersect command and, 222
    Knife tool and, 216
    Line tool and, 64
    Punch command and, 222
    Rectangle tool and, 59
    Selection tool and, 76
    See also keyboard shortcuts
sides (Info Bar), 104
Simplify dialog box, 220
skewing
    by eye, 109
    outline, 109
    with Transform palette, 115
    See also transformations
Skewing tool, 17
    illustrated, 4
    star cursor, 109
    using, 109
Smudge dialog box, 232
Smudge tool, 17, 232

Index

Snap sounds, 41
    folder, 273
    installing, 273
    Preferences, 273
Snap To Grid feature, 40–41
Snap To Guides feature, 38–39
Snap To Point feature, 41–42
Sounds Preferences, 273
special characters, 197–198
    finding/changing, 199
Special Character submenu. See Type menu, Special Character submenu
Special pop-up menus, 199, 200
Spelling checker, 194–196
    Add button, 195
    capitalization errors and, 274
    case-sensitive words and, 274
    Change button, 195, 196
    dictionary, 195
    duplicate words and, 274
    Ignore All button, 195
    illustrated, 194
    opening, 194
    options, 196
    Start button, 195
    Suggest button, 196
Spelling Preferences, 196, 274
Spiral dialog box, 70–71
    Direction icons, 71
    Draw by pop-up menu, 71
    Draw from pop-up menu, 71
    Expansion, 70
    Spiral type, 70
spirals, 70
Spiral tool, 70–71
spot colors
    defined, 123
    process color conversion, 123–124
    See also colors
Square caps, 149
squares, 57–60
    See also Rectangle tool; rectangles
stars, 63–64
straight-to-bumpy paths
    with Bézigon tool, 99
    illustrated, 99, 100
    with Pen tool, 100–101
    See also paths
Strikethrough effect, 185
    applying, 185–186
    colors, 188
    dash pattern, 188
    editing, 188
    See also text, effects
"string of pearls," 153
strokes, 16, 147–158
    applying
        caps, 149–150
        with Inspector palette, 147–148
        joins, 150–151
    arrowheads, 154–156
    attributes of, 147
    Basic, 147–148
    colors, changing, 147
    Custom, 156, 284
    dash pattern, 151–154
    expanding, 225
    Pattern, 157–158, 283
    PostScript, 158
    types of, 147
    weights of, 276
    width, changing, 148–149
Strokes icon pop-up menu
    Basic command, 147
    Custom command, 156
    Pattern command, 157
    PostScript command, 158
Style palette, 10–11
styles, 201–210
    applying, 203–204
    auto-applying, 276
    basing one on another, 207–208
    Child, 207–208
    copying, between documents, 209
    default
        changing, 210
        viewing, 201
    defining, 202, 204–205
        by attributes, 204–205
        by example, 202
    deleting, 210
    duplicating, 209
    name
        choosing, 206
        plus sign (+) by, 205
    Normal, 201, 210
    Normal Text, 201, 210
    object, 202, 204
    organizing, 201
    Parent, 207–208
    redefining, 205–206
    renaming, 203
    selected object, 276
    text, 204
    viewing, 201
Styles palette, 201–210
    highlighted names in, 203
    illustrated, 201
    Options pop-up menu
        Duplicate command, 209
        Edit command, 208
        New command, 202, 204, 206
        Redefine command, 205
        Remove command, 210
        Set Parent command, 207
    See also palettes
submenus. See specific menus
sx (Info Bar), 104
sy (Info Bar), 104

Index

T

tabs
    aligning text with, 174
    changing, 177–178
    default, 176
    deleting, 177
    moving, 177
    setting, 177
    See also text
Taper pop-up menu, 132
templates
    default file, 275
    defined, 29
    making changes to, 29
    saving as, 28
text, 16–17, 165–180
    alignment, 176
    ASCII, 170
    baseline shift, 173
    characters
        holes in, 192
        repeating, 177
        spacing, 172
        width, 172
    effects, 181–192
        applying, 185–186
        Highlight, 184, 188
        Inline, 184, 186
        screen redraw and, 185
        Shadow, 184, 188–189
        Strikethrough, 184, 188
        Underline, 184, 188
        Zoom, 184, 187
    finding, 199–200
    flow direction, 182
    "greeked," 272
    hanging punctuation, 175
    horizontal scale, 172
    hyphens, 173
    importing, 170, 170–171
    inserting away from stroked text block, 169
    kerning, 172
    leading, 172
    lines
        keeping together, 175
        spacing, 172
    linking between objects, 180
    on paths, 183–185
        binding, 181–182
        deleting, 183
        highlighting, 183
        moving, 182, 183
        orientation, 183
        working with, 183–184
    options, 16
    path conversion, 192
    RTF, 170
    selecting, 193
    special effects, 16–17

    styles, 171, 204
    typeface, 171
    type size, 171
    wrapping, 165, 189–190
    See also text blocks; Text Editor
Text alignment pop-up menu, 183
text blocks, 16
    auto-expansion settings, 167
    automatically shrinking, 168
    borders, applying to, 168–169
    boundaries, 268
    changing size of, 166–167
    columns, 178–180
    Control key and, 167
    creating
        by clicking, 166
        by dragging, 165
    deleting, 168, 238
    expanding, 268
    handles, 268
    Link box, 168, 171
    locking, 167
    moving, 169
    positioning, 169–170
    resizing, 167
    rows, 178–180
    selecting, 181
    See also text
Text Editing Preferences, 268
Text Editor, 193–194
    always using, 268
    changing attributes in, 194
    opening, 193
    Option key and, 194
    using, 193
    viewing size, 193
Text Inspector palette, 9, 166–172
    Alignment icon, 176
    Baseline shift, 191
    Character icon, 172, 185
    Dimensions-and-Inset icon, 169
    Dimensions area, 169
    Edit button, 186, 187
    Effects pop-up menu, 185, 191
    Inset area, 169
    Paragraph icon, 174
    Spacing-and-Hyphenation icon, 178
    See also palettes
text ruler, 165
    changing margin indents with, 175
    showing, 175
    See also rulers
Text tool, 4, 165–166, 190
Textured fills, 141
    default settings, 282
    illustrated, 282
    opaque backgrounds, 141
    printing, 141
    scaling, 141
    See also fills

Index

Text Wrap dialog box, 189
TIFF images
    applying Photoshop filters to, 243
    colorizing, 241
    display options, 271
Tilde key (~), 81
Tiled fills, 137–140
    adjusting, 138–140
    angling, 138–139
    applying, 137
    creating, 137
    defined, 137
    moving, 138
    sizing, 138
    transparent, 137
    See also fills
tiling, 254
tint mode, 118
tints
    creating, 125–126
    names of, 125
    storing, 125
    swatches of, 125
title bar, 3
toolbox, 4
    hiding, 44
    illustrated, 4
    tool settings, 4
    Xtra Tools, 70–73, 229–232
    See also specific tools
Toyo color-matching system, 17, 126
tracing, 74
    artwork placement for, 73
    nonprinting layers and, 54
Tracing tool, 4, 15–16, 73–74
Tracing Tool dialog box, 74
transfer function, 258–259
transformations
    copies and, 267
    copying object during, 110
    function application, 110
    group, 267
    mask, 214
    mixing, 116
    Power Duplicating and, 110–112
    storing, 111
    viewing, 112
    See also reflecting; rotating; scaling; skewing
Transform palette, 91, 112–116
    function of, 10
    illustrated, 11
    Move icon, 112
    moving objects with, 112
    opening, 112
    reflecting objects with, 116
    Reflection icon, 116
    rotating objects with, 113
    Rotation icon, 113
    Scale icon, 114
    scaling objects with, 114

Skew icon, 115
skewing objects with, 115
See also palettes
Transparency dialog box, 224
Trap dialog box, 237
traps, 237
Trumatch color-matching system, 126
Type menu
    Bind To Path command, 181
    Convert To Paths command, 192
    Font command, 171
    function of, 8
    illustrated, 8, 171
    Size command, 171
    Special Character submenu, 197–198
        Em Dash command, 198
        Em Space command, 198
        En Dash command, 198
        End Of Column command, 197
        End Of Line command, 197
        En Space command, 198
        Non-Breaking Space command, 198
        Thin space command, 198
    Spelling command, 194
    Text Editor command, 193
    Text Find command, 199
    Type Style command, 171
Type palette
    function of, 10
    illustrated, 11, 171
    opening, 171
    See also palettes

U

Underline effect, 184
    applying, 185–186
    colors, 188
    dash pattern, 188
    editing, 188
    See also text, effects
unit of measurement, changing, 21
units (Info Bar), 104
unsaved work, 275
UserPrep files, 277

V

Variable stroke tool, 67–68
    drawing with, 68
    icon, 68
    plus sign (+) cursor, 68
    pressure-sensitive tablets and, 68
    settings, choosing, 67
versions, reverting to last saved, 30
vertical ruler, 3
View menu, 31
    Edit Guides command, 36, 37
    function of, 7
    Grid command, 39
    Guides command, 34
    Hide Palettes command, 44

Index

illustrated, 7
Info Bar command, 103
Lock Guides command, 38
Magnification submenu, 43
    Fit All command, 43
    Fit Page command, 43
    illustrated, 43
Preview command, 32
Rulers command, 33
Snap To Grid command, 40
Snap To Guides command, 38
Snap To Point command, 41
Text Rulers command, 15, 165

W

White space, 200
width (Info Bar), 104
Window menu
    Color List command, 120
    Color Mixer command, 119
    function of, 8
    Halftone command, 258
    illustrated, 8
    Inspector command, 21
    Layers command, 49
    Other submenu
        Operations command, 144, 218
        Xtra Tools command, 70, 72, 229
    palette diamonds, 44
    Styles command, 201
    Transform command, 112
    Type command, 171
work pages
    active, 275
    arranging, 25–26
    creating, 24–25
    custom-sized, 22–23
    defined, 20
    illustrated, 20
    light-gray line around, 27
    magnification of, 25–26
    multiple, 25
    orientation of, 23–24
    preset sizes, 22
    sizing, 22–23
    thumbnails, 25

X

x (Info Bar), 104
Xtras, 229–238
    defined, 16, 229
    third-party, 17
        adding, 238
        listed, 238
        using, 238
    See also Xtra Tools toolbox

Xtras menu
    Colors submenu
        Color Control command, 233
        Darken Colors command, 234
        Desaturate Colors command, 234
        Lighten Colors command, 234
        Multi-Color Fill command, 144
        Name All Colors command, 235
        Randomize Named Colors command, 235
        Saturate Colors command, 234
        Sort Color List By Name command, 235
    Command-Shift-Plus keyboard shortcut, 228
    Create submenu
        PICT Image command, 248
        Trap command, 237
    Delete submenu
        Unused Named Colors command, 235
        Unused Text Blocks command, 238
    Distort submenu, 236
    function of, 8
    illustrated, 8, 144
Xtras palette
    contents of, 17
    function of, 10
    illustrated, 11
    See also palettes
Xtra Tools toolbox, 229
    3D Rotation tool, 230–231
    Arc tool, 72–73
    Eyedropper tool, 233
    Fisheye Lens tool, 231
    illustrated, 70, 229
    opening, 70
    Smudge tool, 232
    Spiral tool, 70–71
    viewing, 229

Y

y (Info Bar), 104

Z

zip box, 3
zoom box, 3
Zoom effect, 184
    applying, 185–186
    colors, 187
    offset, 187
    three-dimensional, 184
    See also text, effects
zooming, 42–44
    exact amounts, 43–44
    using Magnification submenu, 43
    using Magnifying tool, 42
    See also magnification